Operation Tabarin

Praise for *Operation Tabarin*

'[An] important, solid and well-researched contribution to both the history of Antarctic exploration and the maritime strategic history of that distant region.'

— Professor Eric Grove in *Navy News*

'This well-crafted narrative history makes fascinating reading, whilst providing an invaluable record of the start of the permanent British presence in Antarctica … a valuable and timely addition to the history of Antarctica.'

— *Polar Record*

'Haddelsey brings the little known story of Operation Tabarin to life with his usual blend of narrative drive and thorough attention to detail. Based on extensive research, this volume is a valuable addition to our understanding of Britain's involvement in the Antarctic during this critical period.'

— Heather Lane, Scott Polar Research Institute

'A perspicuous and absorbing history of events from Operation Tabarin to the British Antarctic Survey.'

— Gordon Howkins MBE, Meteorologist, Operation Tabarin

'A timely and very welcome account of an expedition that is vital to our understanding of British Antarctic exploration and the legacy of historic sites such as Port Lockroy.'

— Rachel Morgan, Director of the UK Antarctic Heritage Trust

'Having been one of the crew of HMS *William Scoresby* during Operation Tabarin I have had great pleasure reading this book and remembering the exploits at the bases at Port Lockroy, Hope Bay and Deception Island. Mr Haddelsey deserves praise for bringing it all back so vividly.'

— George James, Wireless Officer, HMS *William Scoresby*, Operation Tabarin, 1944–46

'A well-written book about a little-known but important expedition – very nostalgic.'

— Ian Graham, Lieutenant RNVR, HMS *William Scoresby*, Operation Tabarin, 1944–46

OPERATION TABARIN

BRITAIN'S SECRET WARTIME EXPEDITION TO ANTARCTICA 1944–46

STEPHEN HADDELSEY

WITH ALAN CARROLL

FOREWORD BY HRH PRINCESS ANNE, THE PRINCESS ROYAL

The
History
Press

'What is the reason for sending an expedition of perfectly good fighting men to the South Pole?'

Winston Churchill, 24 April 1944

For Ken Blaiklock
Explorer and friend

Front cover illustrations. Top: A lunchtime halt at the base of the Wall Range during the survey of Wiencke Island, October 1944. (Reproduced courtesy of British Antarctic Survey Archives Service, ref. no. AD6/19/1/A42/1. © Natural Environment Research Council) *Bottom:* Bransfield House, Port Lockroy. (Courtesy of the UK Antarctic Heritage Trust)

First published 2014
This paperback edition first published 2016

The History Press
The Mill, Brimscombe Port
Stroud, Gloucestershire, GL5 2QG
www.thehistorypress.co.uk

British Library Cataloguing in Publication Data.
A catalogue record for this book is available from the British Library.

ISBN 978 0 7509 6746 4

Typesetting and origination by The History Press
Printed and bound by CPI Group (UK) Ltd, Croydon, CR0 4YY

Contents

Author's Note

Many of the diaries and letters quoted in this book were written in circumstances of extreme stress and in a hurry; inevitably, this resulted in an array of spelling mistakes and grammatical errors. For ease of reading, spelling has been corrected and punctuation adjusted where absolutely necessary. Any words inserted by the author for clarity of meaning are identified by the addition of square brackets. It should also be noted that, as a Canadian, Andrew Taylor used American spelling. For consistency and to avoid distraction, all spelling has been anglicised.

All temperatures are given in degrees Fahrenheit and other measures in imperial, as these were the most commonly used during the expedition.

Acknowledgements

Hitherto, Operation Tabarin has received remarkably little attention from writers focusing on the United Kingdom's long and distinguished role in the exploration of the Antarctic continent – and yet this expedition, launched in secret and at the height of the Second World War, would ultimately evolve into the British Antarctic Survey (BAS), one of the most important and most enduring government-sponsored bodies undertaking investigation and research in the region. The expedition also plays a vital part in any attempt to understand and chronicle the UK's territorial claims in the Antarctic and the resulting conflicts with other powers, most notably Argentina. In addition, while the United States and Germany both launched Antarctic expeditions in the years immediately preceding the outbreak of hostilities, the UK would be the only combatant nation to send an expedition during the war itself. This was not coincidental; indeed, the war actually presented the UK authorities with a golden opportunity to reassert claims that had been allowed, through a combination of apathy, timorousness and commercial self-interest, to fall into abeyance.

To tell the story of Operation Tabarin I have relied, to an enormous degree, upon the help and support of a number of individuals. I should like, therefore, to offer my sincere thanks to the following: Ian Graham, Gordon Howkins and George James, the last surviving veterans of Operation Tabarin, for their willingness to share their memories and for proofreading the manuscript. This book is intended to be a tribute to them and to their fellows, and I am extremely grateful to them for ensuring its historical accuracy. Thanks also to Robert Back, son of Dr Eric Back, for permission to quote from his father's papers, now held at the British Antarctic Survey; Gerry Farrington, for making available to me the letters and photographs of his father, 'Fram' Farrington; Justin Marshall, son of 'Freddy' Marshall, for very kindly copying photographs and letters in his possession, and for allowing their use; Martin Lockley, son of 'Jock' Lockley; Sheila Bates and Madeline Russell, daughters of Victor Russell, for permitting use of their father's letters and photographs; Janet Marr, daughter of James Marr; Margaret Cameron, daughter of Jock Matheson; Keith Holmes, for his notes on the naming of the operation; Iain MacLennan, for sharing his research into the life of Jock Matheson; Angela Heck, for facilitating access to the memoirs of Andrew Taylor; Rachel Morgan, Director of the UK Antarctic Heritage Trust, which now manages the Port Lockroy site; Andy Stevenson, for mapping the expedition in so dynamic a fashion; and Ken Blaiklock, for his enthusiastic encouragement, for reading and correcting the manuscript, and for sharing his intimate knowledge of the region, gleaned during his service with the Falkland Islands Dependencies Survey (FIDS) in the years immediately following Operation Tabarin.

In common with my other books, the bulk of this narrative is based very closely upon contemporary sources, including official documents and the letters, diaries and other writings of the participants. However, I should also like to make specific mention of one modern source that was of considerable help to me when describing the diplomatic and departmental wrangling which ultimately gave rise to the operation, and which is described in chapter I of this work. The source in question is an article by John Dudeney and David Walton, 'From *Scotia* to "Operation Tabarin": Developing British Policy for Antarctica', published in the *Polar Record*. I strongly recommend it to anyone interested in learning more about the geo-political background to the expedition. Of the contemporary sources, the vast majority are now held in the archives of the British Antarctic Survey and I should like to thank Ellen Bazeley-White and Joanna Rae for their invaluable assistance in locating and copying these papers. Other papers are held in the National Archives at Kew, at the University of Manitoba and the Scott Polar Research Institute, and I would like also to express my gratitude to these bodies.

Most particularly, I should like to acknowledge the generosity and expertise of Alan Carroll who, in the earliest stages of this project – and on the basis of only a very slight acquaintance – agreed to share with me all the details of his research into the operation, thereby obviating the need for a sizeable portion of the investigative work usually required for a book of this nature. Alan's enthusiasm, his first-hand knowledge of Port Lockroy (where he served as base leader from 1954 to 1957), and his comprehensive list of contacts did a great deal to convince me of the viability of the project. Alan's writings on the early occupation of Base 'A' were also particularly helpful to me when I was shaping the chapters on Port Lockroy – as was his willingness to pursue additional lines of inquiry to help complete the picture. Without Alan's generous assistance, this book would have been much longer in the writing and its final form would almost certainly have been very different. I should also like to thank Jane Carroll, for making me so welcome when I visited their home and for her comments on the manuscript.

I must express my sincerest thanks to HRH Princess Anne, Patron of the United Kingdom Antarctic Heritage Trust, for providing the foreword.

This list is not, indeed cannot, be comprehensive and I hope that those who have not been named individually will not think that their help is any the less appreciated. Every effort has been made to obtain the relevant permissions and I should like to crave the indulgence of any literary executors or copyright holders where these efforts have been unavailing.

As always, my greatest debts of gratitude are to my wife, Caroline, who has striven hard to ensure that I balance writing with lesser activities like eating and drinking – and to my son, George, whose enthusiasm for Antarctic studies reached its zenith when he 'raced penguins' with a real-life polar explorer. But that's another story…

Stephen Haddelsey
Halam, Nottinghamshire

Foreword

BUCKINGHAM PALACE

In February 1944, a party of nine British and Commonwealth soldiers, sailors and scientists landed on a tiny island in the middle of Port Lockroy, off the west coast of the Antarctic Peninsula. In response to incursions by competing powers, their top-secret mission was to establish British sovereignty in the region.

In the seven decades since their arrival, the programme of scientific research and geographical surveying begun by this small group of men under the leadership of Lieutenant Commander James Marr has expanded to become one of the most important and enduring of all government sponsored ventures in the Antarctic.

As patron of the United Kingdom Antarctic Heritage Trust, the body responsible for the conservation of this and many other important historic sites, I had the pleasure of visiting Port Lockroy in January 2007, following in the footsteps of my father, who visited as part of his world tour in January 1957.

With 2014 marking the seventieth anniversary of the expedition's arrival in Antarctica, I am delighted to see for the first time the full story of 'Operation Tabarin', from its inception in the War Cabinet of early 1943 to its evolution into its post-war successors. It is a story of hardship, tension and danger – but also of determination and ultimate victory.

Anne

Prologue

At first glance, nearly four and a half years of war seem to have left only the slightest impression on the Falkland Islands. The low treeless hills, blotched grey and black with boulders and sprouting coarse yellowish grass, continue to support thousands of hardy Corriedale sheep, as they have for the last 100 years. The houses of Stanley, clad in match boarding and roofed with brightly painted sheets of corrugated iron, stand securely rooted around the kelp-strewn waters of the harbour, and Christ Church Cathedral, the most southerly Anglican cathedral in the world, still dominates the town. The ribbons of smoke rising from the chimneys are heavy with the musty aroma of locally dug peat, and the whole scene exudes an atmosphere of domestic calm.

On a typical day, a closer inspection will reveal just a few tell-tale signs of the war. Since 1942, the peacetime population of 2,400 souls has been massively augmented by some 1,500 men of the 11th Battalion of the West Yorkshire Regiment, supported by detachments of gunners, sappers and support services. Khaki is therefore much more prevalent than it once was. Amidst the rocks and scrub, gun pits and embankments have been constructed and the more observant might spot weapon embrasures in some of the buildings. The cemetery also contains ten military graves from the war years: most belong to members of the Falkland Islands Volunteer Force but four, dating from December 1939 and January 1940, are different. These are the last resting places of men mortally wounded in action against the *Graf Spee*. In Sparrow Cove, too, it is possible to see the legacy of the Battle of the River Plate: there are gaping holes in the rusted ironwork of Brunel's SS *Great Britain*, where plates were salvaged to repair HMS *Exeter*.

However, Saturday 29 January 1944 is not a typical day and the signs of war are more obvious than usual – albeit war of a rather novel form.

The grazing sheep look down from their sparse pastures on a scene of unusually intense, even frenetic, activity. Two ships lie tied up side by side in Port William, Stanley's outer harbour, and dockhands and sailors in their sea-going slops swarm over them. One, the *William Scoresby*, is tiny: at just 134ft in length and with a displacement of 370 tons, she is hardly larger than an ordinary trawler – but she has a look of power and strength disproportionate to her size and her bows are reinforced for ice work. Launched in 1925, for most of her career the *Scoresby*, as she is commonly known, has been one of His Majesty's Royal Research Ships, engaged in chasing and marking whales as part of the *Discovery* Investigations into the lifecycle of the great leviathans of the Southern Ocean. In size and shape she closely resembles the swift, steam-powered whale catchers and she is well known both to the Falkland Islanders and to the whalers hunting the Humpback, Fin and Blue whales that teem in the surrounding waters. But now her forward deck carries an antique looking 12-pounder, not the usual 12-bore marker gun, and she is a commissioned, if distinctly scruffy, warship. The second, larger, ship is the *Fitzroy*. Built in 1931 for the Falkland Islands Company, she is 165ft long, with a net register of 853 tons. She is equally familiar to the islanders, having been their most important link with the outside world for the last decade and more. Carrying the bales of wool which form the islands' only export commodity to the 'coast', as the South American ports are known locally, she returns with mail, supplies and occasional visitors. Designed to ride the world's stormiest seas, she too is ruggedly built and a good sea boat, though green-gilled passengers report a tendency to roll sickeningly in stormy seas.

The activity in the harbour has been ceaseless for the last two and a half days, ever since the 14,000-ton troopship, *Highland Monarch*, dropped anchor among the dismasted wrecks cluttering the harbour. With the rattle of her anchor chains echoing around the hills, the erstwhile luxury liner had begun immediately to disgorge soldiers carrying rifles and kitbags: fresh replacements to garrison the islands. Somewhat apart, a much smaller and quite distinct second party had also disembarked, some in uniform, others in civilian dress, and all under the command of a stocky, bespectacled naval officer who gave his orders with an Aberdonian lilt. During their brief stay on the islands, the attitude of these men has been noticeably different from that of their army shipmates, being remarkable for a kind of quiet but enthusiastic expectancy, very much at odds with the dull stoicism of the garrison troops. These are the men of Naval Parties 475 and 476, also known as 'Operation Tabarin', and they are bound for the Antarctic.

As the would-be Antarctic explorers made their way down the gang-plank to report to Government House, *Highland Monarch*'s deck cranes had clattered into life, swinging back and forth to discharge her cargo into the waiting *Fitzroy*. Caught in the cranes' giant nets, crates, sacks and boxes, containing everything from window glazing and stove parts to books and scientific equipment, were swung from the gloom of one cavernous hold, through the crisp, bright air of the South Atlantic, into two rather smaller holds. When the bulk of the cargo had been stowed, the *Fitzroy* moved off to tie-up alongside one of the coaling hulks used by the Falkland Islands Company and the transfer of the bulging black sacks began. To any observer familiar with the bunker capacity of such a ship, it must soon have become apparent that this was no ordinary fuelling stop. Long after the *Fitzroy*'s needs had been met, the coal continued to flow from the hulk, until the ship was covered in a film of choking black dust. Finally, lighters from the *Highland Monarch* ferried over the last few boxes and cases, which were then dumped unceremoniously on top of the coal piled high in the *Fitzroy*'s third hold. Soon she would be ready to sail.

The morning of 29 January had dawned cold and damp and the men gathered on the company's jetty at 6.45 a.m. had stamped their feet and tucked their hands into their armpits to stave off the chill. Despite the fact that the harbour was all but enclosed, its surface looked distinctly choppy, with waves whipped up by the almost incessant winds that scoured the islands. The arrival of the company's trim little launch had raised a murmur of satisfaction, but this turned to frustrated grumbling when the waiting men realised that one of their party was missing, apparently extracting the 'last drop of sweetness from one of those leave-takings which are always so poignant'.[1] At last, he appeared, scurrying round a corner and down the slope towards the jetty. Grinning rather sheepishly in response to the ribald witticisms of his companions, he had clambered into the launch, which then set off across the harbour under an overcast sky.

A few minutes have passed since the boarding party climbed the *Fitzroy*'s rust-streaked sides. Captain Keith Pitt has given the order 'All ashore who are going ashore' and those not sailing are now dashing about completing their last-minute jobs before returning to Stanley. Hatches are fastened, hands shaken, good wishes proffered – and they are gone. The smoke trailing lazily from the ship's single funnel gives way to a steady, thick black plume, billowing in time with the increasingly determined throb of her engines. Pitt gives the order to 'let go': lines are cast off fore and aft, and the water at the stern, coloured brown by the peat of the surrounding hills, begins to froth and boil. The *Fitzroy* sits unusually low in the water and her decks as well as her holds are crowded precariously with canisters and boxes, stacks of timber and a bewildering assortment of items, of every conceivable size and shape. She appears to wallow slightly as she turns, but she steadies quickly as her yeoman exchanges signals with the shore and those on deck wave cheerily in answer to a valedictory hoot from the *Highland Monarch*.

Followed by the *Scoresby*, the *Fitzroy* rounds Cape Pembroke and turns south and then west. For 50 miles or so, they hug the greenish grey shore before reaching Goose Green, where they embark fresh quarters of beef and sheep carcasses, which are then slung from the shrouds on both sides of the ship. Some hens and pigs, bound for South Georgia, are also brought aboard and give the deck the kind of barnyard appearance resented by officers and seamen alike. Finally, at 4 p.m., all is ready and the ships slip out of Choiseul Sound and into the open sea, where a few daring penguins flash in and out of the water beside them, like miniature torpedoes. As the Falkland Islands sink in their wake, the vessels begin to pitch and roll in the heavy sea and clouds of spray dash against the portholes and stream down their faces. With the light fading, the steward arrives to put up the blackout and soon the *Scoresby* and the *Fitzroy* are reduced to two slightly darker smudges upon the rolling blackness of the great Southern Ocean.

1

The Shadow & the Substance

In 1949 Winston Churchill wrote that 'The only thing that frightened me during the war was the U-boat peril'[1] – and no one doubted that his anxiety had been justified. Between 1939 and 1945, German submarines sank nearly 3,000 Allied merchant ships and, at the height of the war, they came within an ace of cutting the supply of raw materials and food that kept Britain fighting. However, the eventual dominance of the U-boats tends to overshadow the fact that, during the very early stages of the conflict, disguised surface raiders, or *Hilfskreuzers*, were thought to constitute just as much of a menace to Britain's supply routes as the fifty-seven U-boats operational in 1939. Between 1940 and 1942, the nine raiders sank a total of 142 Allied vessels and operated over a vast area of ocean stretching from the North Sea to the far South Atlantic. Like the most successful submariners, their commanders combined sound seamanship, great fighting skill, bravery and imagination, and they could expect to be highly decorated by a grateful Führer. Quite inadvertently, they also forged the vital first link in the chain of events that led to Operation Tabarin: the only Antarctic expedition to be launched by any of the combatant nations during the entire Second World War.

From the very outset, the British Admiralty understood the nature of the threat posed by the *Hilfskreuzers* and, determined to tackle it head-on, in 1939 it despatched the long-range *Odin*-class submarine HMS *Olympus* to the sub-Antarctic Indian Ocean. Her mission: to search the Prince Edward Islands and Crozet Island for signs of enemy activity, in particular the establishment of supply depots and fuel dumps. The landing parties from *Olympus* discovered nothing untoward – but the British action would soon prove to be premature rather than misdirected.

Just a few short months after *Olympus* returned to Ceylon at the end of her fruitless search, work began in the German shipbuilding port of

Bremen to convert the 7,900-ton Hansa Line freighter *Kandelfels* into a warship. Armed with six 150mm guns stripped from the obsolete battleship *Schlesien*, one 75mm gun, two 37mm anti-aircraft guns and four 20mm anti-aircraft cannon, the ship also carried 300 mines and two Heinkel 114B aircraft, making her more than capable of overwhelming any unsuspecting Allied merchantman that she might encounter. Given that the auxiliary cruiser's weapons were hidden in order to allay the suspicions of her victims – in much the same manner as the British Q-ships of both world wars – her commander, *Fregattenkapitän* Ernst-Felix Krüder, could also expect to close to devastating range before opening fire. Recommissioned on 2 June 1940, thirteen days later this wolf in sheep's clothing slipped down the River Weser and out into the North Sea to seek her prey. Her intended field of operations was indicated by her new name, *Pinguin*, and over the next ten months her richest hunting ground would be the South Atlantic, her victims the whale-catchers and factory ships of the British and Norwegian Antarctic whaling fleets.

Krüder had good reason to anticipate success. By the end of the nineteenth century, 300 years of intense hunting had all but exterminated the whale populations of the Northern Hemisphere. But the destruction of the whale stocks in the north had done nothing to engender a more rational, conservationist approach in the industry. Instead, recognising that their usual territory was becoming exhausted, the whalers looked for new worlds to conquer. The existence of large numbers of whales in southern seas – particularly Humpback, Fin and Blue whales – had been known for well over a century, having been remarked upon by Captain Cook during his second exploratory voyage of 1772–75, but the logistical difficulty of hunting in these cold and turbulent waters had been a major deterrent to exploitation. With the catastrophic depletion of northern stocks, the waters around the Falklands and those stretching southwards past South Georgia, the South Shetlands and the South Orkneys to the coast of Antarctica itself became the most bountiful whaling fisheries on the face of the globe – and they could no longer be ignored if the industry were to meet the voracious demand for whale products, including whalebone stays and oil for lighting, lubrication and the manufacture of soap.

The first serious attempt at whaling in Antarctic waters was made in 1873 by the German Antarctic Expedition under the command of the experienced Arctic whaler, Captain Eduard Dallmann. In his steamship, *Grönland*, Dallmann was able to harvest some fur and elephant seals, which were beginning to recover from uncontrolled hunting earlier in the century, but his vessel proved unable to match the speed of the larger whales. In the course of this expedition he discovered and named the Bismarck Strait, and the southern entrance to what was later named the Neumayer

Channel by Adrien de Gerlache. Despite his geographic discoveries, however, Dallmann's lack of kills discouraged other whalers from trying to exploit the region for another thirty years.

The next nation to send its whalers south was Norway and by the beginning of the twentieth century the introduction of small but swift steam-driven whale catchers, floating factories and explosive harpoons had made whaling in Antarctic waters an altogether more viable proposition. In December 1904, Captain Carl Anton Larsen built the first whaling station at Grytviken on the British-controlled island of South Georgia, and in no time at all the industry swung into full and bloody life. Within a year, the first floating factory sailed into Antarctic waters and, in less than a decade, a dozen such factories were operating in the region, acting as bases for far-ranging fleets of whale catchers.

In addition to the continuing demand for many of the traditional whale products, the onset of the First World War generated an unprecedented demand for glycerine, a vital component in the manufacture of munitions, and during the whaling season of 1915–16 no fewer than 11,792 whales were slaughtered, generating huge fortunes for the industry's leaders. Although the post-war recession witnessed a massive slump in the price of whale oil, the industry recovered rapidly in the thirties – a resurgence due in large part to increasingly efficient means of hunting and processing, including the invention of the 'whale claw' and the construction of purpose-built factory ships with their own slipways, which replaced the converted freighters and passenger ships previously used. Together, these innovations enabled the whalers to process entire carcasses while still at sea and catches grew ever more colossal. In the season of 1937–38, the industry attained its bloody zenith with some 46,000 whales slaughtered, producing around 3.3 million barrels of oil. It was upon the whale catchers and factory ships engaged in this highly profitable industry that Captain Krüder now focused his attention, turning the hunters into the hunted.

The *Pinguin*'s first engagement in sub-Antarctic waters took place on the night of 13 January 1941, when her prize crews boarded and captured six Norwegian vessels at approximately 57°45'S, 02°30'W. Having monitored the radio transmissions between the incautious whalers, Krüder knew their precise location and approached the factory ships *Solglimt* and *Ole Wegger* from the rear to avoid being spotted by the roving whale catchers, which normally worked ahead of their mother ships. Usually, raiders like *Pinguin* relied upon their innocuous appearance and the careful concealment of their guns to enable them to approach their prey. On this occasion a swirling snowstorm rendered her all but invisible, and Krüder closed to within point-blank range before he swept the decks of the Norwegian vessels with his powerful searchlights, at the same time announcing through his loudhailer that any attempt to use their radio transmitters would invite a devastating fusillade. Caught completely by surprise, the Norwegian skippers had no option but to surrender and within 25 minutes the German prize crews signalled that they had both *Solglimt* and *Ole Wegger* in their hands. Within hours, *Pinguin* added another Norwegian factory ship, *Pelagos*, and seven whale catchers to her tally. The only significant prize to escape was the factory ship *Thorshammer* – but Krüder knew from his radio intercepts that *Thorshammer* had already transferred most of her processed whale oil and some of her bunker fuel to *Pelagos* and *Ole Wegger*, so he decided against pursuit. Between them, *Solglimt*, *Pelagos* and *Ole Wegger* carried a total of 20,230 tons of whale oil, making Krüder's haul the most valuable prize captured by German raiders during the war.

News of the disaster, which first reached the British authorities via a whale catcher despatched to Grytviken by Captain Einor Torp of *Thorshammer*, raised a storm of criticism about the administration of the whaling industry. In particular, it soon came to light that the sailing of the Norwegian fleet at the start of the season had not even been kept secret, its departure being announced – much to the dismay of the whaling managers themselves – during a broadcast in Norwegian from an American radio station. To further compound this criminal lack of caution, the Norwegian whaling expeditions were both unarmed and unescorted by warships. As far as the British Admiralty was concerned, it argued that the collapse of France left Britain standing alone and in need of every gun she possessed in home waters to counteract the threat of invasion. If Norway preferred to commit her defenceless ships to whaling rather than submit them to the risks of freight carrying in the North Atlantic, where they would at least have the protection of British escorts, the responsibility was hers alone. In fact, after *Pinguin*'s raid, the Norwegians would not feel confident enough to despatch another whaling expedition to the Antarctic until January 1944, the month when the vessels of Operation Tabarin headed south from Stanley.

Whatever the Admiralty's opinions might be regarding the protection of the Norwegians, the Naval Officer in Charge in the Falklands could not afford to take any risks with the British whalers. A week after the attack, the 22,500-ton armed merchant cruiser *Queen of Bermuda* sailed from Stanley: her orders, in the words of one crew member, 'to go down south and find out what was what'.[2] As he began patrolling the area between South Georgia, the South Shetland Islands and the Weddell Sea, Captain Geoffrey Hawkins could be confident that his vessel's six 150mm, one 75mm, two 37mm, four 20mm guns and four 533mm torpedo tubes should make her more than a match for any raider. He immediately established contact with the British-chartered factory ships *Southern Empress*,

Svend Foyn II and *Lancing* – which were instructed to add an extra month to their 1940–41 whaling season to compensate for the loss of the captured cargo – and also extended his protection to the lonely *Thorshammer*.

On 1 March, Hawkins received orders to extend his operations still further and on the 5th *Queen of Bermuda* visited Deception Island in the South Shetlands to establish whether the abandoned Norwegian whaling station showed any signs of having been used as a base by German raiders. The shore party found the volcanic island and the derelict whaling factory desolate. To further reduce the military potential of the site, they set fire to a large heap of coal, ruptured the oil storage tanks, severed the supply and discharge pipes serving the tanks, and partly dismantled the abandoned whaling factory buildings. Her demolition work completed, *Queen of Bermuda* returned to protection duties for a further month before accompanying *Thorshammer, Southern Express* and *Svend Foyn II* to Freetown at the beginning of April.

Despite the absence of any signs of German activity on the Prince Edward Islands and Crozet Island in 1939, or on Deception Island in 1941, the Admiralty was right to think that the Germans were using island bases to support their raiders. The *Kriegsmarine* had actually located its supply base in an obscure *fjord* in Kerguelen Island in the southern Indian Ocean, and between 1940 and 1941 it replenished the bunkers and galleys of both *Pinguin* and the most successful German raider of the entire war, *Atlantis*, which had operated off the coast of Sumatra before proceeding into the Southern Ocean. Later in 1941, intelligence reports prompted HMAS *Australia* to mine four suspected anchorages in order to restrict German activity in the region. Consequently, the *Kriegsmarine* abandoned its plans to set up a permanently manned weather station on Kerguelen Island, where, even to this day, some of the mines laid by *Australia* present a hazard to shipping.

As for *Pinguin*, her career came to an abrupt end on 8 May 1941 when the *County*-class heavy cruiser HMS *Cornwall* engaged her near the Seychelles. Despite a gallant defence, *Pinguin* proved no match for a British warship nearly twice her size. At about 5.45 p.m., after a 27-minute engagement, a four-gun salvo from *Cornwall's* 8in forward turrets tore the German ship apart, one of the few survivors remembering that 'the after part of the *Pinguin* was suddenly transformed into a fire-spitting volcano.'[3] An 8in shell had landed among the 130 mines that Krüder had intended to lay in the approaches to Karachi and their simultaneous detonation blew the ship to smithereens. The wreck took just five seconds to sink and she took with her Krüder and 340 members of his crew. Tragically, just moments before the British shells struck, Krüder had ordered the release of 238 prisoners taken from his prizes and all but twenty-four were lost. Of the German crew, only sixty-one survived: four officers and fifty-seven other ranks. During her 357 days at sea, *Pinguin* had sailed some 59,000 miles, more than twice the circumference of the Earth, and she had captured or sunk thirty-two ships, totalling some 154,710 tons.

Pinguin's cruise had more than justified British anxieties regarding enemy activity in the waters of the far south. These anxieties would be heightened still further by the Japanese attacks on Pearl Harbor, the Philippines, Burma and Malaya between December 1941 and January 1942. In particular, the newly appointed Chief of the Imperial General Staff, General Sir Alan Brooke, feared that a Japanese invasion of the Falkland Islands would have disastrous consequences for Allied shipping, as any naval force based on the islands would be able to harry the convoys passing round Cape Horn or seeking to enter the mouth of the River Plate. As one naval officer connected with Operation Tabarin would later remark: 'It is not coincidence that in the first three months of both world wars the South Atlantic squadron fought decisive battles in this very area.'[4]

With hindsight, the idea of a Japanese amphibious assault on the Falklands might seem incredible – but then, on the evening of 6 December 1941, the thought of the Japanese bombing the US Pacific Fleet in Pearl Harbor seemed no less fantastic. With the Falkland Islands defended by a force of just 330 indigenous volunteers with virtually no weapons, consideration of how to bolster their defences became a matter of urgency. In a 'Most Secret' cipher dated 23 March 1942, the Admiralty advised British officials in Washington that 'We view with concern the practically defenceless state of the Falkland Islands.'[5] Given that the impact upon American shipping would be at least as severe as that upon British convoys supplying the Middle East and India, the officials were then asked to:

> ... discuss question of these Islands with US Chiefs of Staff. If they consider the islands should be adequately defended, you should say that we are unable to find or transfer the forces at present but would welcome anything they can do in this respect although we are reluctant to ask US to accept additional burden of defence of British territory.[6]

Not surprisingly, despite the strategic value of the islands, the American response to this plea for them to take over responsibility for the defence of a British overseas territory was lukewarm at best. Even at this stage in the war, America was making it clear that it had no interest in maintaining what the influential American commentator Walter Lipmann called the 'archaic privilege' of empire.[7]

Having previously been advised that it would be impracticable to transfer Commonwealth troops from other theatres in order to defend the Falklands, Churchill had endorsed the approach to the United States. When this was rebuffed, he remained convinced that something must still be done – no matter what the logistical difficulties. On 1 April, he wrote to General 'Pug' Ismay and the Chiefs of Staff Committee:

> It would be a very serious thing to lose the Falkland Islands to the Japanese and no comfort to say that it would hurt the United States more than ourselves ... The islands are a British Possession and responsibility. Hitherto I was told there was no shipping and that it would be much easier for the United States to reinforce them than for us. It is clear this is not so.
>
> In these circumstances a British Battalion should certainly be found, but let me know first how this could be done and what dislocation it involves.
>
> The Falkland Islands are very well known, and their loss would be a shock to the whole Empire. They would certainly have to be retaken. The object of the reinforcement would be to make it necessary for the Japanese to extend their attacking force to a tangible size. This might well act as a deterrent.[8]

From the very beginning of the war, Britain had feared the repercussions of enemy activity in high latitudes. By the spring of 1942 the depredations of the German raiders and the potential for a Japanese invasion of the Falklands had served to turn the eyes not only of the Admiralty but also of the Prime Minister himself to the far southern reaches of the globe. Not surprisingly, Churchill's attention would swiftly be diverted to other theatres, most notably in Russia and North Africa, but in some departments at least the defence of the Falkland Islands and their dependencies would retain its significance. In the minds of the individuals concerned, however, the real nature of the threat to British interests in the region was very different from that which had exercised Churchill, Brooke and the Admiralty. The aggressor, they feared, was not Germany or Japan, but neutral Argentina.

Although she could trace her active engagement in the region back to the 'Heroic Age' of Antarctic exploration (*c.* 1895–1917), Argentina had played only a very limited part in the flurry of activity that followed the influential Sixth International Geographical Congress of 1895. She had launched only two brief Antarctic missions: the first to aid the missing Swedish explorer, Otto Nordenskjöld, in 1903; and the second to ascertain the whereabouts of the Frenchman, Jean-Baptiste Charcot, in 1904 – but she had undertaken no exploratory activity on her own account. Ironically, therefore, her territorial claims were based in large part not upon discovery but upon decisions taken in isolation by a British explorer and a British diplomat at the very beginning of the twentieth century.

The explorer was Dr William Speirs Bruce, leader of the Scottish National Antarctic Expedition. In November 1903 Bruce had established a meteorological station on Laurie Island in the South Orkneys. Keen to ensure that his station would be permanently manned, but lacking any government funding, on landing at Buenos Aires he suggested to the resident British Minister, William Haggard, that he should transfer the station to the Argentine government. Although Bruce himself seemed 'not to have made up his mind whether they [the South Orkneys] were likely to be of any use whatever to Great Britain or no',[9] Haggard saw no reason to block the proposal and he passed it on to the Argentine authorities on 29 December. Within days the Argentines accepted the offer, publishing a Presidential Decree to that effect on 2 January 1904. The British Foreign Secretary, Lord Lansdowne, then gave official sanction to Haggard's actions on 26 April. The Argentine government stopped short of formally annexing the South Orkneys – a policy strongly advocated by elements of the local press – and the Presidential Decree referred only to taking over 'the installation offered by Mr William S. Bruce',[10] but its officials did nominate one member of the newly appointed meteorological party, Hugo Acuña, as postmaster. This appointment clearly implied the assumption of territorial rights. On 22 February, with the members of Bruce's expedition in attendance, the British flag was lowered on Laurie Island and the Argentine raised in its stead, and when Bruce's *Scotia* sailed for the Weddell Sea she carried with her mail bearing the Argentine postmark 'Orcades del Sud, Distrito Rio Gallegos'.[11]

The actions of Bruce and Haggard did not run counter to well-established British policy towards the Antarctic. Although Britain could legitimately claim rights to the South Sandwich Islands, the South Orkneys, the South Shetlands and the Graham Land Peninsula through their discovery by British sailors at the end of the eighteenth century and in the first half of the nineteenth, for decades she had exhibited very little interest in these barren and seemingly unprofitable lumps of rock. Each of the newly discovered islands had been claimed for the Crown by their discoverers, including James Cook, William Smith, Edward Bransfield, John Biscoe, James Clark Ross and George Powell, but no further action was taken. This casual attitude began to change only when Captain Carl Larsen and his fellow whalers began to harvest the immense riches of the southern seas. Although Larsen initially set up Compañía Argentina de Pesca with the backing of an Argentine bank, the canny Norwegian quickly demonstrated that he would deal with whichever country seemed best able to offer security to his enterprise, and by the beginning of 1906 he had formally applied for a lease of land on South Georgia from the

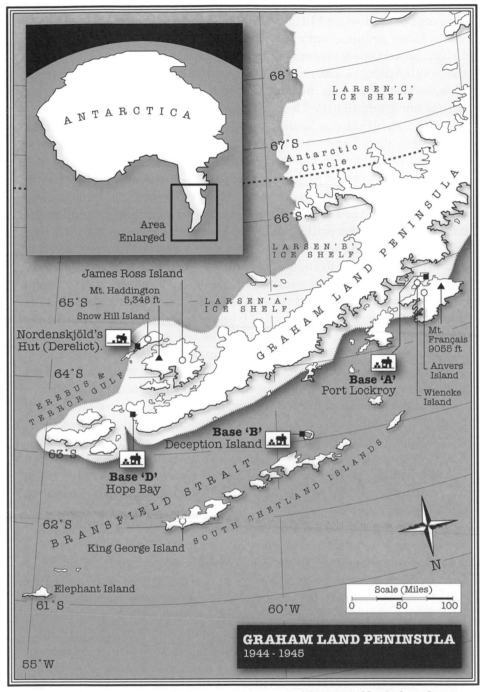

ANTARCTICA

Area Enlarged

68°S

LARSEN 'C' ICE SHELF

67°S

Antarctic Circle

66°S

LARSEN 'B' ICE SHELF

James Ross Island

Mt. Haddington 5,348 ft

LARSEN 'A' ICE SHELF

65°S

Snow Hill Island

GRAHAM LAND PENINSULA

Nordenskjöld's Hut (Derelict).

Mt. Français 9055 ft

64°S

EREBUS & TERROR GULF

Anvers Island

Base 'A' Port Lockroy

Wiencke Island

63°S

Base 'B' Deception Island

Base 'D' Hope Bay

BRANSFIELD STRAIT

SOUTH SHETLAND ISLANDS

62°S

King George Island

N

Elephant Island

61°S

60°W

Scale (Miles)

0   50   100

55°W

GRAHAM LAND PENINSULA
1944 - 1945

Map created by Andrew Stevenson

governor of the Falkland Islands, William Allardyce. With the potential for vast whaling revenues rapidly becoming evident, on 21 July 1908 Great Britain issued Letters Patent in which she asserted that all lands 'situated in the South Atlantic Ocean to the south of the 50th Parallel of South latitude, and lying between the 20th and 80th degrees of West longitude, are part of our Dominions.'[12] These territories included the South Orkneys, the South Shetlands, the South Sandwich Islands, South Georgia and the whole of Graham Land.

The Argentine government had protested British control of the Falkland Islands since 1834, but it passed no comment on the Letters Patent relating to the Falkland Islands Dependencies. Despite this apparent oversight, and possibly as a result of a substantial increase in British activity relating to the administration of the whaling industry, over the ensuing decades the attitude of successive Argentine administrations hardened. This culminated in a claim made in 1927 to the International Bureau of the Universal Postal Union that Argentina's overseas territories included the South Orkneys – where she had maintained year-round occupancy since 1904 – and the South Shetlands, as well as the Falkland Islands themselves. The British government found it extraordinarily difficult to identify a clear and coherent policy to adopt in response to such assertions: on the one hand, the existence of a large British population in Argentina and significant levels of British investment in the country made it reluctant to antagonise unnecessarily. On the other, it needed to maintain its claim to territories which were now far from being profitless; more broadly, any failure to defend its rights could have had profound implications for other parts of the Empire. The policy ultimately adopted was to simply ignore the issue and maintain cordial relations. In the words of the best recent commentary, 'the British response to Argentina's incursions in the island dependencies remained one of letting "sleeping dogs lie".'[13]

With the onset of war, matters went a stage further and bluster at last gave way to action. In 1938, Norway invited both Argentina and Chile to send their representatives to an international polar congress planned for 1940 in Bergen. Although war prevented the congress from taking place, Argentina had started to prepare by setting up a *comisión provisional* tasked with articulating the extent and basis of her Antarctic claims. Not surprisingly, the strongest prop underpinning her argument was Argentina's position as 'the only country in the world which maintains a permanent observatory in the Antarctic regions'.[14] Thus, Dr Bruce's plan to ensure the continuance of his scientific observations in the absence of government funding eventually became the single most powerful element of Argentina's claim to sovereignty over Antarctic territory. 'Had he lived longer,' writes Bruce's biographer, 'Bruce would have been surprised and perhaps amused to see the geo-political consequences of his actions, made in good faith and all in the name of science.'[15]

As a direct result of the work of the Argentine commission – which became the permanent *Comisión Nacional del Antártico* on 30 May 1940 – and no doubt influenced by the course of the war, which unmistakably was going Germany's way, the Argentine government at last decided to stake its claim with something more tangible than words. Accordingly, in January 1942, the naval transport ship, *Primero de Mayo*, sailed from Buenos Aires under the command of *Capitán de Fragata* Alberto J. Oddera. After landing on Deception Island on 8 February, Oddera sailed down the Gerlache Strait and visited the Melchior Islands in the Palmer Archipelago and Winter Island. He surveyed some of the islands and ordered the erection of a navigation beacon on shore. Ice conditions made it impossible to visit Marguerite Bay as planned and so *Primero de Mayo* turned north and reached Buenos Aires towards the end of February. At each of the landings, the Argentine sailors raised their national flag and, in conspicuous places, left notes announcing that Argentina had taken possession of all land south of 60°S and lying between longitudes 25°W and 68°34'W. The following year, *Primero de Mayo* returned under *Capitán de Fragata* Silvano Harriague. On this occasion, the Argentines completed a survey of Melchior Harbour before sailing to Port Lockroy and to Marguerite Bay. They paid another visit to the abandoned facilities of the Hektor Whaling Company on Deception Island and *Primero de Mayo* then returned home.

Learning of the provocative first voyage of *Primero de Mayo*, British officials agonised, in typical fashion, over how they should respond. It very soon became clear, however, that if British claims in the region were to be maintained, 'sitting on the fence' was no longer an option. Perhaps the most influential voice in the debate was that of W. Beckett, a legal adviser to the Foreign Office who opined that, when asserting territorial claims and, in particular, when disputing the claims of other nations, 'the greatest weight is attached to actual physical occupation and use ... If we want to make sure of our title to these islands we must establish something permanently there ourselves, difficult and tiresome as it may be.'[16] Prior to Beckett's memorandum, most officials had favoured a formal protest to the Argentine government; given the supine attitude of previous administrations – engendered in large part by the Foreign Office's reluctance to weaken Britain's cultural and economic relationship with Argentina – it is not surprising that none had supported the idea of physical intervention. Fully appreciating that a robust stance on the issue of the dependencies would send a very clear signal regarding Britain's intention to defend its occupation of the far more important Falkland Islands, their forward-looking governor, Sir Allan Cardinall, welcomed Beckett's advice and suggested that members of his staff should visit the dependencies, courtesy of the Royal Navy. Even more important, the Foreign Secretary, Sir Anthony Eden, also dismissed the idea of relying solely upon protests, noting that 'if we want to keep them [the dependencies] we are not likely to do so by these means'.[17]

Following Eden's intervention, an interdepartmental meeting conceded that, if Britain's claims in the region were to be maintained, it might now be necessary to establish 'permanent, or semi-permanent, settlements in both the South Orkneys and the South Shetlands'.[18] Given that such action could prompt further, and more aggressive, action from Argentina, consideration must be given to whether the potential gains justified the risks involved. The Foreign Office very much doubted it, being particularly concerned that a catastrophic decline in Anglo-Argentine relations could jeopardise the substantial imports of beef from South America. For its part, at the beginning of the century, and in peacetime, the Admiralty had confirmed that, so far as the South Orkneys were concerned, it did not 'attach any importance to the possession of these islands from a Naval point of view'.[19] Having fought the disastrous Battle of Coronel and the victorious Battle of the Falkland Islands during the First World War, and the equally successful Battle of the River Plate in 1939, by the early 1940s the Admiralty was no longer under any illusions regarding the strategic importance of the South Atlantic island groups. This awareness had been further reinforced by the depredations of *Pinguin* and other commerce raiders during 1941. However, while Britain's military interests might still be compromised if a pro-Axis state gained undisputed control of the southern side of Drake Passage, by early 1943 the immediate military threat was considered to be largely extinct. The majority of commerce raiders had been destroyed and, the suspected activity on Kerguelen Island apart, visiting British warships had found no evidence that they had ever used the sub-Antarctic islands for refuelling or repair. This being the case, some – though not all – Admiralty officials considered that there were 'better employments for HM ships in wartime than to visit a distant dependency in order to counter a fictitious claim to that territory by a neutral South American Republic'.[20]

The Colonial Office argued strongly to the contrary. Critically, its officials also realised that, with their wreckage safely mouldering on the ocean floor, *Pinguin* and her sisters could actually be used to serve British interests. In particular, given her lukewarm attitude towards a post-war British Empire, one official suggested that the United States could be told that any British personnel in the area:

> … were there as observers to report the presence of enemy raiders, and mention that at least one had been seen in these waters in recent months

... At the same time, it will provide a useful shield against any Argentine annoyance that may be provoked by our acts. They may get sympathy if they protest against our 'imperialistic designs on their territory', but hardly at British attempts to further 'hemispheric defence'![21]

Two months later, as *Primero de Mayo* prosecuted her second incursion, exactly the same strategy was discussed at a meeting of the War Cabinet chaired by the Deputy Prime Minister, Clement Attlee:

Whilst we hold a title to the Islands [South Orkneys and South Shetlands] by discovery, we have never been in effective occupation and Argentine Government include Islands in their general Antarctic claims and have recently taken various steps to strengthen their claim. An Argentine naval transport, with Chilean naval officers on board, is at present en route to the Islands.

Both Admiralty and Colonial Office attach importance to maintenance of our title to the Islands and prevention of further Argentine encroachments. Foreign Office considers present moment propitious for taking action in view of Argentina's political isolation. It is felt that in default of action now by us situation may arise in which it would be impossible to dislodge Argentina except by force ... [This action] will be described, in reply to any enquiries, as a search for traces of enemy raiders. It is further proposed that permanent occupation should be established next year on all Islands except probably Laurie Island.[22]

The raiders thus became an excuse for an operation actually designed to extract a thorn that had been irritating British flesh since long before the war. Had he lived, the irony would surely not have been lost on Ernst-Felix Krüder.

The action decided upon by the War Cabinet on 28 January was the immediate despatch of the armed merchant cruiser HMS *Carnarvon Castle* to Deception Island. The US Navy was informed of the 'impending tour as a matter of naval routine'[23] but, lacking confidence in the impenetrability of its own ruse, the British government also chose quite deliberately not to tell the State Department of *Carnarvon Castle*'s cruise. Originally a passenger liner of the Union Castle Line, the 20,000-ton *Carnarvon Castle* had been converted to an armed merchant cruiser in Simonstown, South Africa, in September 1939. She had then spent much of her time in the South Atlantic where, on 5 December 1940, she had engaged the 9,200-ton German commerce raider *Thor* 700 miles east of Montevideo. Badly damaged in the encounter, and with thirty-four casualties on board, *Carnarvon Castle* had disengaged and limped to Montevideo, where repairs were effected using steel plate stripped from the scuttled *Graf Spee*. Now under the command of Captain Edward Wollaston Kitson, *Carnarvon Castle* was ordered to proceed to Deception Island where her officers discovered the copper cylinder left by *Primero de Mayo*. In line with British government policy, the landing party obliterated all marks of foreign sovereignty; they hoisted the Union flag and erected four 'British Crown Land' signs at conspicuous points. *Carnarvon Castle* then sailed to Signy Island in the South Orkneys, where the same protocols were followed, before finally making a cordial visit to the Argentine meteorological station on Laurie Island. There, Kitson and his officers again promulgated the fiction of a search for German raiders, but they fooled no one and a month later *Primero de Mayo* returned to Deception Island to destroy the British marks and replace them with those of Argentina.

Clearly this game of tit-for-tat could be played for years without either side gaining the upper hand. As Beckett had articulated in September 1942, possession being nine tenths of the law, the only truly decisive action would be to physically occupy at least some of the dependencies. This requirement was again acknowledged at another interdepartmental meeting on 27 May 1943, and planning for the occupation of the Falkland Islands Dependencies began at last. Although, in the words of one participant, the 'original idea was to send just a party of soldiers … just to sit somewhere in the Antarctic to occupy the place – and that was that',[24] more ambitious objectives soon began to be debated. An Expedition Committee was formed comprising members from the Colonial Office, the Ministry of War Transport, the Foreign Office, the Treasury, the Crown Agents, the *Discovery* Committee and the Admiralty, but the real motive power for the planned expedition came from a trio of highly experienced polar veterans: James Wordie, Neil Mackintosh and Brian Roberts.

Best known for his part in Sir Ernest Shackleton's Imperial Trans-Antarctic Expedition of 1914–17, Wordie's harrowing experiences during the drift of the *Endurance* and on Elephant Island had done nothing to curb his enthusiasm for all things polar. Between 1919 and 1937 he had led no fewer than seven small-scale expeditions to the Arctic and, with fellow Heroic Age veterans Frank Debenham and Raymond Priestley, he had founded the hugely influential Scott Polar Research Institute in Cambridge. Despite being a dour Glaswegian with a reputation for 'great reserve and few words',[25] Wordie had also assumed the role of mentor to a whole generation of aspiring Arctic and Antarctic explorers including, most notably, Gino Watkins, John Rymill and Vivian Fuchs. For his part, as zoologist on the National Oceanographic Expedition of 1925–27, Mackintosh had spent two years studying the dismembered remains of more than 1,600 whales on the bloody 'plans' of the Grytviken and Saldanha Bay whaling stations, becoming in the process one of the great authorities on the life of the Southern Ocean in general and the reproductive cycle of the whale in particular. From 1936 he had been Director of the *Discovery* Investigations, in overall control of the Antarctic research vessels, *Discovery II* and *William Scoresby*. The third member of the triumvirate, Roberts, had served as ornithologist on Rymill's British Graham Land Expedition (BGLE) of 1934–37. From the beginning of the war, he had been involved in research on cold-climate clothing and equipment for the Intelligence Department of the Admiralty and, working with Wordie, he had helped to produce around thirty separate volumes of the so-called 'Blue Books' on cold-climate topics, including geographical handbooks on Iceland, Spitsbergen and Greenland. Although he would not be co-opted onto the Expedition Committee until February 1944, Roberts worked with Wordie on Operation Tabarin from its inception; indeed, he was eventually sacked from his work on the Blue Books because of his willingness to be so diverted without the prior agreement of his boss, H.C. Darby. According to Vivian Fuchs, who rose to become Director of the Falkland Islands Dependencies Survey (FIDS) in 1959 and knew each of them personally, together 'these three were to preside like benign paladins over the general planning and organisation.'[26]

All three shared a keen interest in bolstering British influence in a region which, to their minds, had been sadly neglected for most of the period since the end of the Heroic Age. They were also very quick to appreciate 'that bases established for political reasons could also provide platforms for scientific work'[27] and, from the very outset, they did everything possible to ensure that Operation Tabarin would evolve into a semi-permanent arrangement, incorporating systematic exploration. As early as August 1943, Roberts was discussing the need for Nansen sledges and surveying equipment – items that would hardly be needed if the expedition were to remain a static operation designed solely to reaffirm territorial rights. Put simply, the opportunity to undertake a proper study of the Antarctic Peninsula was just too good to miss. Under the terms of the initial plan, two bases would be established: the first on Deception Island, the second in the vicinity of Hope Bay on the northern tip of the mainland. Naturally, the men on the mainland would enjoy the wider field of operations and their objectives included a journey down the east coast of Graham Land, thereby extending the survey work completed by the BGLE. Both bases would be equipped to send meteorological reports to Stanley and a detailed scientific programme including geology, glaciology, botany, zoology and studies of tidal movements and sea ice was devised by Mackintosh. Depending on the course of the war – and upon the availability of funding – additional bases might be established and the scientific programme expanded still further at a later date.

Initially, the mission as a whole was called 'Operation Bransfield', but, since Edward Bransfield was credited with being the first man ever to set eyes on the Antarctic mainland, this name blatantly failed to comply with the instruction that a mission's code name should bear absolutely no relation to its objective. It also seemed to refute Churchill's assertion that 'Intelligent thought will readily supply an unlimited number of well-sounding names that do not suggest the character of the operation.'[28] As an alternative, Roberts and John Mossop of the Admiralty then suggested 'Operation Tabarin' – and the name stuck. According to Roberts, this name was derived from the 'Bal Tabarin', a nightclub in Paris, 'because we had had to do a lot of night work and the organisation was always so chaotic just as the club and hence the origin of its name.'[29] However, Roberts may also have been influenced, perhaps subconsciously, by an earlier use of the name Tabarin in a polar context. In 1935, Sandy Glen had led the Oxford University Expedition to North East Land in the Spitsbergen Archipelago. In his official account of the expedition, published in 1937, Glen described his winter quarters in memorable terms:

> The ceiling was hung with clothes of every kind and description, windproofs, silk pyjamas, skiing stockings, a sheepskin coat and red-checked shirts, and even a pair of scarlet beach-trousers. They added an impression of gaiety which was charmingly Bohemian; with the gramophone and an imaginary addition of a girl, it might have been a Parisian tabarin.[30]

Although Glen was part of the Oxford polar circle, and Roberts belonged to that of Cambridge, the two groups were far from being mutually exclusive and both Roberts and Wordie had been involved in the Oxford University Exploration Society. Roberts had almost certainly read Glen's book, and its light-hearted picture of living conditions in an expedition hut obviously struck a chord.[31] Given that the real objectives of Operation Tabarin were hidden behind a 'search for traces of enemy raiders', it is also interesting to note that the root of the word *tabarin* is *tabard*, meaning 'little cloak'. This suggests that the name may even have been a rather esoteric hint that the mission's avowed aims 'cloaked' an ulterior motive. Though rather more opaque in meaning than 'Bransfield', 'Tabarin' still broke the rules regulating the selection of code names – but Roberts would not be the last wartime planner to enjoy a somewhat indiscreet in-joke when selecting the name for his pet project.

As well as deciding upon the scope and the name of the expedition, the Expedition Committee also had to identify a suitable leader.

The man eventually chosen was Lieutenant James William Slessor Marr, RNVR. By any standards, Marr's career had been extraordinary – and the vast majority of it had been spent in the field. Born in the village of Cushnie in Aberdeenshire on 9 December 1902, he had studied classics and zoology at the University of Aberdeen and it was while a student that he had been selected from thousands of volunteer Boy Scouts to accompany Shackleton's *Quest* Expedition of 1921–22. After Shackleton's death on 5 January 1922, the expedition failed to reach its most southerly objectives in the Weddell Sea, but it still completed varied work on and around South Georgia, Elephant Island, Gough Island, Tristan da Cunha and St Paul's Rocks. Marr returned from this formative experience to complete his MA in classics and his BSc in zoology, but his studies were interrupted by a series of public appearances designed to repay the debts of the expedition. These involved standing in his Scout uniform outside cinemas where the *Quest* film was being shown and, after each performance, making speeches in order to charm the pounds, shillings and pence from his audiences' pockets. Although he loathed this begging and found it difficult to live down the 'Scout Marr' label and the embarrassing photographs of a full-grown man in shorts, Baden-Powell hat, neckerchief and woggle, these activities did at least introduce him to the fundraising issues inseparable from polar exploration.

During the summer of 1925, Marr took part in the British Arctic Expedition organised and led by Grettir Algarsson and Frank Worsley of *Endurance* fame. Originally, they planned to fly to the North Pole in an airship but when this proved too costly, with unassailable sangfroid they adjusted their programme and decided instead to sail north in an ancient brigantine named *Island*. Once again, in the interests of fundraising, Marr donned his Scout uniform and found himself in the unenviable position of door-knocking through the streets of Liverpool. 'Perfectly inoffensive parsons and genial bishops were led astray,' Worsley recalled with a chuckle, '… At our approach philanthropists, prosperous merchants, brewers, bakers, publicans, and even taxi-drivers fled in all directions.'[32] By the time *Island* sailed, Marr was 22 years old, heavily built, dark and 'with a dour Scots face – like a prize fighter'.[33] He was also physically strong and an accomplished sailor; indeed, Worsley described him as 'our champion at stowing any sail, square or fore and aft, in the ship',[34] and Worsley was no mean judge of a man's sailing abilities. Unsurprisingly, the expedition achieved little except some minor corrections to the charts of the area between Nordaustlandet and Kvitoya. Of his zoological investigations, Marr wrote that they were 'unfortunately, not of a very serious nature. I was utterly new to the game, lack of experience and the conditions under which we worked permitted only of dabbling and, owing to shortage of funds, we had been able to secure only a partial scientific equipment.'[35] Nonetheless, the expedition added to his growing stock of experience; it enabled him to further hone his skills in handling those essential tools of the marine zoologist, the tow-net and dredge, and it gave him the opportunity to describe the plants of West Spitzbergen, Northeast Land and Franz Joseph Land.

In 1927, after a year as Carnegie Scholar at the marine laboratory in Aberdeen, during which he worked up his findings for publication, Marr joined the staff of the *Discovery* Investigations under Dr Stanley Kemp. The forerunner of the *Discovery* Investigations had been formed in 1917 with the specific purpose of advising the Secretary of State for the Colonies on the means by which the economic viability of the Falkland Islands might be sustained, with particular regard to the preservation of the whaling industry. The wholesale slaughter of the whale population had made it abundantly clear to a British government keen to assert its rights in a non-confrontational fashion that controls on whaling must be imposed if the whale, and by implication the revenue-generating whaling industry, were not to be driven to extinction. New laws must be introduced, but to maximise their effectiveness they should be based upon an exact understanding of the whale's lifecycle: of its patterns of migration, feeding and breeding. Such knowledge could only be gained by a properly funded oceanographic research expedition manned by scientists and provided with the latest equipment. These considerations gave rise to the National Oceanographic Expedition of 1925–27, which formed the first part of the long running *Discovery* Investigations, so named because the ship employed for the first two seasons was Scott's veteran expedition ship, *Discovery*.

In the service of the Investigations, Marr took part in three voyages into Antarctic waters: on board the *William Scoresby*, the expedition's subsidiary vessel used for whale marking, from 1928 to 1929; and on *Discovery II*, the purpose-built, steel-hulled replacement for the old *Discovery*, between 1931 and 1933 and from 1935 to 1937. He spent most of his time working on board in the extremely harsh conditions of the Southern Ocean, but during the summer months he also undertook surveys and made biological collections on South Georgia, the South Orkney Islands and South Shetland Islands. His oceanographical work involved a series of long voyages, undertaking multiple 'stations' between the pack ice and the ports of the Falkland Islands, South Africa, Australia and New Zealand. He made extensive collections and, in the process, he not only impressed many of his colleagues – including Neil Mackintosh – with his stoicism and endurance, but also became a leading authority on the collection and preservation of marine animals.

In addition, between his voyage on the *Scoresby* and his first on
Discovery II, Marr had volunteered for the British Australian New Zealand
Antarctic Research Expedition (BANZARE) under the Heroic Age polar
explorer Sir Douglas Mawson. During this expedition MacRobertson
Land, the Banzare Coast and Princess Elizabeth Land were all discovered
and claimed for the Crown by Mawson. The expedition also visited
Crozet Island, Kerguelen Island, Heard Island and Macquarie Island,
adding much to the knowledge of these sub-Antarctic islands. Finally,
between 1939 and 1940, Marr made a further southern voyage in the
whale factory ship *Tede Viken*, this time seconded by the Department of
Scientific and Industrial Research in order to investigate the possible use
of canned or frozen whale meat to augment depleted British wartime
stocks of food. After the whaling expedition he joined the Royal Navy
Volunteer Reserve and served, sometimes on shore stations but latterly
on a minelayer, in Scotland, Iceland, South Africa and Ceylon. Receiving
an urgent recall to London in August 1943 he flew home and presented
himself for interview by a panel of senior naval officers. They explained
the nature and purpose of the expedition and concluded the interview
by offering Marr command of Operation Tabarin, with a promise
of promotion to Lieutenant Commander with immediate effect. He
accepted on the spot. As one contemporary wryly remarked, 'A return to
the south was an altogether more congenial prospect than mine-laying in
the tropics.'[36]

Marr had spent almost his entire adult life at sea, often working in
the most extreme conditions on the cold, wet, windswept decks of
polar research vessels. The somewhat gawky, earnest Boy Scout who had
accompanied Shackleton on the *Quest* was now over 40, balding, bespectacled and deeply lined but with the coveted white ribbon of the Polar
Medal on his breast. A respected field scientist, he had made important
contributions to the published papers of the *Discovery* Investigations,
including a memorable history of the South Orkneys; he was also working on a *Natural History and Geography of the Antarctic Krill*,[37] which would
go on to become, and remain, a definitive work. But the weather-beaten
savant had a lighter side: he retained a pawky sense of humour, enjoyed
inventing jingles, playing his harmonica at barroom sing-songs and performing comic turns to round off an evening's entertainment. He also
drank hard and routinely handed his guests a brimming tumbler of gin
with the toast, uttered in sepulchral tones, 'Let us now mortify the flesh.'[38]

In some ways, the weeks after his arrival in London would prove to
be the most demanding of Marr's entire career. With a fresh half-stripe
stitched onto each sleeve – the new rank of Lieutenant Commander was
designed, in part at least, to confer additional *gravitas* should he have to

confront the Argentine military – he now faced the challenge of recruiting the staff for two bases, finding and procuring all the equipment and supplies for a protracted stay in the Antarctic, and locating a ship capable of transporting the entire expedition to its destination. All this had to be achieved in time for the expedition to establish itself before the end of the austral summer of 1943–44. This would be hugely difficult at the best of times; during a world war it might well prove impossible.

The first task was to find a ship. Flying to Iceland, Marr inspected a Norwegian sealer named *Veslekari*. Built in 1918, she had spent most of her career hunting in the ice-bound waters around Spitzbergen, but she had also been chartered by the American Arctic explorer Louise A. Boyd on four occasions and had been involved in the search for Roald Amundsen when his flying boat crashed in the waters around Bjørnøya in 1928. Since 1940 she had been employed by the Ministry of War Transport. With bows strengthened to withstand the pack and growlers in Arctic waters, a black tarred hull, two masts, ketch-rigged, and auxiliary coal-burning engines, *Veslekari* bore a close resemblance to Shackleton's *Quest* and was one of the largest Norwegian sealers afloat. On cursory inspection, she seemed ideal for the task in hand and, with the authority of the Admiralty behind him, Marr commandeered her and ordered her to London. Once there, work began on a refit and the tired old sealer was also dignified with a new name: HMS *Bransfield*.

Next, Marr must choose the men to accompany him: in theory, all would be volunteers and none would be coerced into becoming Antarctic explorers. While the secrecy of the expedition made it impossible for him to employ the tried-and-tested method of advertising for recruits in the daily newspapers, Marr did enjoy the advantage of knowing many of the more experienced candidates. Moreover, although the exigencies of war had resulted in many being posted to far-flung corners of the globe, the backing of the War Office enabled him to identify the few still in England. As for the remainder, like most Heroic Age leaders, he must accept the necessity of supporting his kernel of experts with enthusiastic amateurs willing to turn their hands to whatever tasks might be allotted to them. In addition, he could rely upon the Expedition Committee to do its best to ensure that the novices received at least some rudimentary training in the specialist work they would be expected to undertake.

As Marr obtained information regarding the whereabouts of each man on his list, he fired off a telegram from his small room in the Colonial Office building at 2 Park Street, ordering them to attend for interview. One early recruit was Ivan Mackenzie Lamb, one of the expedition's few trained scientists. An expert in lichens, in the summer of 1943 the willowy 32-year-old was employed at the British Museum preparing natural history reports on the lichen finds of the BGLE and *Discovery* Investigations:

> This work was well under way when one day in September the Keeper of my department sent up word that he would like to see me at once in his *sanctum sanctorum*. Hastily reviewing in my mind and preparing a defence for all recent sins of commission and omission which might underlie this request, I presented myself before the Presence, whose first action was to impress upon me, by appropriate words and gestures, a solemn warning that the information which he was about to convey to me was of such profound significance and secrecy that the discussion of its terms, even in lowered voices and behind locked doors, almost bordered on the profane.[39]

After a somewhat incoherent and confusing exposition of the project he was being asked to join, Lamb made his way to Park Street for a formal interview. Here he received a rather clearer explanation and, in reply, told Marr that he 'considered it a privilege to be asked to accompany the Expedition in a scientific capacity'.

The experiences of the ship's carpenter, Lewis 'Chippy' Ashton, a veteran of *Discovery II*, also typified the secrecy under which the expedition operated. Having recently been torpedoed in the South Atlantic, Ashton had just joined a new ship in Leith:

> We were due to sail to India via the Cape at daybreak the next morning. At 4 o'clock that afternoon, my new ship's Captain received a wire from the Company's office to the effect that I was to be paid off immediately, and returned to their London office. Another man was en route to replace me, but there was no explanation as to what it was all about. I wondered what I could have done to be rushed off a ship just on the point of sailing.[40]

In London, the bewildered carpenter was escorted through the labyrinthine passages of the Park Street building and ushered into an office where Marr and Mackintosh explained the nature of the expedition and asked if he would join. With his previous ship already en route to India, he agreed. A medical examination by the Colonial Office consulting physician followed and, having been pronounced fit, Ashton was then thrown into a whirligig of activities ranging from manning the office telephone to checking stores, selecting equipment and marking boxes for the shore bases:

> ... they were not slow in finding a use for me where, in a corner of the room a desk was soon decorated with a pencil, a pad of paper, a telephone

and map and I took on the duties of office boy. A great many people completely unacquainted with me called up asking a great many questions
about various subjects and people. I did my best to guess the answers but it
was not long before it was discovered that I was a menace to both security
and public relationship on the end of a telephone.[41]

Lamb and Ashton would become two of the expedition's most trusted and
popular recruits but sometimes, despite Marr's commitment, the process
of selection came close to descending into farce. The 43-year-old William
Flett, for instance, was left in such doubt about whether his qualifications
as a geologist weighed more heavily in the balance than his 'advanced age
and flat feet'[42] that he very nearly missed the ship altogether.

The quartermaster of one post-war expedition would assert that
'Organising an expedition was similar to undertaking all at once the
stocking of a department store, a garage, a hospital, a carpenter's and engineering workshop, a radio station and an hotel'.[43] In the case of Operation
Tabarin, all the usual problems of supply were exaggerated hugely by the
war – and by the departmental bureaucrats who threw up so many obstacles that Ashton christened them 'the block and tackle brigade'. As might
be expected, the sourcing of technical equipment proved especially difficult. The two 'Spitzbergen type' huts had been ordered at such late notice
that the managing director of Boulton & Paul felt compelled to write
to the Colonial Office demanding to know which of his many government contracts, which also included shipping cases for Spitfires and ship
gun turrets, should be given priority. In addition, bicycle wheels for use
with sledging meters had to be fabricated in Chatham Naval Dockyard
and wheel hubs and bearings had to be found for the wind-speed moni-
tors, or anemometers, as all pre-war manufacturing capability had been
switched to the production of war materiel.[44]

By the end of October the preparatory work neared completion, but
the loading of the *Bransfield* had quickly revealed that 'the vessel was
none too big for the job in hand, both as to cargo capacity and passenger accommodation'.[45] As a result, Marr decided that his senior surveyor,
Captain Andrew Taylor of the Royal Canadian Engineers, and the meteorologist, Sub-Lieutenant Gordon Howkins, plus several tons of stores
must travel separately on the *Marquesa*, a meat freighter bound for Buenos
Aires.[46] On 30 October a valedictory party held at the Goring Hotel
turned out to be a rather subdued affair, as the expedition's 'Most Secret'
status made it impossible to invite wives or sweethearts who, in theory
if seldom in practice, were supposed to be kept entirely ignorant of the
expedition's objectives and destination. Worse still, as Lieutenant Eric
Back, the expedition's young medical officer recalled, when he and his

companions left the hotel, 'we were asked to cough up three quid each for the privilege'.[47]

The *Bransfield* had not attracted the admiration of those watching her refit at the Albert Dock. On one occasion a sailor of the Free Norwegian Navy who had served on the *Veslekari* came down to look at the carefully considered improvements being made by Ashton: 'When he saw what "Chippy" was up to, he made a face and shook his head and said very gloomily "No good, no good." Despite that bit of encouragement, "Chippy" carried on with his work, regardless – but it made us think we were in for a dirty passage south.'[48] A few days later, no less a personage than the Hydrographer of the Royal Navy advised Lieutenant Victor Marchesi, the *Bransfield*'s newly appointed master, 'You be careful of these wooden ships – I've had experience of them years ago!'[49] Although they were hardly likely to inspire confidence in the men about to sail, the remarks of Vice Admiral Edgell and the anonymous Norwegian sailor turned out to be amply justified when the discovery of leaking freshwater tanks delayed the departure of the *Bransfield* until the middle of November. Worse was to come.

In order to provide her with some protection from marauding U-boats, the *Bransfield* had been instructed to sail from Tilbury to Falmouth in company with a 6-knot convoy under the escort of a French destroyer. Most Antarctic expeditions sailed with the cheers of hundreds of well-wishers ringing in their ears. On this occasion, the small collection of waving officials prompted an exhausted Marr to observe that 'seldom had an Antarctic expedition sailed with so little send-off fuss.'[50] The events of the next few days, however, would make him very glad indeed that there had been so little fanfare to mark the expedition's departure. Even heavily laden with two years' worth of supplies, the sealer should have been able to keep pace with the rest of the convoy but, by the time she cleared the Downs on 14 November, her two-bladed screw had begun to vibrate so violently that she had fallen far behind: just the kind of lame duck so beloved of submarine commanders. She limped into Portsmouth, where the engineers made repairs before she continued solo. 'On the way,' Marchesi remembered, 'the engineman came up and said we were making water, and he didn't know where it was coming from.'[51] Watching his ship being pumped dry, Marchesi agreed with Marr that, as soon as she had been made ready, they should make for Falmouth, where the Naval Officer in Charge knew of their expedition. En route, the unfortunate ship struck a force 9 gale and she began to leak so badly that the engineer asked permission to stop ship so that the engines could be dedicated to pumping. According to Dr Back, 'it all looked rather unhappy on the whole,'

… and nobody quite knew where we were … Eventually we got into Falmouth, sailing across the minefield – to cries of 'What ship?' as nobody had heard of HMS *Bransfield*. I presume, because we were wooden, we didn't set the minefield off. Going down the Channel Marr thought we were going to get to the Falklands in the *Bransfield* – I don't know if anyone else did. He doled out all the polar clothing but by the time we got to Falmouth it was quite obvious we weren't going to get much further.[52]

They reached Falmouth at 8 p.m., but it had become clear to everyone that the ship could not be expected to proceed. Even without the risk of her falling prey to U-boats, any attempt to sail the length of the Atlantic and into the Southern Ocean would almost certainly result in her total loss.

Leaving the engineer to keep the ship afloat, Marr and Marchesi caught a train to London to consult with the Committee. At one time they had been promised that a minesweeper would be loaned to the expedition if the *Bransfield* proved unsuitable, but by the time they reported her failure, the minesweeper had been allocated to other duties and could not be recalled. Instead, the expedition must somehow find passage out to the Falkland Islands from where the Falkland Islands Company ship, *Fitzroy*, and the *William Scoresby*, with Marchesi as skipper, would transport them to Deception Island and Hope Bay. If successful, this plan would enable them to reach their destination – but it also involved a very considerable compromise, as neither of these vessels would be dedicated on a full-time basis to the expedition and both would have to retreat to Stanley before the onset of winter. But with no alternative available, Marr immediately began to search for a ship that could transport his men and equipment south. His eventual choice – indeed, probably the only available option – was the 14,000-ton *Highland Monarch*, once a luxury passenger liner belonging to the Royal Mail Line, now serving as a troopship. It was fortunate that she could accommodate every member of the land parties, as Taylor and Howkins had also suffered a near-catastrophic mishap and been forced to rejoin the main body of the expedition. Their ship, the *Marquesa*, had sailed from Liverpool on the night of 15 November, but she had immediately struck a submerged wreck which tore out her bottom. By the time the tugs towed her back to port she had 26ft of seawater in her forward holds and was settling fast.

Marr and his men now faced the unenviable task of unshipping all the expedition's stores and transporting them across country from Falmouth to Avonmouth, where *Highland Monarch* lay berthed. One member of the party, however, had had enough. Recent experiences had convinced the expedition's second geologist, a portly middle-aged man named Buck, that he was constitutionally unsuited to polar exploration and he chose this moment to tell Marr that he intended to withdraw. His timing may have been opportune because Marr had far more pressing matters on his mind than the curtailment of his expedition's geological programme. Inevitably, the rushed transhipment of men and materials was chaotic and even the provision of a special train of thirteen trucks and one carriage did little to alleviate the problems, as Back recalled:

> We started off early in the morning and they said, 'We'll send you through just before the "Cornish Riviera Express."' But we didn't get far before the railway seemed to have forgotten all about that and we were pushed into a siding. We trundled slowly across the countryside of the West Country. We stopped on one occasion at Newton Abbot and we all charged out at the signal box to see if they'd make us a cup of tea. We got into Bristol about two o'clock in the morning, whereupon somebody appeared and said, 'Tickets, please.'[53]

At long last, with all its stores and personnel secured, the expedition sailed on 14 December, a full month and a half after Marr's original departure date. The *Highland Monarch* would call first at Gibraltar, where she would disembark a party of Gibraltarian exiles who had been evacuated in 1940 when the threat of invasion seemed imminent. She would then plunge south, bound for Montevideo and the Falklands, where she would deliver a relief garrison of several hundred troops – the legacy of Churchill's instruction of 1 April 1942.

Although he felt relieved at having avoided a lengthy voyage in a ship that had proved so unseaworthy, Marr could not help but be aware that, with the loss of the *Bransfield*, his expedition had avoided disaster by only the narrowest of margins. If the *Highland Monarch* had sailed earlier, or been unable to accommodate the expedition, a full year might have passed before a second attempt could be made – and by then the whole geo-political landscape might have changed and the expedition become redundant. Now, as he paced the boat deck of the huge troopship, so different from the tiny sealer in which he had expected to sail, he could be forgiven for wondering what the future held in store. Over 7,000 miles of hostile ocean lay between him and the Falkland Islands and then another 750 miles to Hope Bay. Moreover, when he reached his destination, he might well find an armed force already in occupation – conceivably German, but more probably Argentine. His was not the first Antarctic expedition to depart in wartime: *Endurance* had sailed on 8 August 1914, four days after Britain's declaration of war on Germany – but all the perils Shackleton had expected to face were natural. Operation

Tabarin was uncomfortably unique in that it confronted not only the dangers inseparable from every polar expedition – ice-choked waters, bitter cold, bottomless crevasses, and wearisome months of darkness and isolation – but also, potentially, an armed and motivated enemy intent on frustrating its every move. Perhaps mine-laying in the Indian Ocean had its advantages after all.

2

The Theatre

Although Marr had been stretched nearly to breaking point in the chaotic days before the expedition sailed from England, by the time the *Scoresby* and the *Fitzroy* left the Falklands six weeks later, he could rest somewhat easier. The voyage from Bristol to Montevideo and thence to Stanley had been trouble-free, with no unexpected 'alarums and excursions', and the loading of the two expedition ships had been completed without mishap. During the two and a half days in Stanley, he had also been able to relax a little as a guest of the Governor, Sir Allan Cardinall. An ethnologist, traveller, author, big game hunter, amateur zoologist and, in the opinion of Marchesi, 'a dear old boy'[1] to boot, Cardinall had been sent to the Falklands in 1941. Having long advocated an unambiguous expression of intent regarding the dependencies, he had greeted Marr's arrival enthusiastically, offering whatever help lay in his power to give: a long way, figuratively and literally, from Whitehall's 'block and tackle brigade'. Cardinall's official residence, Government House, stood aloof from the rest of the town, overlooking the harbour. A rambling mixture of brick and stone, its mullion windows would have given it the air of a comfortable Edwardian rectory were it not for the corrugated-iron roof, which placed it unmistakably on the fringes of the empire. As well as providing a congenial environment in which to draw breath before the real work of the expedition began, the house formed a tangible link with the Heroic Age of Antarctic exploration, because just down the corridor from where Marr slept stood the room once occupied by his old boss, Sir Ernest Shackleton.

The exhausted explorer had reached the islands on 31 May 1916 and it was from here, on 11 June, that he had launched the second of his attempts to rescue his men from Elephant Island in the Uruguayan trawler, *Instituto de Pesca No. 1*. This attempt, too, came to nothing: impenetrable pack ice blocked the ship's path, just as it had blocked that of the whaler *Southern Sky* in May. The marooned men, under the leadership of Frank Wild, had been forced to wait until 30 August before Shackleton finally managed to push through the pack on his fourth attempt, on the Chilean tug, *Yelcho*. His absence had lasted for 128 days and in that time his exploits, particularly the 750-mile small-boat voyage from Elephant Island to South Georgia, had turned him from a 'might have been' into a polar hero.

To any explorer heading south, the saga of the *Endurance* must serve as an inspiration and a warning in equal measure and Marr was no exception. With Cardinall's hearty endorsements ringing in his ears, he was returning to a realm remarkably few men had visited. His familiarity with the Antarctic was considerable – but it had its limitations. Although he had spent years sailing and investigating the Southern Ocean and had visited many of its islands, he had never spent any significant period on shore. And while he had served under three of the greatest Antarctic explorers, Shackleton, Mawson and Frank Wild, and under that supreme polar navigator, Frank Worsley, he had never led an expedition of his own. Moreover, Marr knew full well that on his performance would hang not only the British government's short-term desire to reassert claims that its own negligence had weakened, but also the ambitious aspirations for post-war exploration and study of the 'polar paladins', Wordie, Roberts and Mackintosh. Little wonder, then, if he paced the *Scoresby*'s bridge with an anxiety not wholly dissimilar to that of Shackleton on board the Uruguayan trawler nearly three decades earlier.

As the *Scoresby* began to buck and roll in the gathering swell, Marr could be under no illusions regarding the challenges of the environment in which he now had to prove himself. It was an environment that had left its mark on all the men who had sailed into these waters: all had endured extreme danger and intense cold; many had died and some had run mad. And yet exploration of the area later called the Falkland Islands Dependencies had not begun properly until 1819. In February of that year, while rounding Cape Horn during a trading voyage from Buenos Aires to Valparaiso, the British merchant brig *Williams* had been forced far south by contrary winds. Despite a typically rough handling from the 'Furious Fifties', the *Williams* proved a lucky ship and, having once clawed her way back north, she reached her destination relatively unscathed. Once ashore at Valparaiso, Captain William Smith immediately reported to the senior British naval officer on the South America Station and told him of an uncharted island group sighted in latitude 60°S. Although he considered the claim fairly credible, Captain William Shirreff of HMS *Andromache* expressed his disappointment that Smith had not attempted a landing and judged that he could not divert His Majesty's ships to investigate further without more definite information. After all, Smith might have been fooled by a large iceberg – he would not be the first, nor the last, to be so duped.

Chastened, on his own initiative Smith made two further voyages towards his uncharted islands in search of the evidence required by Shirreff. The first, during his return trip to Buenos Aires in May, he abandoned without sighting land. On the second, in October, he not only saw the islands, he actually made a brief landing. Hearing Smith's latest report, Shirreff was suitably impressed and immediately ordered his ship's master, Edward Bransfield, to charter and take command of the *Williams* and employ its owner and erstwhile captain as his pilot. After an uneventful voyage, in January 1820 the brig reached for the third time what would soon come to be called the South Shetlands. Landing on what would become King George Island, Bransfield took possession of the island group in the name of King George III, blissfully ignorant of the fact that the king had died the day before, and then made a running survey of some 500 miles of the coastline. In the process he discovered the channel – named the Bransfield Strait in 1822 – which separates the islands from the Antarctic mainland. Finally, on 30 January, Bransfield became arguably the first man ever to set eyes on the Antarctic continent itself. He named the coast Trinity Land (now Peninsula), in honour of the Corporation of Trinity House.

Learning of these discoveries, British and American sealers, who were already operating out of South Georgia and the South Sandwich Islands, rushed to take advantage of what soon proved to be extremely rich new hunting grounds. They established their headquarters in the safe harbour of Deception Island and, by the end of 1820, more than fifty-five British and American sealing ships had descended on the South Shetlands, rising to ninety-one ships in 1821. Within four years more than 320,000 fur seals on the islands had been slaughtered for skins and oil. This unprecedented activity in the region quickly led to further geographic finds, beginning in 1821 when the American sealing captain, Nathaniel Brown Palmer, and his English fellow-captain, George Powell, located the South Orkneys, lying 300 miles to the east of the South Shetlands. In the same year and much further to the west, during a double circumnavigation of the Antarctic continent, the Russian sloops *Mirny* and *Vostok*, under the command of Fabian von Bellingshausen, visited Alexander Land (now Island). This island, the largest in Antarctica, lies on the western edge of the giant mountainous peninsula that arcs out from the body of the continent to form the western boundary of the Weddell Sea and the eastern boundary of the Bellingshausen Sea.

This peninsula, the tip of which had been sighted by Bransfield in 1820, was first properly explored by Captain John Biscoe in 1832. The whaling company Enderby Brothers, which had been sealing in southern waters since 1775, had given Biscoe a short but immensely challenging brief: to make a complete circumnavigation of the Antarctic continent in the sealing brig *Tula*, with the smaller *Lively*, under Captain George Avery, acting as a cutter. The voyage proved gruelling. Having crossed the Antarctic Circle on 22 January 1831, the two vessels turned east at 60°S. On 24 February, Biscoe spotted the mainland for the first time and spent a month surveying the coast of what he named Enderby Land, in honour of his employers. After weeks of severe hardship and privation, he decided to make for Hobart, Tasmania to refit. By this point, all but one of his men was suffering from scurvy and the effects of the bitter cold; two had already died on the passage and, according to the account Biscoe later gave to the newly formed Royal Geographical Society (RGS), 'in the helpless state of the crew, and their utter inability to meet any sudden exigency, it was deemed expedient to lie-to every evening until the following morning.'[2]

On 7 May *Tula* attempted to enter the River Derwent but, finding it impossible to make a satisfactory landing, Biscoe diverted to Port Philip in New South Wales. Earlier in the voyage, *Tula* and *Lively* had been separated by a storm and when they met again in August Biscoe learned that the cutter's crew had fared even worse than his own. Under Avery, only three of *Lively*'s complement had survived and they too were on the brink of starvation. Over the ensuing weeks the survivors gradually recovered their strength and Biscoe resolved to continue his voyage. On 10 October 1831 the two ships sailed, pausing en route to hunt for seals between the Chatham and Bounty Islands, but with little success. Having corrected the position of the Bounty Islands on their charts, they resumed the final leg of their Antarctic circumnavigation by sailing south-east on 4 January 1832. In the middle of the following month, Biscoe discovered Adelaide Island and the Biscoe Islands. Four days later, on 21 February, he succeeded in landing on what is now called Anvers Island, just to the west of the Antarctic Peninsula, mistakenly believing it to be part of the mainland.[3] He immediately took formal possession, naming the peninsula Graham Land, after Sir James Graham, First Sea Lord of the Admiralty, and the highest mountain in view Mount William, after King William IV. He then began charting the coast and, mindful of the original purposes of the expedition, he reported that 'the water was so still, that could any seals have been found, the vessels could have been easily loaded … the sun was so warm that the snow was melted off all the rocks along the water-line, which made it more extraordinary that they should be so utterly deserted'.[4]

Now nearing the end of their harrowing voyage, the two ships headed for the South Shetland Islands, where *Tula* narrowly escaped shipwreck after being driven ashore and losing her rudder. Both ships then sailed for

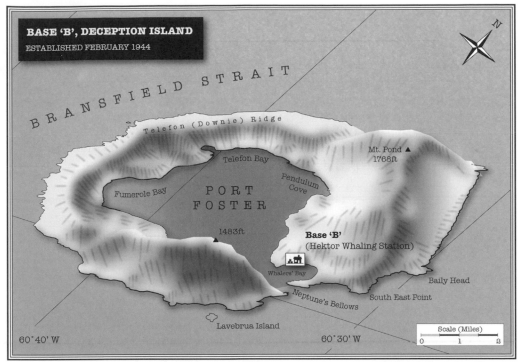

BASE 'B', DECEPTION ISLAND
ESTABLISHED FEBRUARY 1944

BRANSFIELD STRAIT

Telefon (Downie) Ridge

Mt. Pond ▲
1768ft

Telefon Bay

Pendulum
Cove

Fumerole Bay

PORT
FOSTER

Base 'B'
(Hektor Whaling Station)

1483ft

Whalers' Bay

Baily Head

Neptune's Bellows

South East Point

Lavebrua Island

60° 40' W

60° 30' W

Scale (Miles)

0   1   3

Map created by Andrew Stevenson

the Falklands, where *Tula* parted company with *Lively* and made for Brazil. It was here in July 1832 that Biscoe learned of the total loss of the *Lively* at what he called 'Mackay's Island' (one of the Falklands). Her crew had been rescued and taken aboard a cruiser out of Montevideo. Despite this setback, Biscoe finally reached Britain at the beginning of 1833. In recognition of his remarkable achievements, which included becoming the third man, after Cook and Bellingshausen, to circumnavigate the Antarctic continent, the Council of the RGS awarded him their £50 Royal Premium, the precursor of the society's prestigious Founder's and Patron's medals.

Such was the profligacy of the fur sealers that, by the late 1830s, they had virtually exhausted the fertile hunting grounds opened up by Bransfield and his successors. Voyages with an economic motivation then gave way to purely exploratory enterprises. In 1838 the Frenchman Jules Dumont D'Urville discovered Joinville Island – a discovery rather less celebrated than that of the Venus de Milo, which he had unearthed during an Aegean cruise in 1821. Five years later, the experienced Arctic explorer and Royal Navy officer James Clark Ross devoted one of his four Antarctic summers to the region. In his two thick-hulled bomb vessels, *Erebus* and *Terror* – both of which would ultimately be lost during Sir John Franklin's ill-fated quest for the Northwest Passage – he sailed down the eastern flank of

Joinville Island into a gulf which he named after his ships. A large dome-shaped mass of land to the west he called Ross Land (now James Ross Island) and four islands in the near vicinity he named Cockburn, Seymour, Snow Hill and Lockyer islands. With the young assistant zoologist Joseph Dalton Hooker, he landed on Cockburn Island, where they made the first ever collection of Antarctic lichens.

After the departure of *Erebus* and *Terror* it would be nearly thirty years before Dallmann's *Grönland* sailed into the waters around Graham Land in search of whales – and, thereafter, a further twenty-four before the next major exploratory voyage into the area. This latter expedition, led by Lieutenant Adrien de Gerlache de Gomery of the Royal Belgian Navy, and with the Norwegian Roald Amundsen as mate, had been prompted by the Sixth International Geographical Congress held in London in 1895. At the congress the participating nations agreed that the exploration of the Antarctic should be given the highest priority. The 250-ton *Belgica* sailed from Ostend on 22 August 1897 and during the austral summer of 1897–98 the expedition amended charts of the South Shetlands and the north of the Graham Land Peninsula before sailing south down the western coast, where Brabant, Liège and Anvers islands were charted and named. Also discovered were Wiencke Island, named to commemorate a 21-year-old Norwegian seaman, Carl August Wiencke, who had been lost overboard on 22 January, and the Belgica Strait (now the Gerlache Strait). In addition, some 200 miles of the western coastline of the peninsula were charted and named Dancoland (the Danco Coast) after Émile Danco, the expedition's geophysicist. Pack ice blocked the approaches to Alexander Island, and when a ferocious gale sprang up de Gerlache forced his ship into the shelter of the ice. Seeing leads in the pack opening up under the influence of wind and swell, he pushed southwards – against the advice of the scientists on board. The *Belgica* then spent thirteen long months locked in the ice, those on board becoming the first human beings to over-winter inside the Antarctic Circle. The ship did not break free until 14 March 1899 – by that time Danco had died of scurvy and two of the crew had been driven insane by the appalling conditions, the enervating effects of the Antarctic twilight and the poor quality of their provisions.

Of the other expeditions launched in the immediate afterglow of the Sixth International Geographical Congress, three chose Graham Land and its island groups as their primary destination.[5] The first, though little known in England, ranks as one of the greatest tales of heroic endeavour and survival in the annals of Antarctic exploration. In 1902, the Swedish Antarctic Expedition, under geologist Professor Otto Nordenskjöld, entered the Bellingshausen Sea in the 226-ton *Antarctic*. Having rounded the tip of the peninsula and deposited Nordenskjöld and a wintering party of five men and five dogs on Snow Hill Island, Captain Carl Anton Larsen sailed his ship into deep water to the north to undertake biological and other scientific work. When the ship returned in December, ice conditions prevented the recovery of the shore party. Instead, Larsen landed three men at Hope Bay, the closest point to Snow Hill Island that he could reach – and the planned site for one of Marr's two bases. Larsen instructed the trio to sledge to Nordenskjöld's camp and to tell him that the *Antarctic* would try to pick up the entire party at Hope Bay by 10 March 1903.

The ship never arrived; nor did the three-man party succeed in reaching Snow Hill Island, being forced to turn back by open water when almost within sight of their destination. Ignorant of the troubles that had beset the *Antarctic* and of the plans that Larsen had made, Nordenskjöld and his men had no option but to remain at Snow Hill for a second winter. Worse was to come. On 9 January 1903, while making another attempt to reach Nordenskjöld, the *Antarctic* became caught in the pack ice. Like the more famous *Endurance* twelve years later, the steam-driven whaler proved unable to bear the enormous pressure and, her keel ripped out, she sank on 12 February, leaving her twenty-man crew on the sea ice. Over the next sixteen days this party managed to drag their provisions just a mile a day, finally reaching Paulet Island on 28 February.

Meanwhile, aware only that the ship had failed to return as promised, the three sledgers left at Hope Bay were forced to over-winter in a rough stone hut they built from rubble, surviving on the six months' worth of rations they had been landed with and whatever seals and penguins they managed to kill. For eight long months, much of it spent in a depressing semi-darkness, the three men did little more than survive – their plight made all the worse by the realisation that, if the *Antarctic* had sunk as they suspected, then all knowledge of their whereabouts would have been lost with her. It therefore came as a considerable relief when, on 29 September, they were able to make another attempt to reach the party on Snow Hill Island. This time their luck held and, on 12 October, they met Nordenskjöld and a companion sledging on Vega Island. Once the initial euphoria of the meeting had passed, sober realisation dawned. Nordenskjöld and his men had assumed that the *Antarctic* had been forced back by the ice. Her failure even to pick up the party landed at Hope Bay implied a total disaster.

The puzzle was finally solved a little over three weeks later. On 8 November, an Argentine gunboat, the *Uruguay* under Commodore Julián Irízar, arrived at Snow Hill Island, having been despatched as a rescue ship when the *Antarctic* failed to return to civilisation the previous autumn. With spectacular timing, that very evening Captain Larsen and five of his men also showed up, having rowed and sailed from Paulet Island in one of the

Antarctic's surviving boats. Within hours, the rest of the ship's crew had been picked up and the entire party was en route to Buenos Aires. Almost unbelievably, only one man had been lost during the entire expedition: Seaman Wennersgaard had died on 12 June from long-established heart disease.

By the spring of 1903, news of Nordenskjöld's disappearance had reached Europe. Dr Jean-Baptiste Étienne Auguste Charcot, who was preparing for an Arctic expedition, decided to head south instead in order to attempt a rescue. His ship, the *Français*, left Brest on 1 August 1903 with one passenger, Adrien de Gerlache, who was bound for Brazil. During the voyage, Charcot and de Gerlache spent many hours discussing the latter's Antarctic experiences and when, on arrival at Buenos Aires, Charcot learned of Nordenskjöld's rescue, he decided to continue to the western coast of the Graham Land Peninsula, making his first landfall on 1 February 1904 on Smith Island. Sailing down the Gerlache Strait, he landed on Wiencke Island, from where he saw Anvers Island and named the highest point Mount Français. The *Français* entered a harbour on 7 February 1904 and again on 19 February when looking for suitable sites to over-winter. Although this harbour had first been visited by de Gerlache, the Belgian had not thought it significant enough to name. Charcot now corrected this oversight, calling it Port Lockroy in honour of Edouard Lockroy, the politician who had been instrumental in raising funds for his expedition. In forty years' time, Port Lockroy, too, would become inextricably linked with Marr's venture. As for Charcot, after over-wintering on Booth Island, he only narrowly avoided catastrophe when the *Français* struck a reef, causing severe damage near her bows. Major repairs were completed *in situ* and, glad to be still afloat, the expedition limped back to South America.

Charcot returned to the Antarctic in 1908 for a second expedition with his laboratory ship *Pourquoi-Pas?* Reaching Port Lockroy on 27 December 1908 he then sailed as far south as Marguerite Bay and Alexander Island. Learning from the experiences of de Gerlache, he decided it would be too dangerous to over-winter this far south, so he retreated to Petermann Island where four huts were built. By running electricity cables from the ship to the huts, Charcot also ensured that much scientific work could be completed during the winter. After returning to Alexander Island the following summer and naming what he believed to be part of the mainland after his father, Charcot left in January 1910. He dedicated the rest of his career to exploration and research in the Arctic – until he, his ship, and all hands were lost on 15 September 1936 during a gale off the coast of Iceland.

In 1921, just a few months before Marr first saw Antarctica from the deck of the *Quest*, the Australian explorer Hubert Wilkins visited the dependencies as a member of the British Imperial Expedition of 1920–21.[6] Led by John Lachlan Cope, himself a veteran of the *Endurance* Expedition, this four-man expedition had originally planned to fly over King Edward VII Land to the South Pole using old RAF bomber aircraft, but Cope's inability to raise the necessary funds forced him to abandon all ideas of flying. Instead, in order to ascertain if Prince Regent Luitpold Land (the Luitpold Coast) on the western edge of the Weddell Sea was connected to Graham Land, the expedition would trek south overland from Nordenskjöld's hut on Snow Hill Island. Norwegian whalers were engaged to land the party at Snow Hill Island, but adverse weather conditions made this impossible. Amazingly, despite the fact that they had made no provision for a hut, on 12 January 1921 the group was eventually deposited on the edge of Andvord Bay on the western coast of Graham Land.

Realising that the peninsula could not be crossed from this landing point, and that the expedition's primary goal was therefore now unobtainable, Wilkins told Cope that he wanted to abandon the venture as futile. Accepting that his grandly named and wildly ambitious expedition had become a fiasco, a dispirited Cope agreed to leave with him. However, the remaining two members of his party, Thomas Wyatt Bagshawe and Maxime Charles Lester, insisted on trying to salvage something from the expedition and chose to over-winter in a hut made from packing cases and roofed with an old boat abandoned eight years earlier by the whaling ship *Neko*. Except for a supply of *crème-de-menthe* sweets, Bagshawe and Lester had brought very little food with them and they fabricated their primitive cooker from an old oil drum. When the whaling factory ship *Svend Foyn* returned to 'Waterboat Point' the following year, Captain Ola Andersen felt so convinced that the foolhardy young men must have perished that he sent one of his English officers ashore with a prayer book, prepared to read the burial service over their frozen corpses. Contrary to all expectations, the daring eccentrics were not only alive and well but they had also gathered an impressive amount of scientific data including daily weather, tide, ice and zoological observations. Theirs had been an extraordinary adventure and must surely rank as one of the most remarkable, and bizarre, of all Antarctic expeditions. Nor had their privations dispelled their interest in the region, because Lester would go on to serve as an officer on the *Scoresby* during the *Discovery* Investigations of 1926–27.

The newly knighted Sir Hubert Wilkins returned to the Antarctic in 1928 and, on 16 November, he became the first person to achieve powered flight in the Antarctic. Taking off from Deception Island in his Lockheed Vega aircraft, he flew down the eastern coast of the peninsula as far as the Eternity Range. This was followed, on 20 December, by a flight roughly along the meridian of 61°W, crossing Graham Land from Hughes Bay on the north-west to the east coast in 64°S. During this flight, Wilkins flew at an altitude of some 8,200ft to clear the land and, in the process,

became the first man to see the central Graham Land Plateau. The following summer the *Scoresby*, which had been loaned to the expedition by the
Discovery Committee, steamed south looking for an area of flat sea ice so
that Wilkins could attempt to take off and land using the skis fitted to his
aircraft. This modification was thought to be essential so that aerial surveys
could be supported by ground surveys. Unable to find a suitable location, Wilkins eventually replaced the skis with floats and he made several
flights from Port Lockroy, including one on 19 December 1929 that established the width of the Graham Land Peninsula as approximately 25 miles,
measured between Leroux Bay and Richtofen Pass. Before bad weather
brought operations to a close he made further flights, to Charcot Land
(which he proved was an island), to Deception Island and along the west
coast of the peninsula. Wilkins had set a new standard and the next two
expeditions to the region would also make extensive use of aeroplanes.

In 1934 the American millionaire-explorer, Lincoln Ellsworth, arrived
at Deception Island in his ship, *Wyatt Earp*. Also on board was Wilkins,
whom Ellsworth had recruited as a special adviser. Building upon the polar
flight made by fellow American Admiral Richard E. Byrd from his base on
the Ross Ice Shelf on 28 November 1929, Ellsworth intended to fly from
Deception Island to the Weddell Sea and then to become the first man to
cross the continent by flying via the South Pole to the Ross Sea, where he
would await the arrival of the *Wyatt Earp*. He succeeded in making a flight
down the eastern coast of the peninsula but then bad weather forced him
to retreat to the United States in January 1935. The following summer he
returned and, with his British-Canadian pilot Herbert Hollick-Kenyon,
took off from Dundee Island on 23 November 1935. After an eventful
flight the two men ran out of fuel and landed 16 miles short of 'Little
America', the base established by Byrd in 1928–29. They successfully completed the last part of their 2,000-mile journey on foot, but the breakdown
of their radio early in the flight meant that they were unable to report their
landing and their 'disappearance' caused considerable consternation in the
United States. Eventually, after a wait of nearly two months, Ellsworth and
Hollick-Kenyon were picked up from Little America by *Discovery II* on
16 January 1936.

The next British expedition to the region – and the last pre-war British
expedition to the Antarctic as a whole – was the British Graham Land
Expedition, which left London on 10 September 1934. By this point, with
the exception of Shackleton's rather chaotic *Quest* Expedition and Cope's
shambolic British Imperial Expedition, no major British Antarctic expedition had been launched since 1914 and many – including polar worthies
like Wordie and Frank Debenham – believed that, unless bolstered, British
influence in the sphere would rapidly decline. In order to reverse this trend

they first recruited Gino Watkins, glamorous leader of the British Arctic Air Route Expedition of 1930–31. Watkins' plan was hugely ambitious, its primary objective being 'To cross the Antarctic from the Weddell Sea to the Ross Sea, thus carrying out Shackleton's plan for his 1914 Expedition "to secure for the British flag the honour of being the first carried across the South Polar Continent."'[7] But it came to nothing. In the immediate shadow of the Wall Street Crash of September 1929, Watkins' guileless enthusiasm and his tales of the great white wastes to be conquered did little to impress Britain's bruised financiers and by July 1932 he had been forced to abandon his Antarctic ambitions, choosing instead to return to Greenland. A month later the 25-year-old explorer was dead, drowned while seal hunting alone in Lake Fjord.

These events gave rise to a new, less ambitious, but altogether more practicable plan. Under the leadership of the Australian John Rymill – Watkins' second-in-command in the Arctic – the BGLE spent two full years in Graham Land, completing a comprehensive programme of scientific and geographic investigations. In particular, using dog teams and a De Havilland Fox Moth aeroplane, it succeeded in making two major discoveries: 'First that Graham Land is part of the Antarctic Continent and not an archipelago, as was previously thought, and secondly, that a great channel running approximately north and south separates Graham Land from Alexander Land.'[8] Moreover, in most people's eyes, this expedition formed the bridge between the Heroic Age and the modern age of properly equipped, state-funded expeditions. In later years, the experience gained during the BGLE would have a profound influence on future British Antarctic activities. In particular, over the course of the next two decades, the practice of using small boats for scouting ahead of larger vessels when working close inshore, depot-laying by aircraft and hut design were often based on techniques developed by the members of the BGLE.

The last pre-Tabarin expedition to the Graham Land region was not British but American. Sponsored by the US Navy, the State Department, the Department of the Interior and the Treasury, as well as by a few private citizens, the United States Antarctic Service Expedition of 1939–41 (also known as Richard E. Byrd's Third Antarctic Expedition) was only the second official US expedition to the Antarctic and the first since Lieutenant Charles Wilkes' expedition of 1838–42. In accordance with an order issued by President Roosevelt on 25 November 1939, two bases were established. After some difficulty in identifying a suitable landing place, an eastern base was located at Stonington Island in Marguerite Bay. Crucially, Stonington Island is just off the western coast of Graham Land, and therefore well within the Falkland Islands Dependencies. The second base, in the west, was positioned in the Bay of Whales, close to Byrd's Little

America station, and inside New Zealand's Ross Dependency. The main purpose of the expedition was to chart the continental coast from 72°W to 148°W and in this it proved highly successful, completing extensive survey work, including a southward extension of the surveys of the BGLE, as well as conducting an impressive programme of scientific observations into a range of phenomena. Even more significant was the very clear signal that the United States had become a force to be reckoned with in the Antarctic – and that it had very little regard for the prior claims of other nations, including Great Britain.

The United States' position on this subject had been largely consistent since the first quarter of the nineteenth century, when Secretary of State John Quincy Adams had advised President Munro that American sealers should take full advantage of recent British discoveries in the region. According to Adams, Britain's preoccupation with the 'adulteries and fornications' of George IV made it highly unlikely that it would offer any meaningful resistance to such incursions.[9] Almost exactly 100 years later, American policy was more formally articulated by Adams' successor Charles E. Hughes, who refuted the suggestion that 'taking of possession … could establish the basis of rights of sovereignty in the Polar regions'.[10] That, at least, was the United States' public stance. In private, it positively supported the territorial claims made by Ellsworth during his Antarctic expeditions and Byrd's written instructions of 1939 confirmed that 'Members of the Service may take any appropriate steps … which might assist in supporting a sovereignty claim by the United States Government.'[11] Despite its private fury that the United States should choose to encroach on British sovereign territory when Britain was fighting a war against so implacable an enemy as Nazi Germany, the British government's official response was measured, for obvious reasons. Lord Lothian, the British Ambassador in Washington, wrote to the Secretary of State on 17 November 1939, reminding him of the claims of both Britain and New Zealand – but also offering every possible assistance to Byrd's expedition. Not surprisingly, the United States declined the proffered help.[12]

Each of these earlier expeditions would have their lessons for the men of Operation Tabarin, but few had the inclination to read their stories as the *Scoresby* and *Fitzroy* plunged south into worsening weather. In the heavy swell, first one ship and then the other would be lost completely from view: 'The ship laboured along in the heavy seas we encountered in the next three days,' wrote Andrew Taylor, who travelled on the *Fitzroy*. 'Sleet and snow fell occasionally as we sailed through the tempestuous waters just east of Cape Horn. Few of the passengers had any interest in anything but the passage of time.'[13] Unusually for an expedition ship – and even more so for one nominally at war – the *Fitzroy* carried three supernumerary passengers: Tim Hooley, a radio operator bound for South Georgia; his wife, Gladys; and their 14-year-old daughter, Dawn, whose modesty, good manners and happy demeanour made her a welcome addition to the personnel. By the second morning at sea, Dawn recalled, breakfast had become 'a juggling act of holding milky porridge at the right angle so it did not slosh over the side of the dish. The dampened tablecloth, and the boards put up around the table, also the places set but not occupied, told their own story.'[14] By the third day out from Stanley, however, the weather had begun to calm and the empty places at the table began gradually to be filled, so that soon the saloon rang with the varied accents of the expedition's personnel: English, Scottish, Welsh, Canadian, New Zealander and Falkland Islander.

On 2 February, even the prostrated Ivan Mackenzie Lamb felt well enough to crawl from his bunk to watch as the ships closed on the South Shetlands. They entered Bransfield Strait, which separates the islands from the tip of the Graham Land Peninsula, in fog but by the early evening it had cleared sufficiently for them to catch their first glimpse of King George Island: 'huge imposing snow-clad slopes merging with the sky above, and below running down into steep dark cliffs of great height and grandeur.'[15] As if to welcome them, a large iceberg floated serenely by and then calved dramatically, with a scraping whoosh and a cloud of ice smoke. The ships cleared Cape Melville and just as the dark rounded cone of Bridgeman Island became visible above the horizon, a cold south-westerly swept down the channel, forcibly reminding men fresh from the tropics that they were skirting the northernmost edge of Antarctica.

The expedition was now fast approaching Deception Island, where its first base, Base 'B', would be established. Formed from the sea-filled mouth of an active volcano, the island consists of a ring of snow-capped basalt mountains which rise to nearly 2,000ft and enclose a deep lagoon, accessible only through a narrow and dangerous passage, variously called Neptune's Bellows or Hell's Gates. Although the island has long been accepted as one of Antarctica's safest harbours, occasionally it demonstrates its latent power when underwater tremors shake the rocky ring, the black volcanic beaches burst into violent, smoking life, giant boulders hurtle down the hillsides and, most terrifying of all, the waters of Port Foster, the inland lake, begin to boil. During the boom years of the whaling industry, Port Foster was a hive of activity between November and February. Once the surrounding pack ice had retreated, dozens of whaling factory ships would tie-up while their fleets of catchers sped through Neptune's Bellows to hunt in the island-studded seas beyond, returning with a string of bloated corpses bobbing in tow. Before the introduction of laws regulating the industry, the catchers brought in such numbers that the hard-pressed factory ships used only to strip off the blubber, allowing the rest of the carcass, or *skrott*, to float away, dyeing the waters red and littering the interior shores with rotting corpses. One of the most disgusting by-products of the industry as a whole was the stench: the fumes of the blubber boilers corrupting the clean, crisp air of the South Atlantic with an odour memorably described as 'being like a mixture of the smell of a tanning factory and that of fish meal and manure works together with a sickly and almost overpowering odour of meat extract'.[16] At Deception Island, the stink would be even worse than usual, because it was mixed with the smell of sulphur erupting from the black beaches. No wonder the whalers thought it a hellish place.

The island was known to have been visited on a number of occasions by the Argentine Navy and, with its secure harbour and intact buildings, the Admiralty thought it the most probable location for a permanent or semi-permanent Argentine force of occupation. Immediately prior to sailing from England, Marr had been issued with a lengthy set of 'Political Instructions' which sought to give him guidance on how to deal with the inevitable confrontation. The instructions advised him that 'In order that a heated controversy with the Argentine and/or Chilean Government may if possible be avoided … violence should at all costs be avoided.'[17] This was clear enough. The anonymous author then tried to predict every possible action and reaction of the protagonists, so that his instructions came to resemble a comprehensive set of stage directions:

> … it may not always be possible or desirable to avoid the purely technical use of force in such instance as, for example, pushing past a man standing with outstretched arm or vice versa … If the expedition finds Argentines and/or Chileans already installed at a place where it is proposed to land, you should nevertheless make it your object to land also, to establish yourselves, preferably at a suitable distance from the other party, and to maintain towards the latter an attitude of politeness and even cordiality, while making it unmistakably clear that it is your duty to assert and to maintain British Sovereignty over the territory concerned … you should make a formal call on the Argentine and/or Chilean party at which you should take the opportunity to express surprise at finding them there in view of the fact that you were unaware that the permission of His Majesty's Government had been sought and granted for an Argentine and/or Chilean visit …
>
> If an Argentine and/or Chilean party already established on an island show an unmistakable intention of resorting to violent force in order to prevent the expedition from landing on the territory concerned, an attempt should be made to dissuade them tactfully from this intention. Should this fail, however, and violent force be directed against your landing, the

expedition should return under protest to His Majesty's Ship, remain at the island concerned and seek wireless instructions forthwith.[18]

Basically, an attitude of 'live and let live' should be adopted locally, while the larger issues of sovereign rights were debated by the opposing governments. At the same time, however, Marr was ordered to 'take any opportunity which may arise of taking action likely to strengthen the British title to the islands'. The exact nature of such action, and how it could be taken without jeopardising friendly relations, was not vouchsafed.

In the event of a superior Argentine force arriving after a British base had been established, then 'Formal, and possibly a little more than formal, resistance should be opposed … although it should not be carried to a point involving bloodshed, e.g. it should be unnecessary for any foreign party to frog-march any member of the expedition whom they desired to remove physically.' As for flags and other signs of sovereignty, these should be removed whenever possible, though Marr should also 'avoid a situation in which each party takes it in turns to obliterate each other's marks surreptitiously'. Overall, whether intentionally or not, the instructions effectively served to deny Marr any freedom of action in his dealings with the Argentines; reading between the lines – as Marr must surely have done – they also revealed the extent of Whitehall's nervousness regarding the wisdom of the action it had authorised.

The two ships edged through Neptune's Bellows and into Port Foster at 11 a.m. on 3 February, the *Scoresby* taking the lead so that her obsolete 12-pounder might provide at least some semblance of warlike purpose. On both ships there was an air of tense expectancy:

> As we turned the corner, the settlement came in sight; all eyes were anxiously scanning it for any signs of human occupation. On one of the large fuel tanks the Argentine flag had been painted. A door was seen to open and close in one of the buildings, but this was only due to the wind. No human being was to be seen.[19]

With the rattle of the anchor chains still reverberating around the mountains, a landing party rowed ashore to take a closer look. The equipment and by-products of the industry could be seen everywhere: the decayed jetties collapsing into the lagoon; rusting machinery; vats for boiling the whales' blubber down to oil; and piles of ships' chandlery, once used to service the needs of the whale-catchers, but now left to moulder. Whale bones lay all around: enormous ribcages, collapsed in on themselves like the roofs of abandoned houses, piles of wedge-shaped skulls and colossal vertebrae, all long since picked clean by scavenging seagulls which flocked to this charnel house from far and wide. Indeed, so great was the volume of carrion generated by the flensers that one zoologist estimated that millions of seabirds must have been driven to starvation when the whaling station closed in 1931. Also to be seen were sheets of *baleen*, the spiny comb-like material which fringes the mouths of baleen whales, and which they use to strain their staple food, *krill*, from the seawater. In the Victorian age this material carried a high value, being a vital component in the manufacture of corsets, collar stiffeners and parasol ribs. With changes in fashion around the time of the First World War, it became virtually worthless and had been discarded by the whalers. Now it lay in piles, the slimy green algae with which it was covered giving it the appearance of tussock grass.

Of the buildings, those made of corrugated iron were now in the last stages of decay: half filled with snow and ice, their loose cladding clanking mournfully as it flapped to and fro' in the wind. Those of a more substantial construction were generally in a better state of repair and many still contained large quantities of useful equipment, though it lay scattered about as though the last occupants had left in a great hurry. 'The hospital, on the other hand,' Lamb noted, 'was filled with masses of snow and ice and partially wrecked; masses of valuable material, beds, medicines, bandages, operating table, etc, ruined by damp and exposure.'[20] Satisfied that the island remained uninhabited, the landing party hoisted the Union flag and then used red oxide paint to obliterate the Argentine flag. This depressing ghost town would be home to five of Marr's men: William Flett, geologist and base leader; 'Jock' Matheson, bo'sun; Leading Seaman Charles Smith; Sub-Lieutenant Gordon Howkins, meteorologist; and the wireless operator, Norman Layther, from New Zealand.

With the magistrate's building and two of the whalers' dormitories deemed fit for human habitation, unloading could begin immediately without the need to offload and construct the pre-fabricated hut brought from England. Anchored about half a mile offshore, the *Fitzroy* and *Scoresby* unloaded onto a pair of scows that had been roped together and given a false deck of planks. When fully loaded the scows were then towed to the beach by the motor launch so that their cargo could be manhandled 100ft or so up to the buildings. During the process it quickly became apparent that the waters of Port Foster were not always as smooth as might be expected, despite the protection offered by the ring of mountains. On one occasion, Taylor remembered, a strong wind forced the scows high up the beach, making it extremely difficult to dislodge them. Once they were freed, the motor launch struggled to make any headway against the wind and the position of the twenty men on the scows began to look distinctly precarious:

For a few moments it seemed as though the launch would be unable to tow the scows, and as we drifted beam on to the wind, they took on a dangerous heel, all but upsetting. But the valiant little engine chugged away, eventually getting under weigh and pulling us alongside the ship. The scows were rising and falling in the troughs of the waves about six feet, so that one had to judge when they were on a crest, and then leap for the Jacob's ladder which draped down the side of the ship, scrambling up it with agility to make room for the next man coming aboard.[21]

Unloading continued from early morning until late at night and at the end of each day's labours the explorers, unused to such heavy work, crawled to their bunks exhausted, their soft hands made raw.

The wooden building selected by Flett as his headquarters stood at the north end of the whaling station. Like all the other woodwork on the island, its timbers were in surprisingly good condition, free of rot but scoured to a metallic-looking sheen where they were exposed to the elements. Inside, the tables, cupboards, stoves and beds once used by the whalers were also found to be sound and while some of the windows had been broken, either by the elements or by marauding sailors, overall the interior remained remarkably fresh and could easily be made fully habitable. As the building was much larger than the five-man party required, being 100ft long and 25ft wide, they would occupy only its northern section – but there was still space enough for each man to have his own room, of approximately 11ft square. It also had a concrete cellar and a large kitchen with a tiled floor, cupboards and a rather dilapidated cooking range. Once the stores had been piled inside the building, or dumped outside, the men whose home this would be began to scrub and sweep. The two expedition cooks, Smith and Tom Berry, started work on the kitchen, assembling a new range and connecting it to the existing flue, while the radio operators unpacked their rather more fragile equipment.

During the unscheduled transhipping of the expedition's stores and kit in Falmouth, 'Fram' Farrington, the expedition's senior operator, had become very concerned that the repeated jolting would result in his delicate equipment being damaged. His foreboding proved to be well founded: of the twelve 6-volt accumulators, he and Layther discovered that eight had been smashed, with the remaining four also in poor condition. 'The damage,' he wrote, 'was entirely due to the fact that each accumulator had been placed in a wooden box large enough only to take the battery and a few handfuls of wood wool for packing. This negligence almost prevented the expedition stations from going into action.'[22] Fortunately, the ships' masters agreed to donate two of their spare batteries and on 4 February, only thirty-six hours after the ships' arrival, the radio crackled into life and contact was established with Stanley. It was an achievement that Farrington still recalled with pride four decades later.

Outside, other men dug pits in the snow to bury some of the beef and mutton brought from the Falklands and then scavenged round the old factory for anything that might be useful to the party bound for Hope Bay. Timber, corrugated iron, old nails, tables, metal piping, copper wire, iron bars and even an enamelled bath and washbasin were all gathered and transferred to the ships. Outside the magistrate's building, 'Chippy' Ashton found another Argentine flag painted on a metal sheet and, rooting about, he unearthed a brass cylinder that had been buried in cinders piled around the flag support. These 'two interesting souvenirs' Marr asked Marchesi to hand to the governor when the *Scoresby* returned to the Falklands.

By the late afternoon of 6 February, everything was ready. All the stores, personal gear, books, clothing, fuel and Howkins' meteorological equipment had been landed, while the masses of salvage transported in the opposite direction now gave the deck of the *Fitzroy* the appearance of a rag-and-bone man's cart. As the ships prepared to leave, the sailors and members of the Hope Bay shore party bade farewell to Layther, Matheson, Howkins and 'Smitty', then climbed aboard the launch and made their way back to the ships. On board the *Fitzroy*, Flett received his last-minute instructions from Marr and accepted the paraphernalia connected with his new duties as magistrate and postmaster for one of His Majesty's dependencies. According to Taylor, who had shared a cabin with Flett, assuming these onerous duties wrought a profound change in the middle-aged geologist:

> Almost overnight, Flett seemed to grow out of the chrysalis we had known on the trip out. In assuming the title of Magistrate, the old Flett, with his jocular smile was no more, and in his place was an austere despotic looking northern islander encased in an almost unapproachable dignity. His new duties appeared to weigh heavily upon him. As he left our cabin with the remnants of his luggage, we went up on deck with him, to wish him goodbye and good luck. He climbed over the side into the motorboat, and with a cheery wave of his hand, the boat took him off to his new home.[23]

At 6.00 p.m. the *Fitzroy* and the *Scoresby* weighed anchor and a few moments later the battered buildings of the whaling station and the waving figures of the Base 'B' garrison slid from view as the ships rounded Fildes Point and passed through Neptune's Bellows and out into the Southern Ocean.

As he sat down to write his first, brief, informal report to Sir Allan Cardinall, Marr could be very satisfied with the expedition's progress. After so many doubts and anxieties, he had been able to make a completely unopposed landing on Deception Island – the point considered by all authorities to be the most likely flash point; he had established his first base; and his radio operators had even managed to make radio contact with Stanley. 'I am writing in great haste to tell you that (B) has been established,' he told the governor, with obvious relief. 'Everybody is very happy and full of enthusiasm … Things have gone well. I hope they will continue to do so for our other and bigger adventure.'[24] On the deck of the *Fitzroy*, meanwhile, some of the men still lingered at the rails, admiring the breathtaking view of the Trinity Peninsula in north Graham Land and doing their best to ignore the easterly wind that whipped across the waves to scour their hands and faces. Then, as they retreated to the snug, smoky atmosphere of the blacked-out saloon, the two ships swung eastwards, nosing into the wind and the gathering darkness as they set a course for Hope Bay, 150 miles away.

3

The Beachhead

A little before 6 a.m. on 7 February 1944, the *Scoresby* and *Fitzroy* entered Antarctic Sound, the 30-mile-long stretch of water that separates the Trinity Peninsula from Joinville Island. The greyness and turbulence of recent days had at last given way to calmness and sunshine and both sky and sea were a glorious blue. Having seen so little ice between the Falklands and Deception Island, the excited explorers lined the rails to admire the seascape: chunks of ice lay all around, some tiny, others large enough to be described as small bergs. According to Lamb, 'The crannies and cracks in these were of a most wonderful deep cobalt-blue colour, and when the ship passed alongside one of them, one could see the submerged part, coldly green, jutting out far below the surface or sloping sheer down until lost in the darkness down below.'[1] Dwarfing everything was an enormous flat-topped iceberg, 'about the size of Windsor Castle',[2] which must have broken off from one of the glacier tongues or ice shelves and been driven north by tides and the wind or by the westward trending vortex of the Weddell Sea. As the floes and bergy bits grew more numerous, it became impossible to avoid them altogether and pieces of ice grazed noisily down the ships' sides before being left to bob and roll in their wake. Inquisitive Adélie penguins swarmed over the floes, their squawking and excited flapping contrasting sharply with the apathy of the crabeater seals, which basked in the warm sunshine and hardly deigned to turn a dark, moist eye in the direction of the approaching vessels. Twice the black backs and dorsal fins of a pair of whales broke the surface just a few hundred feet from the ships' sides and the entire spectacle made the explorers feel that they were fast approaching the scene of their future labours.

As the *Fitzroy* pressed southward, Taylor remarked that 'the vista ahead of us appeared to be one unbroken field of impenetrable ice'.[3] He was even more disconcerted when, looking to the rear, he found that the track along which the *Fitzroy* had passed so recently had also closed up, 'with the superstructure of the *Scoresby* a half a mile astern being all that was visible above the ice'. In order to cope with the demands of service in the South Atlantic, the *Fitzroy* had been built some 25 per cent stronger than usually required by the Board of Trade — but her cutwater had not been specially strengthened and the masses of fast-moving ice were making Captain Pitt increasingly apprehensive. Captain David Roberts, a representative of the Falkland Islands Company who had accompanied the expedition from Stanley, shared his concerns and together they persuaded Marr to try a different tactic. Since the *Scoresby*'s reinforced bows made her much less vulnerable to the gathering ice, she would reconnoitre the remaining 12 or so miles to Hope Bay while the *Fitzroy* retreated to the comparative safety of Bransfield Strait. At 9.30 a.m., the *Scoresby* drew alongside and Marr, Lamb, Ashton, Back and Roberts transferred to the smaller ship; moments later she pushed on, weaving her way through the ice while the *Fitzroy* turned about and headed north.

Inevitably, as soon as the ships parted company, the ice conditions eased and with Marr directing the steersman from the crow's nest the *Scoresby* made remarkably good progress through fairly light brash. Three and a half hours later she entered the mouth of Hope Bay and dropped anchor 50yd offshore. The bay had been chosen by a committee sitting in the warmth and security of an office in Whitehall, but on closer inspection Marr was relieved to find it a 'most delightful place'.[4] In the foreground a patch of stony ground, about a square mile in extent and stained pink with the ordure of 60,000 penguins, is backed by a wall of jagged black mountains, their hollows and crevices packed with snow. Two of these mountains in particular dominate the scene: on the left, or south-east, a wide snow-filled basin with a rocky rim, named Mount Flora by Gunnar Andersson of Nordenskjöld's expedition. On the right, or south-west, a great round-shouldered bulk, later named Mount Taylor, looms above the crest of Blade Ridge, its brow more often than not topped with cloud, or with streaming plumes of drift snow, which invariably indicate the onset of a blizzard. Between the two, Depot Glacier sweeps down towards a narrow inlet at the head of the bay. To the right of the glacier, Blade Ridge gives way to low ice cliffs, broken by a series of nunataks, which resemble, in the words of one later visitor, 'black rock teeth with cavities stopped with glacial silver'.[5] Most important of all, the site offers relatively easy access to the sea ice running down Crown Prince Gustav Channel, which separates James Ross Island and Vega Island from the east coast of Graham Land. This last feature would enable the expedition to undertake extensive survey journeys, though the absence of dogs meant that the sledges would have to be man-hauled in the style of Scott and Shackleton.

After about an hour ashore, during which they selected a suitable site for the erection of the base hut, scratched about in search of fossils and minerals and laughed at the comical antics of the apparently fearless Adélie penguins, Marr and his companions returned to the *Scoresby* and Marchesi set a course to rendezvous with the *Fitzroy*. In the period since the departure of the *Scoresby*, Captain Pitt had steamed north-westwards as agreed, observing ice conditions all the way. Active Sound, which separates Joinville Island from Dundee Island, was choked with a confused mass of ice, much of it having tumbled from their disintegrating ice cliffs. The southern end of Antarctic Sound, too, appeared to be blocked, while Rosamel Island lay in the midst of a dense belt of pack ice. On the western side of the strait, the sun glanced on the glaciers mantling Mount Bransfield and along the mountain's base the 100ft-high ice cliffs could be seen stretching all the way to Hope Bay. Farther south, a long white carpet of snow led the eye to more distant peaks silhouetted against the blue afternoon sky.

Marr ended the day very well satisfied with his expedition's progress: the Deception Island party had been established successfully and he could now feel confident of being able to build his main base at the preferred location before the end of the austral summer. His optimism proved very short-lived because the following morning Roberts and Pitt told him that the *Fitzroy*'s solo cruise had served only to reinforce their apprehension regarding the dangerous ice conditions. 'I was most anxious to get to Hope Bay,' Marr complained to the governor, 'but both said they could not risk the *Fitzroy* in the ice they had just seen':

> I said if we waited we might shortly find the straits clear of ice but they replied that even under these conditions they could not risk the vessel in Hope Bay for the 4–7 days which might be required to land the stores, since the ice entering Antarctic Sound might be blown into Hope Bay by easterly winds and they might not be able to get out. They emphasised this most strongly and it was abundantly clear that *Fitzroy* could not be got into Hope Bay in any circumstances … I was bitterly disappointed.[6]

Recognising Marr's profound frustration, Roberts suggested that the *Scoresby* might be used to transfer the expedition's cargo from the *Fitzroy* to the landing site, but Marr felt 'convinced it would have taken weeks owing to *Scoresby*'s poor carrying capacity'.[7] Marchesi, too, thought the proposal impracticable: 'Even if I wanted to ferry the stores in, I doubt very much if we should have been able.'[8]

Marr's problems did not end there. According to his original plan, having established Base 'A' at Hope Bay, he would retain HMS *Bransfield* so that Marchesi could survey the islands in the region. In addition, the ship would be used to transport survey teams to designated points around the coast so that they could then sledge inland. With the ship over-wintering alongside the base, this work could have been extended well into the autumn and recommenced very early in the spring. When the *Bransfield* had been condemned as unseaworthy after her troubled voyage to Falmouth, Marr had hoped that this plan could still be carried out using the *Scoresby*, but this was not to be. The ship's lengthy period of mothball-ing after the declaration of war meant not only that she now had a very limited range, but also that her sounding gear, vital for hydrographic work, had seized up. Quite simply, though seaworthy, she was no longer fitted to the purposes of the expedition. While this fact made it impossible to undertake all the journeys that Marr had planned, by itself it would not have totally compromised his expedition's objectives so far as surveying was concerned. But now that his preferred base site, with its excellent access to sledging routes, had been rejected, his entire survey programme was in jeopardy.

Nonetheless, with Pitt and Roberts adamant that they would not risk their company's ship in Hope Bay, Marr had no option but to look for an alternative site, pushing south-westwards down the Graham Land coast. His own disappointment soon affected the mood of the expedition as a whole and enthusiastic anticipation quickly gave way to fretting and impatience. Some on board simply felt frustrated that they could not begin the work for which they had been selected. Others, like Farrington, questioned the decision to abandon Hope Bay: 'In my own opinion, the various conditions were as good as one could reasonably expect here and I think we could have completed the job. However, the ship's people would not run the necessary risk and so we are looking for another place.'[9] Farrington was not speaking from ignorance. Born in Northern Ireland in 1908, as a young man his one ambition had been 'to visit the distant parts of the world [and] to find a way to be paid for doing it'.[10] Qualifying as a marine wireless officer in 1929, he had spent six years with the Merchant Service before an irresistible urge to visit the polar regions compelled him to apply for a job with the *Discovery* Investigations. For the next three years he had served with Marr on the *Scoresby* and between 1937 and 1938 he had not only visited the South Orkneys and the South Shetlands, but also cruised down the west coast of Graham Land – the scene of the expedi-tion's current trials. His knowledge of ice navigation, therefore, though not particularly extensive, exceeded that of many on board and lent his opinions a certain authority.

Matters were made worse by the weather. The ideal conditions of 7 February now gave way to dense fog; with icebergs and uncharted rocks all around, Marchesi and Pitt had no choice but to lie-to for two whole days. Completely invisible to one another, the two ships became separated and, desperate to re-establish contact without risking a collision, Pitt ordered that the *Fitzroy*'s siren should be sounded at regular intervals. For long hours, they heard nothing in reply but the slap of the water as it struck the ship's side and tension continued to mount until, at last, late on the afternoon of 9 February, they heard an answering blast. Soon afterwards a ghostly looking *Scoresby* hove into view, causing Dawn Hooley to remark that 'she was a comfort to see, knowing we were not alone in this white wilderness'.[11]

On the 10th the fog lifted, giving way to a clear, sunny but windy day, and the two ships immediately got underway. As they picked their way slowly down the coast, it quickly became apparent even to the uninitiated why Hope Bay had been chosen as the best possible landing point for the expedition. Marr observed that the entire coast 'is fringed by almost continuous ice-cliffs broken only here and there by rocky headlands on which one might possibly gain a foot-hold but certainly not access to the interior as they are so precipitous.'[12] Moreover, the steep incline of the rock surfaces would have made the erection of the base huts hugely challenging at best. Sailing westwards and south-westwards, from the neighbourhood of Antarctic Sound to Andvord Bay in the Palmer Archipelago, they failed to identify even a single suitable site. The impossibility of landing was made abundantly clear on the evening of 10 February, when Marr and five others lowered the motor launch in order to put up a 'British Crown Land' sign at Hughes Bay on the Danco Coast. Ice debris and small bergs encumbered the 2 miles of water between the ships and the shore and in many places it became necessary to fend off the larger lumps with spades and boat-hooks. When the landing party reached the mainland, it was confronted by rocks so sheer that the water rushed from them like a waterfall when the 6ft swell subsided, making any attempt to gain a foothold little short of suicidal. Thwarted, Marr and his companions turned about and pushed and nudged their way back to the waiting *Fitzroy*.

The following morning, Marr accepted that he could put off a decision no longer. With the *Fitzroy*'s fuel dwindling and the end of the season fast approaching, the expedition had to make for the nearest point known to offer a fairly safe anchorage and a flat area sufficiently large to accommodate the huts – that meant Port Lockroy, the harbour first visited by de Gerlache in January 1898 and then by Charcot in February 1904. In good visibility the two ships continued in a south-westerly direction along the Gerlache Strait, with the spectacular west coast of Graham Land on their port bow. 'Here and there,' remembered Taylor, 'the sun shone down upon the black and white of the scene, throwing the icy facets of the mountains into glistening relief. The exposed rock faces were covered with a light frost, which made the scene one that might have come from a fairyland.'[13] Every now and then, one of the ice cliffs would calve, sending a cascade of ice rubble tumbling into the sea to then bob back to the surface as brash or small bergs. Seabirds wheeled and screeched overhead, the great, grey curving backs of whales broke the surface and, when the sun broke through the clouds, it seemed again that the certainty of a clear objective had given the expedition renewed optimism and purpose.

With the sun glinting from the ice cliffs, the ships continued to feel their way southward, skirting the coastline of Anvers Island but carefully avoiding the Schollaert Channel between Anvers Island and Brabant Island. The brash ice thickened in Lion Sound, but they managed to push through to the comparatively clear waters of the Neumayer Channel, which separates Anvers Island from Wiencke Island, without incident – despite the frequent roar of ice plunging from the faces of the ice cliffs. Steaming down the channel, it seemed at first as though the ships had entered a cul-de-sac, but then after a series of twists and turns they found a bay opening up between Damoy Point on Wiencke Island and the north shore of Doumer Island. This narrow *fjord*-like anchorage, studded with small islands and with high mountains and ice cliffs rising on three sides, was Port Lockroy.

The ships entered the harbour through a passage to the north of the islands and almost immediately evidence of previous human activity came into view. Since the beginning of the century several sealing ships had visited the harbour and as many as eight whaling vessels and three large cargo ships had anchored there in February 1911.[14] The Norwegian factory ship *Solstreif* had spent a number of summers in the area between 1911 and 1931 with several attendant whale catchers, though there can be very little doubt that their choice of location stemmed as much from the safe anchorage as from the availability of whales. During their visits the whalers had been industrious, and the remains of a large flensing plan, wooden flumes built to collect melt-water for use in oil processing, mooring bollards and the wrecks of two wooden scows and a blubber boat could all be seen. The huge bleached bones of whales flensed on the northern shore of Goudier Island, and at Jougla Point and Alice Creek, also bore silent testament to the whaling activity of the last four decades. Rather less depressing was the graffiti left by previous visitors, including the *Discovery II* and the *Scoresby* on Goudier Island and the Wilkins expedition, daubed in large white letters upon boulders at Besnard Point at the eastern end of the harbour.

With cables hitched to the bollards, Pitt ordered that two anchors be dropped so that the mooring lines could be tightened. Marchesi then brought the *Scoresby* alongside. At 4 p.m., after the ships had been made fast, Marr, Taylor, Ashton, Lamb and Back went ashore in the dinghy and the motor launch. Navigating through a narrow belt of brash, they landed at Lécuyer Point, a promontory of dull grey stones worn smooth by the ceaseless action of sea and ice. The point stands on the south side of Port Lockroy and is the site of a small rookery of Gentoo penguins and cormorants which, for all its stench and noise, gives a welcome touch of life to an otherwise desolate scene. Soft, wet snow covered the lower stones of the point and as they climbed from the boats the members of the landing party sank to their knees with every step. With the temperature below freezing and a strong east wind blowing the loose surface snow into their faces, they could be forgiven for thinking that 'the prospect of our new home was anything but inviting'.[15]

Depressing though the first survey might have been to the landsmen, to a sailor's eyes Port Lockroy would have seemed perfect. In particular, Pitt and Roberts could feel confident that their thin-hulled ship was much safer in the lee of Wiencke Island than she would have been in Hope Bay, where the chunks of brash joggled for entry. The prevailing winds at Port Lockroy would tend to drive ice away from the *Fitzroy* and, if the wind changed direction, Pitt would have a choice of three exits – to the north, south or west. There was also ample space to build the hut and the penguin colony would supplement the expedition's tinned food with fresh meat and eggs.

But the harbour was not without some very significant defects. In particular, since the Gerlache Strait seldom freezes over because of strong currents, access to the mainland for survey work would prove well-nigh impossible – a fact that completely justified Marr's fears about abandoning Hope Bay. As well as severely reducing the work that the expedition could undertake, this limitation could be very detrimental in terms of morale. Throughout the history of polar exploration, the importance of keeping expedition personnel active and usefully employed has been demonstrated again and again. Naturally enough, most expedition members were fit young men who had volunteered in order to explore – and this meant sledging in the periods before and after the darkness and bitter cold of the long winter months. When winter brought an end to outdoor activities, the men could occupy themselves in writing up their sledging journals; plotting their surveys; completing their scientific reports; and in repairing and improving their clothing, sledges, tents and other equipment ready for the next season's travelling. Denied the opportunity to undertake sledging journeys, the men of Operation Tabarin might well struggle for occupation and, when added to the psychological and physiological reaction to prolonged periods of semi-darkness and isolation, known colloquially as 'cabin fever', this inactivity could prove extremely damaging. The condition, which is marked by restlessness, irritability, irrational frustration, disturbed sleep patterns and paranoia, had been observed on previous polar expeditions – most notably on de Gerlache's *Belgica* expedition – and is now known to result from a lack of sunlight, which in turn accelerates the pineal gland's secretion of melatonin. The most effective cures for the ailment are a change of scene and sunlight, but many expeditions had found that another important tonic was the care and companionship of sledge dogs or, in the case of Shackleton's *Nimrod* Expedition and Scott's *Terra Nova* Expedition, ponies – but here again Marr's men were at a distinct disadvantage.

Marr was certainly not blind to Port Lockroy's flaws and this awareness caused him to return again to what he saw increasingly as a very personal failure to establish Base 'A' at Hope Bay as he had been instructed. With the implications of his failure constantly nagging at his peace of mind, he wrote to Cardinall:

> I do not doubt but that we shall be able to carry out some useful work, both scientific and otherwise this coming winter, but I feel that I have failed miserably in my task which was to get to Hope Bay. I feel exasperated and ashamed that I could not persuade *Fitzroy* to follow me into Hope Bay …
>
> I am most anxious not to have to spend more than a winter here and I should like at the earliest possible date next season to be moved to Hope Bay which is scientifically one of the most interesting places in Antarctica besides being a base from which extensive sledge journeys could be made in all directions.[16]

A key requirement of polar exploration – any exploration – is pragmatism: an ability to accept circumstances that cannot be avoided and to make the best of them. A classic example of such an approach was Shackleton's decision, during his *Nimrod* Expedition of 1907–9, to establish his winter quarters in McMurdo Sound, thereby breaking an ill-advised promise he had made to Captain Scott prior to sailing south. Shackleton knew that his actions would be criticised in some quarters; he carefully documented the unforeseen circumstances that had forced his decision – then he moved on. Understandable though Marr's frustration might be, his apparent inability to put the past behind him and devote all his mental and physical energy to the task in hand may have caused Cardinall some anxiety.

More positively, there was also ample evidence that establishment of a base at Port Lockroy would not run completely counter to the main purpose of the expedition: to reinforce British territorial claims and to undermine those of Argentina. The previous visitors to the harbour had included the *Primero de Mayo*, which had stopped here during her tours of 1943. In his official report, Marr noted that 'On the rocks of the penguin rookery a few hundred yards from the base the name *Primo de Mayo* [*sic*] was splashed in large red letters along with other names which evidently belonged to some of her crew'.[17] A sign with the Argentine flag painted on it had also been erected on Goudier Island, the largest of the rocky islands guarding the inner anchorage, but Marr observed with obvious satisfaction that this 'had been poorly guyed and had fallen down'. Finally, a brass cylinder containing the usual proclamation had been found close to where the flag had originally stood. Given this evidence, Marr thought it possible 'that the Foreign and Colonial Offices may find some consolation in our being here … this is a locality which the Argentines are most likely to re-visit and it is going to give them a lot to think about if they find us here as well as at Deception.'[18]

Whatever its pros and cons, given the time of year and the *Fitzroy*'s inability to cope with anything but light brash, Port Lockroy had now to become Operation Tabarin's main winter quarters and a building site had to be chosen. Initially, Marr considered Alice Creek, but its proximity to the tail of a glacier and the fact that nesting Gentoo penguins occupied the majority of the exposed rock eventually resulted in its rejection. Attention then turned to Goudier Island, which, as well as being the largest island, had the advantage of lying closest to the shore. An area of gravel on the low north-west corner of the island was discounted because, without tide tables, no one knew whether the site might be subject to flooding; however, a flat site about 40ft above sea level seemed ideal – not least because it stood some distance from the malodorous penguin rookery on Jougla Point, with its ankle-deep droppings. By evening this area had been carefully surveyed and the consensus of opinion was that it would provide just enough space for the proposed buildings.

With the decision made, the process of unloading the ships began at once under the supervision of the *Fitzroy*'s efficient young first officer. The two wooden scows, which normally served the *Fitzroy* when collecting wool from sheep stations in the Falkland Islands, were once again lashed together and a temporary wooden deck fitted between them to facilitate the unloading of stores. This contrivance enabled the crew to bring ashore some 15 tons of stores and equipment on each journey. Once they had been loaded, the launch towed the scows through the shallow passage separating Goudier Island from Jougla Point and round the west side of the island to a position near one of the old mooring chains left by the whalers. Deep water allowed the scows to approach the narrow ledge of rock that formed the shore, but from there it was necessary to manhandle the cargo up the steep rock face to the base site. Taylor found it very hard work:

Each case of goods which came ashore was handed up the slope from man to man … To those of us who had enjoyed the comfort of the voyage out from England, the constant lifting and wrestling with the endless stream of cases that seemed to flow inexorably up from the loaded scows made an exhausting task, and told better than words of our poor physical condition. Davies called this part of the islet 'Heartbreak Hill.' Many a case of fresh potatoes or tinned goods slipped from a pair of tired hands in this odd bucket brigade, spewing its contents down the grey rocky slope into the sea.[19]

The unloading continued until 10.30 p.m. and with the weather sunny and calm the flat top of Goudier Island was soon littered with a mass of crates, cases and sacks. Fortunately, the next day a navigable route was found to the more gently sloping north side of the island, obviating the need to drag every item up the rock face and thereby reducing both the effort required and the risk of damage to the precious stores.

Delivered to the summit in an indiscriminate heap, some semblance of order was established when the stores were separated into two piles: one for food and the other for articles required immediately, including radio parts, building materials and tools. The frozen mutton carcasses brought from Goose Green were hauled up as well and buried in a patch of snow at the south of the island for future use. Even Dawn Hooley lent a hand, melting snow or icicles 'as big as a man's arm'[20] in order to maintain a constant flow of hot tea for the labourers. The most important task was to build the expedition's Boulton & Paul hut and Taylor noted that 'No time was lost after landing in pouring [concrete for] the piers required for the foundation of the 16 by 28½ foot prefabricated house.'[21] By the close of 14 February the industrious Ashton had erected three of the walls and lifted the rafters into place. Unlike buildings later supplied by the company for Antarctic use, cladding timber for the Tabarin hut came in stock lengths, not pre-cut to size – though this may have resulted from the short time allowed for its manufacture. This meant that each section had to be measured and cut to suit. In addition, some of the markings on the prefabricated sections had been obscured in transit, while others were hidden by snow. All of this made construction unnecessarily frustrating and time consuming and eventually, in order to expedite matters, Ashton decided to ignore many of the pre-cut mortise and tenon joints, resorting instead to the 'plain carpentry' at which, as an experienced ship's carpenter, he was so adept. Of the hut as a whole, Back wryly observed that 'the exact plan was suitable for putting it up in the English summer but not in Antarctic blizzards. So, although they were all marked, Ashton put them all in the right place, but he did them all with six-inch nails and it was a very nice hut.'[22] The doctor would not be the last polar explorer to pass rather derisory comment on the designers and manufacturers of expedition accommodation.[23]

The following day they raised the 40ft tubular metal aerial masts, one to the north and the other to the south of the hut, each secured with cod-line stays and concrete foundations. The aerial itself was then strung between the two masts. Tim Hooley helped and when the masts seemed secure, Dawn performed an impromptu 'maypole dance', Ashton recording this unique event for posterity with his own cine camera.[24] Although building work was progressing well, the members of the shore party still ate and slept on the ships, giving them a comfortable environment in which to write letters to their loved ones. The opportunity to send these home came when Back and Berry opened a temporary post office in the lounge of the *Fitzroy*. The provision of a postal service continued to be accepted as an important means by which to underpin a territorial claim and Marr carefully reported to his masters that 'Although we are established on an island, in view of its proximity to the mainland I have considered it part of Graham Land and have accordingly stamped our official and private correspondence with the Graham Land stamp and postmark.'[25] At the time of the expedition, English law forbade postmasters from operating on a Sunday; however, Back and Berry were either ignorant of the restriction on Sunday trading or they felt that their isolation gave them immunity because they stamped a number of the items passing through their hands with the date of Sunday 13 February 1944. In wartime, they could not afford to be quite so relaxed about censorship and Marr duly appointed Farrington as official censor. Clearly, he took his new-found responsibilities seriously, because he signed and placed the 'censored' stamp on every item of outgoing mail – including his own. The permanent post office would eventually be opened in the main base hut on 23 March.

On 15 February the expedition reached another important milestone when the Canadian Johnson 'Chore-Horse' generator burst into noisy life, providing sufficient power to enable Farrington to establish radio contact with the Naval Officer in Charge at Stanley and, a day later, with Norman Layther at Base 'B'. For the first three months, radio traffic would be restricted in order to minimise the risks to security and Farrington encrypted all messages before sending them in Morse code. With the bases at Deception Island and Port Lockroy now in contact with Stanley, with each other and with the ships, the expedition's radio objectives had all been achieved, and relief and satisfaction filled Farrington's next letter to his wife:

All our stores – lashings of them, for we picked up a lot more on our journey out – are ashore and our hut is rapidly nearing completion … I don't think I have ever worked so hard before but it has been grand and I am feeling fine. The whole party is beginning to work like a team and that is all to the good. The beauty of our surroundings is beyond description and if only you could be with me I could be content here for a very long time ... Even the weather has been excellent since we arrived here and we have had days when it was too warm to be comfortable.[26]

Though he may not have realised it at the time, over the coming months Farrington would be one of the few members of the party whose work remained largely unaffected by the expedition's inability to undertake sledging journeys in the area around Port Lockroy. Responsible for both the maintenance of his radio equipment and for sending and receiving messages, sledging would never have been more than an unofficial adjunct to his duties and its loss rather less of a disappointment.

With the departure of the *Fitzroy* and the *Scoresby* now imminent, inevitably some of the men began to dwell on their impending isolation. Counting Goudier Island as a part of the Antarctic mainland, the nine-man party at Port Lockroy would be the only human inhabitants on a continent of some 5 million square miles. It was a daunting prospect and with this in mind Farrington suggested to Marr that some informal radio contact might be kept with the Argentine weather station at Laurie Island. Apart from the two Operation Tabarin bases, the Argentines' was the only other occupied base in the whole of the Southern Ocean below South Georgia. However, without clear instructions to the contrary, Marr decided that this would not be permissible. Had he known that the officer commanding at Laurie Island was a native of an Allied nation, the Norwegian Aage Johanssen, rather than an Argentine national, perhaps he would have thought differently.

At 3 a.m. on Thursday 17 February Marr and his eight companions gathered their kitbags and, after a cup of tea and 'one for the road', clambered down the *Fitzroy*'s side and into the motor launch to be ferried ashore. For much of their stay the weather at Port Lockroy had been gloriously fine and warm with blue skies and a sea 'as smooth as glass'.[27] Now it was depressingly drear and grey and as the boat approached the island a sudden gust of wind whipped what Taylor described as 'the only pork pie hat in Antarctica'[28] from Ashton's head and dropped it into the water close to the ice cliffs. Declining to recover his lost headgear on the grounds that it might be unlucky to turn back, the carpenter steered the boat towards the little cove and then the nine men walked up the slope to their still incomplete hut to obtain the best possible view of the retreating ships.

Forty feet below, the capstans began to turn noisily, drawing the rusty anchor chains through their hawseholes until the anchors thudded against

the ships' plates. The clatter of the engines gradually increased and seconds
later the *Fitzroy* and the *Scoresby* put to sea, ready to dash north through
the gathering pack. As they turned their noses towards the harbour mouth,
the base handyman, Kenneth Blair, broke a Union flag from the top of
the flagstaff on the summit of the island and the men cheered. The ships
sounded their sirens in reply and those crewmen not immediately occupied with the task in hand joined Captain Roberts and the Hooleys in
waving farewell. 'We shall be comfortable enough and everybody is in
high spirits and working well,' Marr had assured the governor in his last
letter, while Farrington sought to allay the anxieties of his wife and young
son by telling them that 'we are all set for our little sojourn in these parts.'[29]
From her position at the rail, the 14-year-old Dawn Hooley was neither
sentimental nor inclined to gloss over the raw emotion of the moment.
Watching as the members of the shore party disappeared from view she
thought that they 'must have felt very alone in the world'.[30]

4

Island Life

With sleet and snow sweeping across Goudier Island, the shore party could not afford to stand still for long and the ships' upper works had hardly been lost to view before Marr and his men returned to work laying the hut floor. Since their first landing, they had laboured from 6 a.m. until 10 or 11 p.m. every day and on the night of 16/17 February they had enjoyed less than four hours' sleep. All felt close to exhaustion and Taylor commented that:

> Under these conditions, perhaps it is understandable that our new home presented an unprepossessing appearance at half past three that morning … There was a roof on it, but we had no floor. The windows were merely tacked in and were threatening to blow out at any moment. We had no heat, fire or chimney, but Berry was bravely trying to cook in a small enclosure built of crates and boxes just outside the door of the building, his shelter roofed with a couple of sheets of corrugated iron weighted down with stones.[1]

In these primitive conditions, Tom Berry, who had served as Chief Steward on *Discovery II*, managed to prepare a welcome breakfast of bacon, eggs, bread and jam. The nine men wolfed down the food and then, fully clothed, rolled themselves in sleeping bags and blankets and settled down for a few hours of well-deserved sleep. When they woke, Berry cooked another meal of bacon, eggs, sausages and tea, and work began on the installation of the largest of the expedition's stoves, nicknamed 'Big Bunty', its temporary chimney projecting horizontally out of a window. Although this arrangement quickly raised the temperature and made the hut much more comfortable, it also had its disadvantages as a change in wind direction filled the hut with dense, acrid smoke – a problem not entirely eradicated until they replaced Big Bunty with a smaller 'bogey' stove whose chimney was permanently routed through the ceiling. Towards the end of the day 'Doc' Back prepared several basins of hot soapy water so that the men could have their first wash for several days, and later he attended to their cuts and blisters using Elastoplast dressings. Finally, after supper, the party toasted the future in sherry and gin and 'turned in for the night, tired out but contented with life on the whole'.[2]

Work progressed well over the next few days, though the weather proved unpredictable. Sometimes the men could labour in shirtsleeves with the air still and the sun warm on their backs. At others, a bitterly cold east wind whipped across the building site, tossing loose snow about and making frost nips a real danger. When the wind rose to gale force, Marr ordered that the roof of the near-complete main hut should be secured with 1.5in wire stays, with stanchions driven into clefts between the rocks.

Despite the worsening conditions, by 22 February attention could be turned to building two extensions on the newly christened 'Bransfield House', one on the north side and the other along the galley end. The extension to the north would eventually serve as the expedition's mess room and dormitory, but while it was under construction everyone slept in the rather barn-like Boulton & Paul building, using the iron bedsteads brought from Deception Island. Davies, Back, Lamb and Taylor occupied bunks on one side, Ashton and Berry slept on the opposite side, while Marr and Blair were located next to the galley. Only Farrington enjoyed any degree of privacy, telling his wife with obvious satisfaction, that 'I am to have a little corner room to myself in the hut and there I will have the wireless gear and my bed complete with spring mattress if you please. I will be able to arrange my books and other little treasures as I please.'[3] Building work would continue with minor interruptions until the end of April, expanding to include a porch and a third substantial extension to the main hut. This last section of the building would run east to west and project at a right angle to the rest of the structure, giving its floor plan a squat L-shape. It would provide space for general storage and accommodate a bathroom, incorporating the cast-iron bathtub salvaged from the Deception Island hospital and the lavatories. Although luxurious in some respects, by the time of its completion, the hut's design and its interior layout would have seemed familiar to most veterans of the Heroic Age of polar exploration.

Since all but two of the men came from either the Royal Navy or the Merchant Service, nautical terminology became the accepted lingua franca during the building phase, much to the confusion of the non-sailors, Taylor and Lamb:

The floor became the 'deck'; the front was the 'forepart', and the rear was 'aft', whether talking about a boat, a building or a board; boards were sawn either 'fore and aft' or 'athwartships'; partitions were 'bulkheads' and the ceiling the 'deckhead'; the outer edge of a piece of wood was its 'outboard' side; posts or columns were the 'stanchions'; and pieces of wood and other supplies which were lying strewn around and outside the house were 'overboard', while if they became lost they were 'adrift'. The kitchen was ... the galley, rooms were 'cabins' and any kind of cupboard was a 'locker' in which one's 'gear' was 'stowed'.[4]

Fortunately, this unusual phraseology did not discourage them and, along with Back, Taylor and Lamb, became two of Ashton's most enthusiastic assistants – though the fastidious carpenter reserved the right to finish each element of the work himself.

Language was not the only challenge faced by the craftsmen. The timber retrieved from Deception Island had warped over the years, while the African hardwood originally used to floor some Nissen huts on the Falklands proved so tough that, when they were hammered in, the salvaged Norwegian nails bent into a variety of shapes known colloquially as 'coat hangers'. The ambitious nature of Ashton's modifications also meant that the supply of wood rapidly began to dwindle and the workmen soon found themselves foraging among the scraps previously discarded as useless. A scarcity of tongue-and-groove match boarding made it necessary to line the corrugated iron lavatory annex with sections of packing cases and the partitions between the permanent two-man sleeping cubicles in the main mess room extension were made from 'beaver board', a material which, Marr observed, 'has not been used in the Antarctic before but has been widely used in the Arctic during this war'.[5] For all its usefulness, however, the board proved neither wind nor sound proof.

Another cause of the shortages was the men's decision to 'liberate' precious building materials for their own purposes, and homemade bookshelves, cupboards, tables and other items of furniture appeared miraculously in each of the cabins. With the addition of books, photographs and an official issue of small rugs to soften and brighten the floor, the hut gradually began to take on a more homely feel. And yet it was impossible for the men not to be aware of their isolation and inaccessibility; of their distance from their nearest neighbour; and of the essential fragility of their new home. Suffering from a minor stomach disorder, prior to the completion of the toilet block, one night Lamb left the hut to relieve himself. During those few solitary minutes, he was struck as never before by the sheer hostility of the environment in which he and his companions now dwelt:

... there was a vague glare of moonlight behind the ruffled clouds, the wind was whining desperately, and the landscape looked so savage and inhospitable that I was seized for a moment with a sort of fear, and I was glad to get back to my bunk again, thinking that even this, so warm and comfortable, was separated from [the elements] only by four inches of wood and paper.[6]

Putting these natural but largely unspoken fears to one side, the general consensus among the inhabitants was that Bransfield House provided 'very comfortable and commodious'[7] accommodation. Indeed, Taylor felt that the expedition could claim to be 'much more comfortable in this house than many people are in much more civilised localities'.[8] As for Marr, while he agreed that the hut made a 'fine residence' and went to some lengths to acknowledge 'the energy, genius and craftsmanship' of Ashton, he also considered that the sheer size of the modified building could serve to support the political objectives of his expedition:

Doubtless we could have done with a less elaborate building than we eventually built, but bearing in mind the political background from which the expedition started and the possibility of the permanent occupation of this base which might entail I considered we had good reason for erecting as imposing a structure as we could.[9]

Despite this confidence, he and his companions might have been surprised to discover that their hut would still be standing, and in regular use, seventy years after Ashton drove the first nail home.

Once the main structure had been made secure and weatherproof, some of the explorers could begin to focus on jobs other than construction work. As well as taking six daily meteorological observations, during these early days of the expedition Back found that his medical practice was far more extensive than might have been expected in the pure, germ-free atmosphere of the Antarctic. In early March Lamb and Blair both contracted tonsillitis and other members reported colds and other minor ailments, giving rise to speculation regarding the possibility of germs having been transported south in the packing cases and bedding. Farrington noted that though the party was 'in good spirits ... most of us are suffering from effects of overwork'[10] and Back attributed much of the illness to a combination of lack of sleep and hard physical labour. 'It can hardly be due to diet deficiencies,' opined Lamb, 'for we have a rich and varied diet, still largely fresh, and supplemented by a daily issue of vitamin C tablets.'[11]

Immediately before disembarking from the *Fitzroy* on 17 February, an understandably nervous Back had delivered an impassioned speech 'on the merits (to say nothing of the ethics) of building up a medical

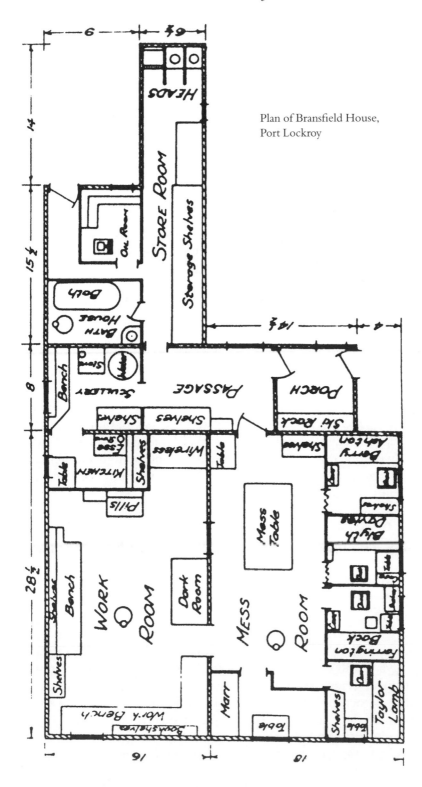

Plan of Bransfield House,
Port Lockroy

practice in his new territory in such a manner as this'.[12] In later years, he felt able to describe his general lack of preparedness with rather more amusement:

> As far as medical stores were concerned, I was told, 'You can order anything you like but you aren't allowed to talk to anyone about it.' I had a very brief visit with Surgeon Commander Bingham[13] who gave me two bits of advice; one was true and one was not. He said: 'Deception Island is like England,' which is not true, and that, 'Resinol is excellent treatment for frostbite,' which it is. The Navy provided a very good medical library for junior Medical Officers, so I ordered that, but somebody left it on the jetty at Montevideo, so the whole time I was down South, the only book I had was *Aids to Tropical Diseases*, but I don't think my colleagues knew that, and they all thought I was quite a good doctor.[14]

In addition to *Tropical Diseases* by Mansol Bahr, the medical library, left so carelessly on the jetty at Montevideo, would have contained such works as *Venereal Diseases* by Burke, *Diseases of the Eye* by Parsons, *Naval Hygiene* by Shaw, *Common Skin Diseases* by Roxburgh and *Anaesthetics Afloat* by Woolbron. It should also have included *Emergency Surgery* by Hamilton Bailey but, surprisingly for a book in such high demand at this stage of the war, it was 'out of print'.[15] Fortunately, Back felt competent to operate on Farrington's septic finger without reference to its pages, though he later admitted that he had '… awful visions, actually, that with a septic finger, something would go wrong: you'd first have to amputate his finger, and then half his arm and the rest of his arm. [One] wasn't quite certain how you were going to end up.'[16]

Another vital job was to get all the stores under cover. Most had been only roughly sorted and still lay on the summit of Goudier Island, protected by nothing more substantial than a tarpaulin. The expedition's stores officer, Gwion, or 'Taff', Davies, a 26-year-old Welshman from Mostyn in Flintshire, had taken his Tripos in Natural Sciences at Cambridge before the outbreak of war – but he had also sailed before the mast on the schooner, *Merry Miller*, and during the Antarctic whaling season of 1939–40 he had worked with Marr preserving, freezing and canning whale meat. This last experience had given him a profound respect for Marr and he had jumped at the chance to join the personnel of Operation Tabarin. Now the two worked closely together, scratching a reference on each tin of food so that its contents would not become a mystery in the event of rust or damp causing the label to become detached. In Marr's opinion, 'The whole life and work of an expedition such as this hangs upon the protection and maintenance of its vital stores and it is not generally appreciated what a vast amount of hard, unspectacular and often thankless work that this entails.'[17]

One foodstuff that proved impossible to preserve was the meat brought from the Falklands. Due to a lack of cold storage, during the voyage south the mutton and beef had been suspended from the shrouds of the *Fitzroy* in a fashion tried and tested during previous polar expeditions. This means of transportation had given to the ship the appearance of a butcher's stall and threatened to drip gore on the unwary in warmer weather, but it had also provided the men with a source of easily accessible nourishment and many had hacked lumps of fat from the carcasses and eaten them raw in an attempt to combat the cold. On arrival at Port Lockroy they had buried the meat in a bank of snow, but after four weeks of unseasonably warm weather it had started to decay. Its hiding place had also been discovered by the predacious brown skuas and giant petrels, and eventually it was dragged down and left on the beach so that the birds might eat in peace. 'These repulsive birds were soon gorging themselves with the rotten meat,' noted Lamb, 'and I was able to film them from a distance of from 15 to 10 feet [sic].'[18]

The last item to be brought ashore had been the 38 tons of coal for heating and cooking, all in bags weighing about 200lb each. Carrying the coal to the hut had been physically demanding for the tired men, and so unpopular had the job become that fetching a sack had been introduced as a forfeit for anyone heard swearing at the mess table. But the penalty did not produce the desired effect; Lamb commented soon afterwards that 'our only anxiety now is that the entrance to the hut may get obstructed by the accumulation of coal'.[19] With this stockpile so conveniently located, Davies became the 'expedition miner', responsible for chipping the daily ration from the frozen heap: 'you had to mine it with a crowbar and it was quite a job getting every sack out … Anyway, I was pleased to do that, 'cos it gave me a job, didn't it? Everybody had his own job, you see.'[20]

On 19 March the shore party's lonely vigil was briefly interrupted by the welcome arrival of the *Scoresby*, which had sailed from Stanley a week earlier. The following morning Marchesi came ashore with Flett, the Base Leader from Deception Island, who had been invited to discuss progress with Marr and, in the absence of a geologist at Port Lockroy, to advise him on local rock formations. A variety of requisitioned items, including Ruberoid roofing felt, were also brought ashore, together with a small amount of mail from Stanley. That evening, four of the ship's complement joined the shore party for dinner, followed by an increasingly boisterous gramophone concert, which continued long after the departure of the guests at 11 p.m.

Over the next few months the gramophone, with its accompanying 150 records, would come to be seen as a mixed blessing. On the one hand, as Farrington told his wife in a typically homesick letter, a familiar piece could remind the men of a world far removed from the one they currently inhabited: 'As I listen to the record being played here, eight thousand miles and more from home, I picture you and me sitting there facing each other across the supper table in the little kitchen where we have known so much happiness.'[21] On the other hand, the constant rep-etition of personal favourites caused extreme irritation to unwilling ears. According to Taylor, who often buried his head in his bedclothes in order to muffle the oft-repeated tunes, 'we found ourselves anticipating every note and inflection as some tunes wore deeper and deeper grooves into the same records night after night.'[22] At times, the desire to destroy the offending records must have become almost irresistible, but on this occa-sion proceedings were halted not by smashed shellac but by a broken leg, sustained when Berry slipped and fell awkwardly during an impromptu fan-dance.

In the sober light of day, Back confirmed his diagnosis and confined Berry to bed until the fitting of a plaster cast rendered him more mobile. In the meantime, Blair would deputise as cook, assisted by John Blyth, a Falkland Islander who had just arrived on the *Scoresby*. Blyth's arrival could not have been better timed. Even before the departure of the two ships in February, Marr had become convinced that Blair would be inca-pable of coping with the duties allotted to him, and he had dispatched a message to Sir Allan Cardinall asking him to find a suitable replacement. On the *Fitzroy*'s return to Stanley, the post had been advertised, candidates interviewed, and Blyth appointed and given a berth on the *Scoresby*, all within thirty-six hours. Blyth had told his interviewers that he:

> … could make bread and cakes, had done some cooking at home, had done some carpentry … And that I had seen the film of Scott's journey to the South Pole,[23] read many books about southern explorers, and thought this a good opportunity to see a part of the world that I'd always wanted to see.[24]

These limited qualifications, along with his seemingly boundless enthu-siasm, would soon prove more than sufficient to make the 20-year-old Blyth a highly valued member of the expedition, Marr noting that 'Temperamentally and physically he is well suited to this sort of life.'[25]

As well as helping to resolve this pressing personnel issue before the onset of winter, the *Scoresby*'s reappearance provided Marr with a wel-come opportunity to address other matters. In particular, the *Scoresby*'s visit would enable him to assert British claims over an area wider than that of Port Lockroy. Along with Ashton, Back, Blair and Lamb, he boarded the ship after an early breakfast on 22 March and by midday all five were scanning the shoreline of Flandres Bay, a deep indentation in the Graham Land coastline off Gerlache Strait, in search of a suitable landing place. Eventually, Marr decided on Cape Renard, a remarkable conical rock which appears to spring vertically out of the sea to rise to a height of 2,624ft. The ship stood off as he and a small landing party rowed ashore, carrying a metal Union flag and a wooden board on which the words 'British Crown Land' had been painted. Standing in the bows of the dinghy as it rose and fell in the 8ft swell, Marr took the painter in his hand and then, judging his moment to perfection, leapt for a rocky ledge just above sea level. Covered in a slimy growth of blue-green algae, the ledge provided only a very insecure foothold and for a moment it looked as though he would slip off into the sea, but years of working on deck in the turbulent waters of the South Atlantic had given Marr a finely tuned sense of balance and he managed to cling on with hands and knees before climbing higher to secure the painter around a knob of rock. Next, he hauled in the boat so that the rest of the party could land without recourse to gymnastics. Together they gouged out a foundation using pickaxe and shovel and then raised the sign, securing it with guys and with stones packed around its feet. The first 'British Crown Land' sign had been placed on the Antarctic mainland.[26]

To celebrate this achievement, on the voyage back to Port Lockroy Marr asked Marchesi if he might use the *Scoresby*'s facilities to take a warm saltwater bath, since the bath salvaged from Deception Island had not yet been installed at the hut. Unfortunately, his ablutions proved somewhat less relaxing than he might have hoped. As Marchesi picked his way back towards Base 'A', he found himself navigating a channel studded with tiny, snow-covered islands, each about 40 or 50ft long and closely resembling chunks of pack ice. 'I was on the bridge,' Marchesi remembered:

and the Officer of the Watch was leaning over the side ... there were a few bits of ice hanging around and looking ahead I saw what looked just like a piece of ice; I didn't pay much attention until suddenly the Officer of the Watch said 'My God! I can see the bottom!'

Fortunately we had spotted this just in time to put the engines full astern, before the ship hit the rock amidships thereby reducing the impact. This sent a loud 'CLANG!' through the ship – the next thing I knew was Jimmy Marr, stark naked and dripping with water, arriving on the bridge. He thought we were damaged and sinking, but luckily all was well, so he retired to take another hot bath. We returned to Port Lockroy with a very clean Jimmy Marr at about 17:30, when he and his party were put ashore.[27]

The *Scoresby*'s steel cladding gave her sufficient strength to withstand the impact amidships and she sustained no serious damage. Marr left no account of whether his modesty had received a more serious dent – though the better part of twenty years at sea had probably ensured that his skin was at least as thick as the ship's.

The next day witnessed the erection of another sign: that of the Port Lockroy Post Office. With stamps on sale again, some of the ship's crew collected lumps of rock and packed them into bulky parcels so that they could send the largest possible assortment of stamp denominations to philatelist friends in the UK. Back and Berry, the latter propped up on pillows and blankets, then stamped and franked this weighty correspondence so that it could be dispatched with the returning *Scoresby*. At the time, no one appears to have commented on the apparent anomaly that, while radio communications were restricted and encrypted for reasons of secrecy, letters could now be posted from the expedition's two bases with Falkland Islands stamps bearing the franking legend 'Graham Land, Dependency of'.

On 24 March the *Scoresby*, carrying Flett and Blair, sailed for Stanley via Deception Island. As soon as the ship departed with what everyone assumed to be the last outgoing mail, work began on a Nissen hut brought from the Falklands. Using a sheet of corrugated iron as a makeshift sledge, Lamb, Taylor, Marr, Davies, Back and Farrington dragged about 7 tons of rock from the beach for use in the foundations. Next, they erected the steel framework, but when this blew over in a violent storm, shearing all the bolts in the process, the builders had no option but to start again from scratch. Finally, with the skeletal frame re-erected, they could attach the curved corrugated iron sheets with J-bolts and begin to transfer the stores inside. Prior to the completion of the Nissen hut, the stores could only be accessed by prising up the corner of the frozen, snow-covered tarpaulin and crawling around underneath until the required case could be identified and manhandled into the open air. It was, in Davies' words, 'a job for a bed bug'.[28] Those cases not so protected were frozen into a solid block of ice and snow and required even more effort to free. Once cleared of the accumulated snow, the boxes were stacked down each side of the hut, with a passageway left along the middle. Racks loaded with lengthy items such as skis and sledge runners were then suspended from the steel ribs of the ceiling.

Most polar explorers have struggled against the incursion of drift snow, which can enter with the force of a steam jet through the tiniest aperture, and Davies found that the completed Nissen hut became the scene of one of his hardest-fought battles. Inevitably, the structure had suffered during its demolition, transportation and re-erection, but all the visible damage had been repaired and the gaps in the cladding sealed. And yet every blizzard filled it with drifts, 'big as a double sofa, some of them'.[29] Puzzled, he examined every inch of the building until, with a blizzard in full spate, at last he found the points of entry: scores of tiny, unplugged bolt-holes dating to the hut's first erection on the Falkland Islands. He tried manufacturing plugs with paper and rags, but these blew out. He experimented with flour paste, but this froze solid before he could apply it. Finally, proving the old adage that necessity is the mother of invention:

> out of disgust or desperation, I spat on 'em and of course that froze them up … It stopped the holes! I went round then, spitting at all these scores of little holes, wherever I could find one. And, you know, it stuck and it stopped the problem – and that's how we kept the snow out![30]

Around the same time, Lamb observed: 'There is no doubt that winter is now approaching; there is a sharp nip in the air all day … and it gets dark already about 1830hrs.'[31] However, the landscape could still reveal itself as breathtakingly beautiful, especially when at sunset Mount Français was fringed with a deep rose colour against a darkening purple-blue sky.

Even Farrington, who thought longingly of his home and family, found that he was not immune to the bewitching spectacles of the Antarctic. On 5 April, in a letter to his wife, he described Port Lockroy as it appeared in the light of the full moon:

> She had just sailed out in all her beauty from behind a snow-clad mountain. And our surroundings became like a delicate silver etching. I stood out alone and it was so calm and quiet that I thought the little waves breaking on the shore might be the same as those we listened to on summer evenings at Rhoscolyn. A bird calling as it flew away beyond the house might have been a thrush. Overhead little wisps of silvery clouds traced delicate patterns across the sky and the bright stars peeped out of the dome of night.[32]

Seven days later he was thrilled to hear that his nostalgic word picture would reach home much sooner than he had anticipated. Prior to sailing from Port Lockroy, Marchesi had expressed doubt about being able to return before the onset of winter, 'but said he would do so if possible'.[33] On 12 April news came through that the *Scoresby* would pay one last visit to Deception Island and that the Naval Officer in Charge at the Falkland Islands had told Marchesi to use his own discretion when determining whether to push on to Goudier Island. 'We had previously been informed that it was too late for her to come down here,' Farrington wrote, 'and I can assure you that we were feeling pretty sore about it … This will be the first mail we have received since leaving home. I am as excited as can be.'[34] Confident in Marchesi's determination to reach the base, Marr immediately sent another coded invitation to Flett at Deception Island so that the two could continue their discussions about the work at Base 'B'.

Having encountered very little ice in the Neumayer Channel, the *Scoresby* arrived at 2.35 p.m. on 17 April and anchored to the west of the island. Flett and Marchesi came ashore in a dinghy, together with some bicycle wheels to be used as sledge meters, mutton carcasses and yet another cast iron bath salvaged from the derelict hospital on Deception Island.[35] Much to the delight of the men of Base 'A', they also brought the mail and newspapers from home and silence descended on the hut as the explorers retired to read their letters. 'It is wonderful what a difference it makes here to have mail from one's loved ones at home,' Lamb wrote gratefully, 'and to be able to send back a reply.'[36] The arrival of the mail clearly lightened the mood because Lamb also noted that, after a fine dinner prepared by Berry and Blyth, 'proceedings became lively', the usually staid Flett performing a dance with Berry, still in his plaster cast, to the accompaniment of Blyth's accordion. Presumably Back believed that this exercise would aid his patient's recovery because he joined their gambols, which continued until the party broke up at 10.30 p.m. with a rendition of *Auld Lang Syne*. The *Scoresby* sailed north at 6.30 the following morning, but the excesses of the night before meant that she departed without fanfare; indeed, none of the shore party left their beds to wave her off.

If an unexpected postal delivery could act as a potent tonic, an unanticipated interruption to the mail service could produce equally powerful negative effects. On 23 April Marr received a signal telling him that the combined Town Hall and Post Office in Stanley had burned to the ground on the 16th and that all the letters sent north on 24 March had been destroyed. This devastating news meant that for seven long months the only letters that the explorers' families would receive would be those sent on 17 February and 17 April. The only additional communications they could hope for would be short, coded telegrams which used set formulaic phrases approved by the censor.

The residents of Goudier Island might have been surprised by the importance attached to their private correspondence by individuals other than its intended recipients. The Foreign Office, ever an unwilling participant in the operation, had vigorously opposed the franking of mail believing that it would advertise the expedition's existence and accelerate a damaging confrontation with Argentina – but the Colonial Office had insisted upon it as the best and most traditional means by which to underpin sovereignty claims. Now, with the expedition's franked mail passing through Montevideo, the Foreign Office mandarins had to accept that 'the question of publicity has become unavoidable'.[37] They also had to decide on how to acknowledge formally the expedition's existence to the wider world. The obvious answer was an official press release and on 24 April 1944, *The Times* carried a brief article with the headline 'Antarctic Research', in which it revealed that 'arrangements have been made for scientific research and survey work to be resumed in some of the most remote British possessions'.[38] The same day, the BBC reported the existence of the expedition during one of its Overseas Service broadcasts to North America. Although the broadcast stopped short of identifying the precise location of the bases, it did assert that the expedition was primarily concerned with 'protecting vital interests and safeguarding the whaling industry'. This last claim caused much amusement at Port Lockroy when Layther, who heard the broadcast at Deception Island, relayed its contents to Farrington. Just three days later, the *Daily Sketch* published an article on the issue of the overprinted stamps, with the *London Evening News* following suit on 6 May. Given that the statement released by the Colonial Office referred to 'administrative officials' and to the fact that the expedition 'expected to remain in the Antarctic for a long time', Argentine and Chilean officials would have been left in absolutely no doubt regarding the expedition's motives.

Of course, the Argentines were not the only readers of *The Times* nor the only people to listen to the BBC's Overseas Service. On the same day as the broadcast and the publication of the article, Winston Churchill wrote to the Foreign Office asking:

> What is the reason for sending an expedition of perfectly good fighting men to the South Pole? If you are seeking to establish our claims as against the United States, the fact might at least have been kept secret during this period of preparation for solemn events.[39]

When the decision to launch Operation Tabarin had been taken early in 1943, Churchill had been in Casablanca with President Roosevelt discussing the planned Normandy landings and the escalation of action in the Far East. In his reply to the brusque memorandum, Anthony Eden reminded the prime minister of his absence from the meeting of the War Cabinet and of the fact that, subsequent to the meeting, 'you approved this decision.'[40] He then went on to reassure Churchill that 'The object of the action which we are taking is to reaffirm our title to the Falkland Islands Dependencies and is not aimed against the United States, who have no claims over this territory, but against Argentine and Chilean claims and encroachments.'[41] As First Lord of the Admiralty, in August 1914 Churchill had responded to Shackleton's offer to surrender the *Endurance* and her crew to the war effort with the curt order, 'Proceed.'[42] His concern, thirty years later, with the assignment to Antarctica of 'perfectly good fighting men' provides an interesting contrast with his earlier indifference. But it is even more arresting because it reveals Churchill's acute awareness not only of the need to avoid offending the United States' sensibilities at a critical juncture, but also of his ally's very real interest in the region.

With the existence of this once covert operation revealed in newspapers and on the radio, from this point on a greater volume of coded wireless transmissions was permitted – but the men knew that the brevity and strictly limited number of their personal radio telegrams would do little to allay the anxiety of their loved ones. In the absence of any incoming post, the BBC's shortwave service, especially the nine o'clock news and programmes like 'Music While You Work', provided a very welcome link with home and Farrington recalled 'the nostalgic thrill it gave us to hear the sonorous sound of the bells drowning the noises of the storms outside – it seemed to bring our dear ones nearer'.[43] But the immediacy of this link also had its disadvantages. On one occasion, the men could clearly hear the boom of London's anti-aircraft batteries as Big Ben's chimes faded away and Farrington clearly remembered 'the depression that settled on us all at the thought of family and friends at risk'.[44]

At the beginning of May, survey work began when Marr rowed Taylor, Davies and Lamb, with a plane table and rangefinder, to Alice Creek. Climbing to an altitude of 360ft on Harbour Glacier, Taylor plotted points on the plane table, while Lamb used the rangefinder to measure distances between the observed landmarks. This done, they roped themselves together in case they encountered crevasses, and proceeded to a rocky outcrop at the foot of Jabet Peak, where they collected rock samples. The following day, they repeated the visit in order to set up the camera to produce panoramic views for use as part of the survey, but defective equipment meant that the work took much longer than planned. The expedition's decrepit Cirkut No. 6 survey camera dated to the early years of the century and, according to Taylor's official survey report, 'two films were spoiled before any results at all were obtained from it', and even those required 'the expenditure of much profanity and patience ... The motor seemed to lack the power necessary to turn both the camera and the film simultaneously, resulting in stoppages, overexposures and vertical streakiness in the pictures.'[45] Over the following months, the camera would be practically rebuilt, with its covers refitted, the motor stripped and cleaned, the starting switch repaired, the shutter cleaned and reground, and the tripod legs refitted. Fortunately, other elements of Taylor's work proceeded more smoothly. On the evening of 25 May he and Lamb set up the theodolite in order to calculate the position of Goudier Island. They sighted the instrument on known stars in each of the four quadrants of the hemisphere, a total of some fifty stars, and when the star appeared exactly on the cross hairs of the theodolite, they noted the time from the chronometer and logged the angles. A few days later they repeated the observation to confirm their original readings.

Inside the hut, things were beginning to assume a much more workmanlike appearance and Farrington, always anxious to send reassuring messages to his wife, could tell her that 'We are rapidly getting things more and more shipshape and now we are finding more time for the little inside jobs, which though not much in themselves, add greatly to our comfort.'[46] Many of the shelves and other fixtures were finished; leftover timber had been sorted out and stacked; and outdoor clothing hung up so that it would be ready-to-hand when anyone needed to work outside. Davies made a 'cellar' out of empty boxes in the space underneath the corrugated iron extension and the items still piled in the dumps were sorted and rehoused. Meanwhile, Ashton built his own bench in the shared workshop and installed a carpenter's and machinist's vice and a grindstone with which he could sharpen his cherished tools – many of which were his own private property – before hanging them in specially constructed racks. 'To such a craftsman as he is,' Taylor observed, 'the sight of the band of "wood butchers" losing and breaking these tools of his must have been a heart breaking experience … So one can readily understand the gratifying delight with which Ashton eventually approached the problem of constructing a workbench for himself.'[47] An equally sympathetic Lamb added the finishing touches by gathering together all the loose nails, screws and bolts and meticulously sorting them into tins, which he placed on shelves above the tool racks.

More important for the comfort of the hut's inhabitants as a whole was the completion of the indoor lavatories, which 'were gravity operated and were not installed without great deliberations by a specialist'.[48] Although these deliberations resulted in nothing more sophisticated than two buckets on a 'sledge' made of corrugated iron to aid the process of emptying them on to the sea ice, the colder temperatures made the addition of this facility a very welcome development. Nonetheless, many thought emptying the latrines one of the worst chores and Blyth noted that, since the contents of the buckets soon froze and had to be chipped out with an ice axe, 'it was advisable to wear goggles and cover the mouth.'[49]

On 22 May the sun sank behind the massive bulk of Mount Français to the north. It would not reappear for over two months and in the intervening period the best that the men could hope for would be a chill semi-darkness. Taylor wrote that:

For a few weeks following the loss of the sun, its disappearance had no perceptible effect upon our spirits, but by the end of June, the continuous series
of drab grey days, many of which were made even more gloomy by gales
which blew for days at a time, had become monotonous in the extreme.[50]

For his part, Farrington thought:

[the] worst feature was the lack of daylight in the wintertime when we had
to remain in the house with the lamps and fires going all day. It used to get
very warm and stuffy as we were unable to open any windows ... The sun
was out of sight for about eight weeks and in the middle of the day we only
had about four hours of twilight.[51]

With the men now largely confined indoors, Marr knew that the next
few weeks could prove to be the most trying of the entire expedition. In
an attempt to minimise the depressing effects of incarceration, he not only
ensured that each of the men had a useful occupation, but also introduced
a routine which would help to give order to their lives. Davies thought
this routine 'very varied ... you'd think, being down there, you'd be wondering what to do with yourself. But actually, there was more work than
you could manage, almost ... Really, you're working from the time you
turned out to the time you turned in.'[52]

So far as Marr was concerned, one of the most important jobs was to
prepare both men and equipment for sledging: 'There was a great deal
to do as there had been no time in London to give any attention to this
side of our work.'[53] Skis and tents were checked; harnesses and covers
for sleeping bags sewn; ration boxes and ski-bindings manufactured; and
sledging rations measured and packed. A 12ft Nansen sledge, which had
been delivered ready for use, was unpacked and Marr, Davies and Taylor
assembled two 6ft Nansen sledges. These had arrived as kits and required
fastening together with lashings made of rawhide and rope. In the manner
developed by the Inuit, the strips of rawhide, previously soaked in water,
were passed through holes in the wood, drawn tight and fastened with
small screws. As it dried the rawhide contracted and hardened, making a
firm lashing. Since the expedition did not possess a sledge meter to record
the distances travelled, Ashton 'contrived an ingenious substitute' using
one of the bicycle wheels brought down by the *Scoresby*. Of course, this
equipment would be useless unless the men learned how to travel in polar
conditions and so, whenever the weather permitted, Marr drilled them
in skiing until 'they were able to move about comfortably and quickly
over all types of surface and country'.[54] As well as giving the men a skill
that would facilitate the completion of their fieldwork, the practice also

provided much needed and pleasurable exercise. Even Farrington, who was not renowned for his physicality, remarked that it was 'an exquisite joy almost akin to flying'.[55]

Lamb, whose 1942 doctoral thesis had examined continental movement as evidenced by lichen flora, concentrated on the study of how lichens survived under Antarctic conditions. He was, Back thought, 'the best botanist to go down since Hooker, if not even better than him',[56] and his enthusiasm for his rather arcane subject proved surprisingly contagious. According to the doctor, 'he encouraged the most uninterested of his companions to an interest in lichens … He would go around and survey some little growth about half-an-inch long, and this would be described as "luxuriant vegetation" and he really inspired everybody.'[57] As well as grasping every possible opportunity to collect lichen samples, in the preceding weeks Lamb had undertaken a range of environmental experiments and prepared more for the winter months. He had made a 5ft-tall snow gauge to record snow accumulation and had borrowed a low-temperature thermometer from the doctor so that he could observe ground surface temperatures under the snow. He had also dug into the 'miniature glacier' to the south of the hut to locate bands of ice in the granulated snow, which demonstrated the processes of snow accumulation and subsequent thawing. He had also tunnelled into a snowdrift to ascertain the distance light would penetrate through freshly fallen snow. He crawled into this tunnel, removed snow from above his head until he could see light and then, thrusting a ruler upwards, he measured the depth of the remaining snow. Recording a thickness of 23in, he surmised that mosses would receive sufficient light to survive despite being buried under a considerable amount of snow, although only from the green and blue end of the visible spectrum. 'I am convinced,' Marr wrote in his scientific report, 'that, restricted as his field has been, his meticulous and painstaking work here has already gone a long way towards clearing up the somewhat confused taxonomy of the Antarctic lichens'[58] – a conviction fully supported by Lamb's discovery of several unknown species, including *Verrucaria surpuloides*, the only true marine lichen in the world.

Back, who traced his fascination with meteorology to his schooldays at Marlborough College, proved equally conscientious and had started his six daily meteorological observations on 1 March, an achievement which he considered 'not bad as we only landed in February'.[59] His readings indicate that they experienced their coldest day in August 1944, when the mercury fell to −12°F, and their warmest in early January 1945, when he recorded a temperature of 45 degrees above zero. Taylor, who had endured winters of −40°F in his home city of Winnipeg, was derisive of such temperatures, noting that 'Back once hung a thermometer on the wall of the house …

and it immediately climbed up above a hundred.' However, he also acknowledged that 'if the slightest breeze springs up, such heat is gone in an instant,
and the chill of the atmosphere is felt immediately.'[60] Back also recorded the
wind patterns – noting that it blew for 80 per cent of the period of their
stay, peaking at 80mph in November – and the mean temperature of the sea,
which fell from 35°F in March to 28°F in August. Although some members
of the expedition bemoaned the fact that their doctor seemed far more passionate about meteorology than about the practise of medicine, Marr was
convinced that Back's enthusiasm for his scientific duties could pay real div-
idends. Referring obliquely to the Argentines' claim to Laurie Island, and
to the legitimacy given to that claim by their uninterrupted programme of
meteorology, he asserted that Back's work would serve to 'strengthen our
political position, if strengthened it need be, should our sovereign rights
over these territories again be questioned by a foreign power'.[61] In this context, he might be forgiven for thinking Back's prioritisation of science over
the treatment of sprains, cuts and frost nips more than justified.

The onward transmission of Back's readings to Stanley constituted one
of Farrington's most important tasks; indeed, Marr considered it so significant that he later wrote that Farrington 'has done the expedition, and all
it stands for, a greater service than any other member'.[62] For the first three
months, wireless communication continued to be restricted to the minimum necessary to maintain contact between the two bases and Stanley,
with all messages encrypted using five-figure cipher groups. With even
the lengthy requisitions for the next season's stores, which often exceeded
1,000 groups, dealt with in this way, the work proved both tedious and
exacting. However, according to Farrington:

> Only on one occasion was I made aware of a mistake arising out of this
> system. That was when a request for 30 gallons (a year's supply) of rum for
> 1945 resulted about five months later in a delivery to Hope Bay of 300 gal-
> lons of rum. I was never able to prove whether the error occurred due to
> faulty mental arithmetic by Doc and myself, a mistake in signalling or a kind
> thought by a sympathetic dispatch clerk in Naval Stores.[63]

The work became somewhat less onerous when, on 18 July, the Admiralty
tacitly acknowledged that the expedition's whereabouts had become
common knowledge and issued instructions that messages should henceforth be transmitted using the international code. In November, the
meteorological reports would be increased to three per day, with the
weather information from Port Lockroy and Deception Island incor-
porated into the Naval Fleet Synoptic Reports for the South Atlantic,
broadcast from Stanley.

Although each member of the expedition had his own special responsibility, everyone, including Marr, shared in the more unpleasant but routine tasks. According to Davies:

> He had reason for wanting to scotch any notion that such jobs were beneath the dignity of officers, and to extol the virtue of useful work of all kinds. There was no need for him to worry about that sort of thing with our crowd, as we all got on well together, shared the same food and living quarters, with no 'officer' privileges or apartheid. We made it our business to get on well together, make the best of each other and help one another – we had to, to survive down there – a contrast to the competitive way of life which 'civilisation' forces on us.

Not everyone shared Davies' rose-tinted views. Taylor, in particular, recorded a number of instances of what he considered to be incompetence, laziness and obstructiveness very much at odds with both Davies' utopian vision and the complimentary personnel reports written by Marr. Back, though helpful as an assistant carpenter and conscientious in his meteorological work, he thought prone to 'Farrington's influence to laziness'. Davies, while 'most anxious and willing to tackle any job', he considered largely incompetent and his energy 'uselessly misdirected'. But the worst offender in his eyes was Berry, whom he thought 'a gossiping rumour mongering mischief maker, whose mouth never stops flapping from morning to night.'[64] Inevitably, such views became difficult to conceal at times and Marchesi noted on his return visits that 'Sometimes you thought there was a certain amount of friction going on between various people,' though he also acknowledged that 'this is understandable after six months with nothing else to do.'[65]

Marr, too, though respected by the majority, attracted his fair share of criticism. Davies remembered how Marr drove himself.

> Whenever there was a miserable job to do; for instance, say one of the windows blew in during a blizzard, he was the first man out, tacking up canvas and all that sort of thing with his cold hands. And if ever there was a miserable, horrible job, or a dangerous job he was there in the thick of it … "Never lay back" he said, "Never lay back." And you felt … it wasn't the thing to do, to take things easy – you've got to do a proper job, do it to your utmost, for the rest of your life, really, as far as you could; not lay back and take it easy.[66]

However, Back thought that this work ethic also had its negative aspects: 'if there were two ways to do any job, he would choose the difficult way.

He seemed to revel in doing things the hard way, which sometimes was a bit difficult if you were working with him.'[67] Many members of the expedition had begun to refer to their leader as 'The Boss', a slightly tongue-in-cheek reference to Marr's mentor, Shackleton, whose men had given him the same nickname; but, in a humorous allusion to his uncompromising drive, Farrington also described him as 'the Führer'.[68]

Despite his reputation for occasional conviviality and his penchant for 'barroom singsongs', Marr appears to have been regarded by many as 'a loner, very much so'.[69] This trait was no doubt exacerbated by his position of command and the need to prevent a familiarity which, in some circumstances, might undermine his authority. 'Marr kept his own counsel,' opined Back:

> he obviously had secret orders. Presumably he knew what we were supposed to do; if he was, he was the only person who did. I've no doubt the instructions were 'That these are top secret and you keep them to yourself.' So that with those instructions he was to some extent like the captain of a ship: he was on his own and he couldn't have any confidants.[70]

It is possible that the deep-seated disillusionment resulting from his inability to establish Base 'A' at Hope Bay also tended to make him somewhat morose or taciturn. Even the admiring Davies, who was perhaps closer to Marr than anyone else, admitted that 'normally he wasn't a smiling sort of person at all; I think he was naturally a bit dour. But, apart from that, I think just the sheer anxieties of what he had to do, and the whole expedition … told on him.'[71] His apparent inability to conquer or to at least better disguise these feelings was unfortunate, because it limited Marr's success in diverting his men from similar thoughts and inevitably, trapped by force of circumstance on a tiny island, with limited opportunities to conduct scientific and survey work, some began to question the purpose of the expedition and their part in it. Without doubt, Marr's harshest critic was Taylor, who would go on to express serious reservations regarding his leader's character and achievements – though these comments may have been influenced, in part at least, by dissatisfaction with his own treatment by officialdom after the end of the expedition. Most significantly, he asserted, albeit only in a much later private memorandum, that Marr's drinking had begun to reach disturbing proportions and rumours regarding this weakness would continue to circulate long after the expedition.[72]

Conditions in the bunkroom area during cold weather were far from ideal and sometimes added to the strains of living in such isolation. In particular, with the drop in temperatures condensation began to form on the ceiling, producing an irritating 'indoor rain'. To solve the problem, Ashton fitted an additional roof of corrugated iron, using *Sisal Kraft* paper as insulation between the two layers. Another frustration was lack of privacy. Five cabins had been built in the bunkroom extension, each 6ft x 7ft and fitted with a window. Apart from Marr's, which doubled as an office, each cabin accommodated two men, and was furnished with a two-tiered bunk bed brought from the whaling factory at Deception Island and a folding chair. But there was only enough room for one man at a time to change his clothes, while attempts to heat the sleeping area at night had to be abandoned due to fumes building up during periods when doors could not be opened on a fairly regular basis.

In such circumstances, personal traits and habits which might have seemed harmless or amusing elsewhere now became a source of irritation. On one occasion, Farrington, who had now moved into a cabin with Back, noted that:

> I have turned in now. Doc is having a bath but he is making noises as though he will be coming to bed at any moment. He is a noisy lad … He is terribly untidy too – this morning he put on one of my socks by mistake and then we couldn't tell which was his and which were mine. Luckily I had bathed last night and was getting out a clean pair in any case. Here he comes now, so I'll have to say goodnight.[73]

Fortunately, even Taylor, who was not of a particularly forgiving nature, acknowledged that while there 'were occasional flare-ups of temper, and we had our likes and dislikes among each other … no altercation assumed any serious proportions'.[74]

So far as the quality of their food was concerned, the men had remarkably few complaints. In Back's opinion, 'We had very good food; a bit monotonous, and the tinned milk all froze and it was pretty disgusting. But on the whole, the food was excellent.'[75] Moreover, whatever his faults as a hut companion, no one questioned Berry's skills as a cook. In his official report Marr tended to avoid criticism and to concentrate on his team's strengths, writing that 'We have lived well, indeed luxuriously, on the excellent cooking and baking of A.T. Berry who has found an able and willing assistant in Blyth.'[76] But even Taylor, who loathed Berry, became almost fulsome in his praise:

> We were fortunate in having such a good cook as Berry turned out to be. Under the circumstances in which we had plenty of food supplies of a very limited variety, I do not think that anyone could have served up better meals than those which were supplied us by Berry and Blyth. In my own experience with survey cooks and army cooks, I have never eaten so consistently well as I did at Port Lockroy.[77]

He also agreed with Berry's insistence on regular mealtimes on the basis that 'regular meals and regular habits … give the body its best chance to function healthily.'[78]

Tinned foods included beef, carrots, peas and asparagus, while beetroot, potatoes, cabbage and beans had been provided in dried form. But these products were supplemented with turnips, which seemed immune to the cold, and with 'seal meat, fish, shags and just lately the eggs of penguins, shags and gulls'.[79] Welcome though they were, some of these fresh supplements to the preserved foodstuffs proved difficult to source – a fact that prompted Marr to remark that 'chickens and pigs could be kept at these bases. They do well enough at South Georgia.'[80] Fish were scarce and since the explorers managed to shoot only four Weddell seals for the pot, their flesh, too, became something of a delicacy:

> The steaks and livers are excellent. We have also tried the heart – stuffed. It is very palatable and indistinguishable from the stuffed heart commonly encountered in restaurants at home. Shags (*Phalacrocorax*) were occasionally eaten. They were usually served *en casserole* and very palatable they were too.[81]

The shags could also be roasted and Blyth carefully recorded Berry's tried and tested method of preparation: 'First you kill it, that's most important, then gut it and wash it out in the sea, then put an onion in its throat, and hang upside down for two hours, the onion will take away the salty taste, then skin it, stuff it, and roast it.'[82]

For drinking water, the expedition relied upon the chunks of freshwater ice littering the harbour – a supply constantly refreshed by thunderous avalanches from the surrounding glacier faces and ice cliffs. However, harvesting the ice presented its own problems. In the poor light of the winter months it proved difficult to distinguish freshwater ice from sea ice and Davies remembered with a chuckle that:

> sometimes somebody'd make a mistake and when it came to "tea-oh!", we'd all be sitting down smiling with hot tea in front of us. All of a sudden everybody's face would go very serious and sour because they'd got sea-ice, you see. Nobody likes salty tea very much … So that fellow's name was mud for the rest of the day.[83]

Alcohol, too, was available in quite surprising quantities, with sherry, rum, gin, beer and whisky all featuring at the regular Saturday night gatherings when the men relaxed together, singing songs to the accompaniment of Blyth's accordion or Marr's mouth organ, telling stories, performing a sketch, or, if the weather permitted, competing in a race on snow shoes.

On special occasions the alcohol-fuelled after-dinner entertainment could become boisterous, Farrington noting on his birthday that 'Doc has just been singing some ribald songs and now Blyth is giving Taylor a lesson on the accordion! Sounds like somebody learning the Morse code.'[84]

Another milestone that more than justified a celebration was Midwinter's Day on 21 June. This event, which marks the sun's furthest declension and the beginning of its long, slow climb back towards the horizon, constitutes the single most important date in the Antarctic almanac. Since the beginning of the Heroic Age it has been celebrated by every party over-wintering on the continent and Operation Tabarin was no exception. The day dawned cold but fine and in the traditional manner all but vital routine tasks, such as bringing in ice for drinking water and coal for the stoves, were postponed until the morrow. Having enjoyed an unusually long lie-in the men devoted the rest of their day to pleasure. With the exception of Berry and Blyth, who concentrated on cooking, and Lamb, who had twisted his right leg in a skiing accident on 10 June, the entire party spent the afternoon skiing around the penguin rookery before returning to a slap-up meal of hors d'oeuvres, purée of pea, fried pilchards, asparagus *au beurre*, York Ham, potatoes (baked and croquette) and garden peas followed by plum pudding, *Macédoine fruit en jelly* and mince pies, all washed down with 'a few drinks to enliven the proceedings and coffee'.[85] Lamb took three photographs by flashlight to record the event for posterity, but there was little likelihood of Marr requiring such an *aide-mémoire*. At the height of the proceedings Farrington, who had been exchanging compliments with his opposite number in Stanley, entered the mess room with the news that Marr's wife had given birth to their second child and their first son – an event that quickly generated a congratulatory message from the party on Deception Island: 'Scotland 2; the rest 0.'

The entire party felt buoyed up by the realisation that winter's end was now in sight: soon, sledging would be a viable prospect, and harnesses and ration boxes would become vital equipment instead of so much clutter. The weather remained somewhat variable, but whenever possible everyone practised their skiing in readiness for the planned survey journeys, their favourite spot being the relatively gentle slopes of the Rookery. By mid-July the sun had risen high enough to send its beams down the Neumayer Channel to light Doumer Island right down to the water's edge, though the great mass of Mount Français still blocked the direct sunlight from reaching Goudier Island. On the 24th Lamb recorded that the sun 'at last returned to us today, being visible for a short time from the door of the hut'.[86] It had been absent since 22 May.

As with so many over-winter expeditions in the Antarctic, the plans for the forthcoming sledging journey now became an obsession for men whose movements had been restricted for so long and Taylor observed that 'Plans for it, always a bit sketchy, were at their best on a Saturday night, following one of Berry's special dinners, when the "arm chair sledgers" gave their imagination free rein.'[87] In the early days, before the onset of winter and despite Marr's gloomy predictions, many had continued to hope that the sea would freeze and allow them to sledge across the whole of the Graham Land Peninsula. But, with the sea stubbornly refusing to oblige, even the most sanguine were soon forced to admit that their range would be far more limited. In fact, traversable sea ice never formed in the Gerlache Strait during the period that Port Lockroy was permanently occupied, and in the summer season of 1944–45 the explorers found that they would be restricted to travelling along the glaciers of neighbouring Wiencke Island. Although this journey would fall far short of the ambitious programme that Marr had aspired to when he accepted leadership of the expedition, for most of the men who took part this first experience of polar travel would be quite unforgettable. For some it would prove near fatal.

5

Wiencke Island

Sledging began on 18 September, when two teams, Marr and Davies in one party and Taylor and Lamb in the other, dragged their 12ft Nansen sledges across the sea ice to Wiencke Island. Each sledge boasted a semi-circular 'cowcatcher' to protect its bow; a pair of wooden handlebars at the stern; and rope brakes, which ran beneath the runners when applied. A key task of the winter months had been the preparation of the sledging rations, which consisted of staple foods known to combine high nutritive values with a minimum of weight: pemmican, biscuits, fats, sugar, oats, chocolate, milk, cocoa, pea flour, tinned bacon and marmite. These items had been packed into ration boxes weighing 50lb each, of which 35lb was food, and each box was expected to last two men for seven days. On paper, with four such boxes per sledge, the parties' maximum period of sledging would be approximately four weeks; however, Marr believed that the rations could be made to last much longer. Taylor 'was told at the time they were being assembled that they were based on the ration schedule used by Scott in 1913, though ours had been increased in amount from the 33.3 ounces per man day of Scott's to about 41.'[1] Given the fate of Scott's polar party in March 1912, it is uncertain whether this news increased or lessened his confidence. In addition to food and fuel, the sledges carried the two-man pyramid tents, Primus stoves, cooking utensils, shovels, skis and survey equipment, bringing their total laden weight to nearly 700lb each.

On an overcast, windless afternoon, with the temperatures hovering just below freezing, the party made good progress across the half mile of sea ice separating Goudier Island from the Gentoo penguin rookery at the foot of Wiencke Island. But as soon as they began to ascend the slopes of the Rookery it became clear that the sledges were simply too heavy for two men to pull uphill and they were forced to double up in order to reach the base of 'Knife Edge Ridge'.[2] This snow ridge connects the

Rookery with the Channel Glacier, which the sledging party intended to use as their route into the interior of the island. It consists of a frozen wall of ice with a slope of some 45 degrees on one side and, on the other, 200ft cliffs which drop into the sea at the entrance to the Peltier Channel. The condition of its surface varies considerably: after a heavy fall of snow it can be climbed in a zigzag traverse on skies; at other times, steps have to be kicked or cut with an ice axe. At the foot of the Knife Edge, Marr and his team began the tedious process of unloading before hauling the empty sledges up the steep slope and then 200ft along its narrow spine to reach the lower slopes of the glacier. Next they brought up the ration boxes and tents and reloaded them before returning to base for the night.

The following morning the weather had deteriorated, with a gusty wind, light snow and patches of fog. In the hope that the conditions would improve as they climbed towards the glacier, Marr decided to proceed and the four men skied back across the sea ice and ascended the slopes to where they had left the sledges the evening before. But the weather worsened and Taylor noted that 'by the time we had reached the point on the glacier at which we had left the sledges, the falling snow had thickened, and the wind was driving it to such an extent that it had become impossible to see beyond a couple of hundred feet'.[3] Continuing the journey would involve travelling blind along the edge of the 200ft-high ice cliffs and Marr had no option but to abort the journey until visibility improved. Disappointed, they skied back to the hut with a cold north wind scouring their faces and with the driving snow reducing visibility to practically nil.

On 20 September, with the assistance of Ashton, Back and Farrington, who would take charge at the base in the absence of Marr and Taylor, they hauled the sledges, one at a time, to an altitude of 600ft above sea level and about 2 miles from the base. Although the surface had begun to level out, it had become clear that the sledges were simply too heavy for the four-man party to manage. 'Accordingly, we decided to travel to the east side of Wiencke Island, where our first survey camp was to be established, with one week's fuel and rations instead of two as originally planned, and at the same time to jettison everything that could reasonably be spared.'[4] By the time Marr and Davies had sorted through the stores, determining what would be left at the depot and what would be carried on the two sledges, a thick fog had descended and the temperature had dropped to 23°F. Cold and tired, they enjoyed 'a light lunch of tea and coffee, which Ashton thought far too light for the work he had done',[5] and skied back to the base, arriving at 5 p.m.

The next day thick fog made it impossible to take the compass bearings necessary for the computation of the course followed, so the party did not return to the sledges until the 22nd, once again accompanied by

Ashton, who would help push the heaviest. The fog remained so dense that, after picking up the sledges, now reduced in weight to approximately 450lb each, the five men struggled on almost blind for a mile up the glacier. Then it suddenly cleared and at last they could set a course across a gentle slope, making for the entrance of a narrow ice-filled valley that led over a 1,000ft pass to the other side of the island. Just as the sun began to break through, they were joined by Back, who had skied from the base. He immediately began to push at the second of the sledges and, with his short, quick strides, his Norwegian snowshoes, or *truger*, 'threw up a continual spray of snow behind him like the water from the stern of a Mississippi paddle-wheel steamer'.[6]

The party maintained a rate of approximately 1½mph across an area riddled with crevasses of indeterminable width and depth, caused by the buckling and splitting of the glacier as it collided with the nearby mountains. Despite the thickness of the snow, the echo of their footsteps in the hidden caverns was disconcertingly audible and Taylor observed that 'it was like putting one's foot ashore to hear the echoless crunch of the snow after we had passed them'.[7] At 1 p.m., they stopped for lunch at a point about half a mile from the foot of the Wall Range, overlooking the Peltier Channel and a snowfield, on the far side of which stood Savoia Peak, a 4,642ft mountain named by Charcot and scaled by members of his *Français* expedition. 'We were looking at what is beyond doubt some of the finest scenery in the world,' wrote Marr:

> To the south lay the narrow passage of the Peltier Channel with its 200-foot ice-walls and flanked by the superb range of the Sierra du Fief [now gazetted as the Fief Range] to the east. The channel was open except for some thin and apparently navigable ice at its northern end. To the west lay Lockroy harbour with the icy peaks of Anvers [Island] beyond. To the north the broad snow field of the harbour glacier leading northwards to the dog-leg corner of the Neumayer Channel; and to the east the sheer sides of Wall Mountain and Luigi de Savoia [Savoia Peak] with the narrow ice-filled valley up which we were to travel in between.[8]

Intending to enter what they named the Luigi Glacier (an unadopted name), they began to descend a sloping col of snow jutting out from the base of the Wall Range. Beyond the col the gradient became much steeper and the descent more precipitous, but with Taylor guiding the nose of the first sledge and Lamb and Ashton roped up behind to prevent a headlong dash downhill, they managed to navigate down the slope without accident. Attempting a more direct route, Marr, Davies and Back also made it down, but as they reached the glacier their sledge broke through a snow

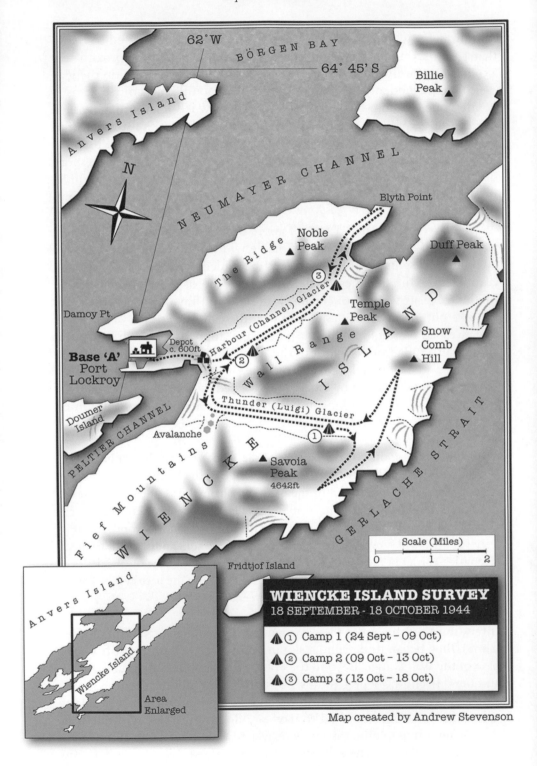

Map created by Andrew Stevenson

bridge and came to an abrupt halt with one runner resting on the surface and the other hanging over a hidden crevasse.

Tying a 50ft alpine rope to the traces, the six men tried to haul the sledge free: 'on this line we all gave a heave to shift the sledge out of the crevasse when … snap! The curved cowcatcher on the front of the sledge parted and broke and the sledge settled even more deeply into the hole.'[9] The sledge was now so firmly jammed that they had no option but to unload; however, with the bridge already weakened, Marr decided that it would be unwise to risk burdening it with more than one man's weight. He immediately roped up and then inched his way towards the lopsided sledge so that he could pass the boxes, one by one, to Taylor, who then passed them to Lamb. Once he had retreated to safer ground, the empty sledge moved easily and the six men could at last see that the crevasse was some 30ft deep and 2½ft wide, with smooth walls of blue ice: small by the standards of many crevasses, but still large enough to have caused serious damage to the sledge or to anyone unfortunate enough to have fallen into it.

With the sledge once again on terra firma, at 4 p.m. Back and Ashton decided to ski back to base, leaving the sledgers to continue their journey alone. Tired after their labours, and struggling with soft snow and a steep gradient, the four men made slow progress. After just a quarter of a mile, Marr decided that they must again double up and so he and Davies left their sledge with its cargo of camping equipment and joined Taylor and Lamb to begin the long, steady pull up the glacier. Laden with the survey instruments, the sledge was heavy, but they continued to trudge steadily upwards to an altitude of 800ft above sea level. They followed a broad ridge leading towards the centre of the glacier, gradually increasing the distance from the base of the Wall Range and approaching Savoia Peak. Flanked by these impressive features, Davies felt that the party 'seemed absolutely minute – like little bugs almost, crawling up the glacier – these mountains were so huge!'[10] And soon the mountains' ability to crush such puny insects would become frighteningly apparent.

At about 5 p.m. they found their path strewn with large blocks of ice, which seriously impeded the progress of the sledge and made it impossible for the sledgers to follow a direct course. When Taylor remarked on these giant lumps of ice, Lamb casually suggested that they were probably the debris of avalanches from the Wall Range:

… we looked up and sure enough, there was a huge hanging glacier of blue ice precariously perched on the top. We now realised that we were in a dangerous position, and exerted our strength to get further up and out of it with all speed; but it was too late. Less than a minute afterwards there was a report like a gun above us, followed by a terrible rumbling like thunder, and from the summit at which we had been looking up a moment before we saw hundreds of tons of snow and ice hurtling down 2,000 feet of cliff face to our left.[11]

For what was probably no more than a matter of seconds, the four men stood rooted to the spot in their harnesses, 'gazing in a kind of fascination at the destruction coming down to overwhelm us'.[12] Then, with the white wall dropping at ever-increasing speed, and with colossal, bouncing blocks of ice fleetingly visible in the billowing white cloud, the instinct of self-preservation took over. With one accord, they turned and ran obliquely down the slope away from the approaching danger – but almost instantly they were halted by their sledge harnesses. Desperately they fumbled with the straps, but their chilled fingers would not function properly and for all their frantic clawing they could not free themselves. 'We couldn't get out of them,' Davies recalled, 'our fingers were too frozen to let go so, instinctively, I think, we just lay down on the snow, "head to sea" as it were, as you might in a small boat.'[13]

A tremendous gust of displaced air blew over the prostrate men and a cloud of fine snow enveloped them, blocking out the light and forcing its way into their eyes, ears and mouths. 'I remember clearly,' Marr wrote, 'that in that instant my fear went away and the only thought that passed through my mind was that in a second or two I should receive a crack on the head that would finish me. I think I wondered vaguely if it would hurt.'[14] For his part, Lamb 'covered my face with my hands and thought of the ice blocks which I had seen coming down; surely it was our finish. Then I became aware that the wind had dropped, the terrible thundering noise had ceased, and one could see again.'[15] By some miracle, the full force of the avalanche had missed them and only snow smoke reached them, despite the 2,000ft downward rush of hundreds of tons of glacier ice. When they stood up, shaken and covered from head to toe in powdered snow, they and their sledges were unscathed. Taylor observed that, judging by the size of the lumps of ice that had skittered to a halt just feet away, 'this had been a small ice fall compared to some of the previous ones. We hitched ourselves to the sledge again, and trudged on at an accelerated pace for the centre of the glacier and the summit.'[16] From this point on, the scene of their incredible escape would be known as 'Thunder Glacier'.

Keeping to the middle of the glacier, the tired but thankful men trudged on. As they gradually gained height, the 'sun gilt cap of a flat topped peak' slowly rose ahead of them, followed by a panoramic view of the Danco Coast, with a belt of mist hanging suspended over the Gerlache Strait. They reached the summit of the glacier at 6 p.m., having covered a couple of miles and ascended several hundred feet since the avalanche so nearly

overwhelmed them. In Marr's opinion, they 'must have covered that distance in record time, stopping only twice to rest when utterly played out'.[17]
It was cold, darkness was gathering fast and a searching wind whipped
through the narrow throat of the glacier to the west. Influenced by his own
poor physical condition and that of his men after their winter of inactivity – and also by the shock of their recent close shave – Marr decided that
the party was in no fit state to haul up the second sledge, with its cargo
of camping gear. Instead they should return, yet again, to the main base.
Starting back at 6.15 p.m., they paused briefly at the sledge abandoned
earlier in the day to recoup their strength with some frozen chocolate and
biscuits, and then Lamb and Taylor took on the role of trailblazers, skiing
along at a rapid, mechanical pace and following their outward tracks in
the gathering dusk. By the time they all reached the depot it was dark
and they made their way with some difficulty down towards the Knife
Edge, Marr admitting that he and Davies only narrowly escaped tumbling
over the 200ft ice cliffs into Lockroy harbour. Finally, they skied down
the Rookery slopes and across the sea ice to Goudier Island, which they
reached in near-total darkness just before 9 p.m. – much to the surprise of
the hut's inhabitants.

Instead of recommencing their journey, the following day Marr and
Davies worked on an ingenious quick-release mechanism for their harnesses. Satisfied that they would not again find themselves hitched
to seemingly immoveable 500lb sledges in a crisis, at 10.30 a.m. on
24 September they began again. Although Taylor noted that, after so many
false starts, 'some of the other chaps were still sceptical … and would have
been less surprised to have seen us that night again than they had been the
night before,'[18] the party made good progress. Having reached the sledge
left by Marr and Davies two days before, they pulled it into the centre of
the glacier, well clear of the avalanche zone, and stopped for lunch. By the
time they finished, a dense bank of fog had begun to roll down the glacier
towards them and within minutes of starting again they were in the thick
of it. Fortunately, there was just enough visibility for the party to find the
tracks they had made on the afternoon of the 22nd and they followed
these to the summit. From that point, Marr and Davies continued down
the other side of the glacier, while Lamb and Taylor halted in the hope that
the fog would clear and enable them to undertake the survey that Taylor
had planned. They waited for an hour, but the fog showed no signs of
lifting and eventually they gave up and followed their companions' tracks
downhill until, at 4.30 p.m., they made out the ghostly outlines of their
tents pitched at an altitude of 500ft above sea level.

Marr and Davies, who had pitched the two tents a few yards apart on
a level snowfield, were already well established, but the new arrivals had

to unpack their bedrolls, a ration box, cooking utensils and their pressure stove and pass them through the round entrance funnel before relaxing. The two-man tents issued to Operation Tabarin were of a standard design for polar work, being of a pyramid shape and roughly 6ft sq. Each tent consisted of four 7ft bamboo poles, over which two skins were fastened: the inner skin being made of a light, white balloon fabric, and the outer of heavy dark-coloured canvas. The outer skin possessed an apron about a foot wide, on top of which snow and ice could be piled to prevent the whole structure from blowing away in a gale. Standard practice among veteran sledgers was to leave the four poles laced to the tent's covers so that it might be unfurled like a giant umbrella, but this process was far from easy in a stiff wind: the tightly woven canvas would flap and snap like a sail and require a vigorous effort on the part of exhausted travellers to control its wayward motions. All in all, in Taylor's opinion, the tents 'provided very serviceable, though cramped, quarters, and having a relatively small cubical content, they were easily and quickly heated'.[19]

Once they had raised their tents, experienced sledgers would follow a carefully devised routine, the whole system designed to maximise comfort and to make best use of the available room. First, the 'inside man' would crawl through the entrance funnel to receive the ground sheet, the bedding rolls and the cooking and ration boxes from the 'outside man'. Having secured the sledge, skis and other equipment to be left outside, the latter also climbed inside, brushing the snow from his clothes and boots in the space between the inner and outer skins. Once inside, both men would remove their outer garments and hang them up to dry, so that a plume of steam would soon be seen issuing from the ventilator at the apex of the pyramid. Most men sat in their sleeping bags to cook, eat or write, still wearing underwear, shirt, pullover, socks and trousers. This was partly for warmth and partly because the only alternative was to kneel, a posture that soon became distinctly uncomfortable.

At this stage of the expedition, however, experience was sorely lacking among the sledgers and on this, his first night under canvas, Lamb dolefully observed that 'everything seemed to be hopelessly muddled and cramped, for we had not yet learned the technique of arranging things so as to exist in comparative comfort.'[20] In the half-light provided by the paraffin safety lamp and the Primus stove, they melted snow and prepared their first meal of cocoa followed by a mixture of pemmican, pea flour and biscuits. In different circumstances this thick brown sludge, with its meagre flavouring of pea flour or curry powder, would seem distinctly unappetising to most people, but after a hard day's manhauling, tired sledgers thought of it very differently: 'we couldn't get enough of it,' Davies remembered. 'It was marvellous! It was great, you know if you're hungry.'[21] Having eaten, they pulled in the radio box and listened to the 9 o'clock BBC time signal and news, which they heard quite clearly. Afterwards they rolled over in their sleeping bags to rest, though Lamb wrote that 'the unaccustomed environment and the hard lumpy snow beneath us did not make for a sound sleep'.[22]

The evening of the 24th became a battle of elbows and knees as Lamb and Taylor vied for space in their badly organised tent, and the next morning things were no better: 'everything we needed seemed to always be in some box which was outside the tent, and there was a constant traffic through the round aperture which constituted the entrance.'[23] To cap it all, just as they prepared to make their long-awaited breakfast of cocoa and porridge, Taylor knocked over the pot of laboriously melted snow and, while neither man was scalded, they had to begin again. Tent companions have argued over far more trivial incidents but, as a grateful Taylor remarked, 'Lamb showed a patience which is typical of him on this occasion when he remarked "what a pity!" or words to that effect.'[24]

After breakfast, all four men crawled from their tents to discover a fine, sunny day and at 10 a.m. Taylor and Lamb skied back to the summit of the Luigi Glacier to make another attempt at their survey. Apart from a bank of fog over the Gerlache Strait, the air was clear and the two quickly got to work using plane table and rangefinder before taking compass bearings of features along the Danco Coast. From their elevated position they could see that the Gerlache Strait remained free of fast ice, once again emphasising the difficulty of accessing the mainland in order to undertake more extensive sledging. Marr and Davies, meanwhile, tidied the campsite and repaired the damaged sledge using a replacement cowcatcher brought from the base.

The next day the weather was still fine but dull and the temperature had risen to 23°F, or 9 degrees below freezing. Taylor and Lamb immediately set out to continue their survey work down the eastern side of the Fief Range, traversing the Luigi Glacier at an elevation of between 300 and 700ft above sea level. They stopped at a point where they could enjoy a particularly good view of the jumbled icefalls and sheer rock faces of the Fief Range and also look down upon the snow-capped Fridtjof Island. After completing a series of observations, they turned back, following a route which took them close to the rock buttress at the base of Savoia Peak. Here they collected some geological samples of fine-grained basalt. For their part, Davies and Marr reconnoitred the area east of the Wall Range and climbed a glacier flowing between the range and a feature they later named 'Snow Comb Hill'.[25] From the top of this divide they obtained a view towards the northern reaches of Wiencke Island and identified what appeared to be two navigable routes heading in that direction. The first lay across Channel Glacier, while the second, more difficult path, followed the spine of the island east of the Wall Range and Nemo Peak.

For the next fortnight appalling weather prevented any examination of the routes seen by Marr and Davies and the party was mostly tent-bound. The temperature fluctuated considerably, but seldom rose above freezing, while the wind often gusted at well above 50mph, sometimes making normal conversation quite impossible. If the men poked their heads through the entrance funnels, they were blinded by a whirling, wind-whipped vortex of driven snow and on the few occasions when the wind dropped dense fog prevailed. In Taylor's view:

> ... to experience such a storm, in such tiny quarters in the midst of what one knows to be such massive surroundings, with the tearing driving roar of the wind ceaselessly in one's ears for hour after hour, leaves a never-to-be-forgotten impression of man's true insignificance, and the mantle of humility rests readily upon one's shoulders in the presence of such inexorable power.[26]

With the canvas walls bellying and flapping and the stout bamboo poles bending at crazy angles before the blast, Marr admitted that the gale had 'reached a pitch of violence that made me wonder if the tents would hold. We had not bargained for such weather.'[27] If the tents failed then the four men would be forced to make a desperate journey back to the depot: the distance was not great, but disorientated men without a tent easily succumb in such conditions.

They spent the majority of their time lying in their sleeping bags to keep warm, using their Primus stoves only for cooking in order to conserve fuel – in much the same fashion as their predecessors during the Heroic Age expeditions. These periods of enforced inactivity have been the bane of sledging expeditions since time immemorial and even the most mundane task was seized upon as a means by which to help pass the time. Lamb sorted and labelled the geological specimens collected from Savoia Peak, Taylor plotted his observations on the plane table sheet and Marr and Davies wrestled with a broken Primus. Like the tents, the stoves issued to the expedition were of a standard type used by most polar explorers of the period. Weighing about 4lb, they burned paraffin oil and the most common problem was the blocking of the flame jets, a fault only partially resolved by straining the paraffin before use. In attempting to change a blocked jet with a double-jointed spanner, Davies had sheared the brass fitting. 'Well, that was trouble,' he recalled penitently. 'We'd got no way of cooking our food. I knew Taylor and Lamb were in the next tent but then, in a gale of wind, you didn't feel like humping over there.'[28] Davies and Marr had little success, but eventually Taylor managed to effect a temporary repair by filing down a nail and jamming it into the hole. This produced only a smoky and feeble flame – but it did enable them to cook. When not occupied with such distractions, 'We took our met readings every few hours, listened to the radio occasionally, and ate and slept, for that was all there was to do.'[29]

A gap in the weather on 30 September allowed Taylor and Lamb to do a limited amount of surveying and photography while Marr and Davies trekked back to the dump at the summit of the Luigi Glacier for fresh supplies, including a new Primus to replace the damaged one. They returned with the supplies, including cheese and dried potatoes, and some personal messages left at the depot by the men at the base. These included a radiogram from Lamb's wife and another addressed to Marr from the Governor of the Falklands confirming that he supported the idea of a survey of the coast of Graham Land to be made from the planned base at Hope Bay and that the *Scoresby* could be used to support the work. For Marr this was particularly good news: although the final decision did not lie with the governor, it indicated that he continued to harbour ambitious plans for the future and that his enthusiasm for the work of the expedition had not been dampened by its limited successes to date.

During the first five days of October anything but very local travel was impossible and the men were reduced to watching 'the shadows of the drift snow racing up and round the outer tent fabric like dancing snakes or flames'.[30] On the 4th the usual monotony was disturbed by an unfortunate accident. While Lamb was preparing the cocoa to accompany the evening meal, the pot slipped from the 'patent potholder' and emptied its contents over his stockinged feet. He rapidly removed his socks and applied petroleum jelly from the medical kit, but his feet were severely scalded. As well as being acutely painful and rendering him temporarily immobile, the injury substantially increased the risk of frostbite. And, of course, there was another essential activity, 'unavoidable business'[31] in Lamb's terms, which made frostbite a very real danger. When sledging, explorers usually attempted to time their bodily functions to coincide with the routine stops during the day. In reasonably clement weather, the shelter in the lee of a sledge gave adequate protection from frostbite, while the pemmican-based diet tended to generate large, soft and easily passed stools, limiting the time that the men were exposed. During enforced lie-ups, except during the very worst blizzard conditions, the men would still seek to excrete outside – even though, as Taylor recalled with a shiver, the 'wind-chill of our "southern exposures" was extremely great, and we re-entered the tent with our trousers full of snow.'[32] However, on those mercifully rare occasions when a man was rendered immobile, perhaps by dysentery caused by contaminated pemmican, conditions inside a tent could become appalling.

By 6 October, Marr could hardly contain his impatience at the interruption to the expedition's work:

> This wretched weather and the enforced inactivity which it brings is very
> trying. Since we began relaying the first loads up on to the harbour gla-
> cier [Channel Glacier] nearly three weeks ago we have had only five good
> working days. Of the twelve days spent in this camp all but three have been
> spent largely in our sleeping bags.[33]

Lack of exercise and the cramped conditions left the men feeling weak
at the knees and when the sun at last broke through on the morning of
7 October they stumbled from their tents desperate to make the most of
the clear, calm day. Lamb was still unable to walk any distance so he stayed
behind to complete 'household duties' while Marr, Davies and Taylor
started surveying about a mile to the north of the camp, where they could
enjoy a fine view of the Danco Coast. At midday the clouds closed in
again and they were forced to take cover, but not before Taylor had succeeded in taking a photograph of the distant coastline with the panoramic
camera. The following day dawned sufficiently clear for them to continue
their work and Lamb felt able to accompany Taylor to a knoll a couple of
miles from the camp. Here, on an exposed face of Snow Comb Hill at an
altitude of 1,200ft above sea level, he was delighted to find a growth of
lichens which seemed to be thriving despite the violence of the prevailing
north-easterlies.

Davies and Marr, meanwhile, used a steel tape to measure the distance
between their camp and the point at which the survey had been conducted the previous day. The line they followed could then be used as a
baseline when plotting the positions of the features observed on the mainland. According to Davies, this process involved 'pulling out this chain …
and then putting in a little marker flag. Marr would come up to it and
then I'd go ahead and put in another marker flag in a dead straight line
and so on.'[34] The two men had been labouring for some hours when a
horrified Davies realised that he had forgotten to insert a marker flag at
one of their earlier stops. When he suggested that he could guess where
the flag should go, Marr's answer was uncompromising: 'No, it was not
good enough: we had to go back to the very beginning again and do the
whole thing again. We were cold and hungry towards the end of it … and
didn't I feel a fool.'[35] In the opinion of Davies, whose admiration for Marr
was unstinting, 'He was absolutely dead right: he didn't say much, he said
we'd got to do it again. It just shows how thorough he was, conscientious.'[36] Given that Marr's programme of fieldwork had been so severely
curtailed by circumstances beyond his control, this unyielding insistence

upon accuracy might be interpreted as a compelling need to ensure that whatever could be done should be completed to the very highest standard. Of course, Back, who viewed Marr as a glutton for punishment, might have taken a rather different view.

At last, on 9 October, Lamb could record that 'It being fair and calm this morning, although with poor visibility, we decided to break camp'.[37] They loaded the instruments, specimens and everything else not essential to camp life onto the survey sledge and dragged it back to the summit of Luigi Glacier, which they had last visited on 25 September. They then skied back to the camp, where they struck the tents. This proved to be a difficult task, as both tents had to be dug out of deep drifts. Their external aprons were firmly frozen to the surface and could only be broken free with considerable effort. When they rolled back the ground sheets, they also discovered that over the course of the previous two weeks their body heat had thawed the snow below so that, by the end of the period, to all intents and purposes they had been sleeping in manmade troughs. With the tents collapsed, they and everything else, including bedding, rations and stoves, were loaded onto the second sledge and then hauled to the summit.

On the far side of the glacier the surface was so hard and smooth that rope brakes were needed to prevent the sledges from running away. Taylor was also having trouble with the quick release mechanism on his harness: 'it let me escape several times most inopportunely, creating delays which were most exasperating as we watched a couple of small avalanches reminding us that we were not far distant from the scene of our earlier adventure.'[38] When they reached the bottom of Luigi Glacier and began the ascent around the base of the Wall Range, the hauling became much more difficult: the snow was softer, the sledge began to plough a furrow, and it was not long before all four men combined their strength to pull one sledge at a time, beginning with the heavier sledge loaded with the camping equipment. In Taylor's opinion, 'few methods of transport invented by man stand lower in any scale of efficacy than does man-hauling,' and his description of their labours would have struck a chord with every man who accompanied Scott, Shackleton or Mawson earlier in the century:

> With the weight of the sledge arranged by the harness upon one's diaphragm, one foot is placed mechanically before the other in a lunging stride, with an action in parts not unlike that of a hula dancer … As one weary leg glides forward after the other, the body in a lather of sweat, even in temperatures well below zero, one's entire attention becomes focused upon the little group coupled to the sledge, and one wonders if perhaps the other chaps are not pulling as hard as they were, if perhaps they are deliberately leaving more of the job to their partners, if the leader is never going

to stop for that rest which one feels so sincerely to have earned … In such a condition, one could blandly stride past a wall of gold without noticing it, so eagerly is one's attention focused upon the need for a rest halt. Yea, for pure soul destroying labour, it must be difficult to beat manhauling.[39]

When they reached a fairly level part of the Channel Glacier about three-quarters of a mile higher up, they decided to camp, leaving the survey sledge to be collected the next day. Exhausted, they pitched their tents, prepared a scratch meal and turned in for the night at 10 p.m.

Feeling suitably refreshed, they dragged up the survey sledge the following morning and then Marr and Davies set out for the depot 1.5 miles away to obtain fresh supplies. In addition to luxuries such as jam and tea, they returned with an important radio message that had been left by the men at the base. It was from the governor and the Secretary of State and to Marr's delight they had agreed to proceed with the original plans for the establishment of a base at Hope Bay early in 1945. A 550-ton, ice-strengthened Newfoundland sealer, the *Eagle*, had been chartered to support the expedition and sledge dogs would also be provided. Marr noted that 'As the signal was now a week old and requested an urgent reply it was clear that I should have to get back to the Base without delay.'[40] Accordingly, at 3.30 p.m., he set out alone on skis, heading for Port Lockroy and hoping that his business would take no more than a day or so to complete. In the meantime, he would send Blyth to take his place until he was able to return. 'I had a good run down arriving at six in time for dinner,' he reported. 'Farrington and the others had spring-cleaned the house in our absence and it was looking very well with floors, tables and benches scrubbed and everything stowed away shipshape.' After weeks of hard pulling and tent-bound discomfort, it was not very surprising that he thought it 'a very pleasant house'.[41]

Back on Wiencke Island, the next day Taylor, Davies and Lamb pulled the survey sledge 2 miles to the north end of the Channel Glacier, where it terminates with the Neumayer Channel. There they planned to camp for a few days. Visibility was poor, but the excellent surface enabled them to make good time and having found a suitable campsite they were able to begin their return journey to collect the rest of the equipment and the tents immediately after lunch. They found Blyth waiting for them, but any hopes of establishing the new camp were dashed by a thick snowstorm which had blown up during their descent. There seemed little point in attempting to travel unnecessarily in the worsening conditions, so instead they made themselves comfortable, listening to Blyth's account of life at Port Lockroy and enjoying his delicious omelettes and hash, made with the provisions that he had brought with him.

The conditions did not improve until 13 October and by then 18in of snow had fallen. Leaving a cache of 100lb of food to save weight, the four men loaded their sledge with the tents and camping equipment, donned their harnesses and began to pull. Deep, fresh snow now carpeted the excellent surface of two days before and their progress was agonisingly slow: 'We would rest a few moments and then, after a series of terrific tugs in unison, would succeed in getting our heavy load on the move again, only to stop in another hundred feet, ready to drop from sheer exhaustion.'[42] Even after they reached the glacier's summit and had begun to descend, they found it necessary to pull every inch of the way, for the sledge runners and their own skis were sinking deeply into the soft, powdery snow. At last they reached the survey sledge – but the day's work was still not done. As well as the surplus foodstuffs, some essential cooking utensils had been left at the old campsite and Taylor, Davies and Lamb set out once again to collect them. A cold wind was blowing from the west and it was snowing fairly heavily, but they reached the cache without accident and, having loaded all the additional food as well as the utensils onto a small lightweight toboggan, they headed back up the glacier. By this time visibility had decreased to just 50yd, and the party relied upon frequent compass bearings to complete their journey. Though much lighter than the Nansen sledges, the toboggan proved nearly as difficult to pull through the thick snow and it capsized repeatedly and had to be righted. By the time they reached their tents, the party felt completely exhausted and after a welcome meal of sausage meat, potatoes and scrambled eggs prepared by Blyth, they collapsed into their sleeping bags.

After such a strenuous day, an enforced lie-up on 14 October was not entirely unwelcome, the four men resting in their sleeping bags, enjoying some of the tinned delicacies brought from the cache the day before and listening to the radio. With the ingenuity common to most field expeditions, Taylor had rigged up a primitive loudspeaker by removing the radio set's earphones from the headband and fitting them into an empty biscuit tin, thereby allowing everyone to hear the broadcast. They found that the small portable set had to be 'cooked up' to 65°F before it would perform satisfactorily, but otherwise:

> it worked well, and we had little static except that occasionally created by the abrasion of the snow particles being carried past us by the wind … The biscuit tin was tied up to the peak of the tent by a shoelace, and the entire box vibrated as a diaphragm, giving all its emanations a decidedly tinny effect.[43]

On 15 October Lamb and Taylor roped themselves together and skied north, downhill and towards a headland, which they subsequently named

Blyth Point (an unadopted name), overlooking the Neumayer Channel. The distance to the point was about 1.5 miles and involved negotiating a field of 'tremendous square shaped and cavernous crevasses, about a hundred feet square, and bottomless from our aspect'.[44] Having passed through this zone without incident, they planted a survey flag at an elevation of 700ft above sea level and took a photograph looking northwards up the largely ice-free channel. From this point, they decided to ski towards a rocky buttress overlooking Börgen Bay, about 300ft higher up and a mile to the south on the west coast of Wiencke Island. Below this buttress they discovered a gentle slope with easily accessible rocks and stones recently exposed by the spring thaw. 'We examined this lower part,' Lamb enthused, 'and found there a rich lichen flora, the chief components being *Neuropogon, Umbilicaria* and a number of crustaceous lichens.'[45] Returning to their camp, Lamb immediately set to work drying off his precious lichen samples by gently heating them in a tin lid over the pressure stove while Taylor studied a copy of Marr's reply to the governor, delivered to the camp that afternoon by Back and Farrington. In his message, Marr requested that the *Scoresby* should pick him up as soon as possible so that he might confer with Sir Allan regarding the plans for 1945. Inevitably, this meant that it would be impossible for him to return to the survey party, so Blyth would remain as the fourth man until the whole group returned to base.

Low cloud prevented much surveying the next day, so Taylor and Lamb measured a survey baseline to the east of the camp, and from the ends of the line Taylor took theodolite angles on Noble Peak and on the point at which the flag had been placed the previous morning. In the afternoon Marr and Farrington appeared, having taken four hours to haul a toboggan load of food from the base. Their day trip had clearly been undertaken as much for exercise and for a change of scene as for anything else because, as Taylor remarked, 'By this time, we had with us sufficient food and paraffin to have sustained us for a month, had it been necessary.'[46]

When the men crawled from their tents on 17 October, they found the conditions sunny and fairly clear, the temperature about 10 degrees below freezing but a strong north-east wind carrying 'fine drift snow like sugar along the surface'.[47] At 10.30 a.m. all four set out with a lightly loaded sledge hoping to complete the survey work around Blyth Point. Initially, despite the favourable conditions, the sledge dragged badly and when they unloaded it and turned it over they discovered lumps of ice frozen to its runners, which they cleared with a knife. Then, at an elevation of about 700ft above sea level, while traversing the heavily crevassed area around Noble Peak, they encountered a windswept surface of treacherous hard blue ice and the sledge became quite unmanageable, threatening to slip down the 40-degree slope to their right. 'Had we but started slipping down,' Taylor noted, 'we would have had a Hobson's choice between ending up at the bottom of one of these crevasses, or in the icy water of the sea.'[48]

In order to stabilise the sledge, Lamb and Taylor continued pulling from the front while Blyth and Davies kept its stern lined up with their chosen course. This was made particularly difficult by Davies' *truger*, which gave very little grip on the slope. As his feet slipped out from under him, he instinctively grabbed at Blyth or the sledge, risking a headlong slide for all three. Eventually, he unlashed a shovel and drove its blade into the surface so that it supported the lower edge of the sledge runner. When the sledge had moved forward a few feet, he drew the shovel out and then drove it in again at the front of the runner, so that the sledge could slide forward, resting on the blade, for another 10ft or so. 'It was painfully slow and extremely dangerous progress that we were making,' Taylor observed, 'with the sledge momentarily threatening to swing below us like a pendulum, before tugging us after it, if we made but one false step.'[49] They continued in this fashion for some time, but they all knew that if the sledge started slipping when the shovel was pulled free, it would be very difficult to stop. Lamb therefore suggested that they should unload and manhandle the survey equipment to a more secure spot before returning for the empty sledge. Each man made two trips before everything had been carried to a relatively level stretch of snow. Then, they recovered the empty sledge, which they could now move with only minimal effort, reloaded it and dragged it to the point where Lamb and Taylor had planted the survey flag on 15 October.

With a brisk wind blowing a good deal of snow around, conditions were far from ideal but as he doubted that they could expect an improvement any time soon, Taylor immediately set to work exposing panoramic photographs, taking a series of theodolite angles and plotting prominent landscape features on the plane table. Lamb recorded the angles and worked the rangefinder while Blyth and Davies excavated a pit in the snow, which they hoped would provide a shelter in which they could all enjoy their lunch. This scheme failed because the wind constantly blew drift snow over them as they dug and then, when they climbed out of the hole and ran around in order to warm up, both plunged through concealed snow bridges. First Davies went in up to his waist, but managed to claw his way out, then Blyth fell into another just yards from where they had been digging their temporary shelter. 'These two events had a most sobering effect upon their subsequent behaviour,' Taylor noted.[50] The surveyors completed their work at 6 p.m. and two hours later they reached their camp. 'Blyth soon produced an excellent hot stew for us all,' wrote a grateful Lamb, 'and for my part, I do not remember ever having enjoyed a meal more.'[51]

Wednesday 18 October was the last day of this, the expedition's first major sledging journey. During the morning, Lamb and Taylor completed a round of theodolite angles and took a panoramic photograph and then they packed their equipment, leaving one sledge, one tent, two bedrolls and all the extra rations in a depot so that their work could be resumed at a later date. By 3 p.m. everything was ready and the four men began the homeward journey, dragging the survey sledge and the toboggan towards the Channel Glacier. The surface snow was well packed and they made very good time, pausing at the crest of the glacier to enjoy the views to the south and to take photographs, before heading for the depot established on 20 September. From the depot they made their way towards the Knife Edge, braking the sledge with ropes. As they descended, they were relieved to see that the sea ice remained firm and that they would not have to wait at the Rookery while the men at the base dug out a boat in order to collect them. Confident that they would not have to pitch their tent while they waited to be picked up, they secured the sledge above the steep slope to the Rookery and then proceeded downhill with just the toboggan, loaded with their notebooks and other essentials needed at the base. After an easy trek across the sea ice, they reached the hut at 6.30 p.m. and Lamb recorded that 'It was very pleasant to arrive back, where a warm welcome awaited us after an absence of 24 days.'[52]

By the time the team finally returned to base, only the extremities of Wiencke Island still needed to be surveyed, so they had been largely successful in meeting their objectives.[53] In addition, as an introduction to sledging, the expedition had served its purpose and the men had learned first to endure, and then to make the best of the difficult conditions inseparable from manhauling. Nonetheless, as senior surveyor, Taylor was under no illusions regarding either the limitations of the methods adopted or the results achieved:

> Travelling along the glaciers which fringe the shoreline is certainly not the ideal method of surveying for these coasts, as one is forced to attempt to plot the position of a shoreline of which one seldom catches a glance; it is to be surmised that it lies vertically below the edge of the ice cliff which verges the course one is following, but it is not always convenient to ascertain this point. In the summer time, with the long spells of fine clear weather which are occasionally encountered, a thousand times more work could be accomplished by a single plane photographing every tortuous sinuosity of the coasts with an amount of detail which cannot be approached by any other method. Shore parties, certainly, are needed for the establishment of the ground control required by triangulation and astronomic observing, collecting such specimens of geological, botanical and zoological interest as

each landing affords. But this type of country cries out for the use of aerial photography, and the use of other methods is merely playing at the job to produce very inferior results compared to that which might be attained.[54]

Given the extent of the aerial surveys undertaken by Wilkins, Rymill and Ellsworth in the years between the wars, no one could seriously argue with Taylor's point of view. An aeroplane had never been considered as a realistic proposition for Operation Tabarin, but the departure of both ships in February, combined with the absence of navigable sea ice, had been little short of disastrous so far as Marr's plans for lengthy coastal surveys were concerned.

The impacts of adverse weather had also been profound: survey work was completed on just twelve days out of twenty-four spent in the field. Of these twelve days, only one had been truly clear, and another five just good enough to permit some work of value. During the remaining twelve days the party had either been battered by violent blizzards or enveloped in dense fog, and analysis of Back's meteorological log reveals that they had experienced one of the longest spells of continuous bad weather during the entire year. All in all, as Taylor later wrote:

It was an interesting journey to have partaken in, giving one an insight into the laborious methods and equipment which explorers had been forced to use in the early part of the century. But it is not a method which should be followed today, especially along such a coastline as that of western Graham Land.[55]

A Waiting Game

During the sledgers' absence, Farrington had initiated a thorough spring clean of Bransfield House. The linoleum floor had been scrubbed so that its original colour became visible for the first time in months, plans had been laid for painting the exterior of the hut and Back, in particular, had taken 'a keen delight in throwing out the accumulation of empty cigarette tins, boxes of old nails, bits of sealskin and other oddments which people had kept in case they "might come in useful someday"'.[1] This flurry of activity made the hut seem more homely and gave the explorers a renewed pride in their dwelling – but, taking place at the beginning of the sledging season, it also served to emphasise just how far their location on Goudier Island, the absence of a suitable ship and the lack of navigable sea ice had curbed their ambitions. Had the expedition been able to establish its winter quarters at Hope Bay as intended, its members would now be forging new routes along the coast of the Graham Land Peninsula or up into its mountainous interior; instead, they were reduced to wielding mops and brooms.

Any feelings of futility which these restrictions might have engendered were alleviated by the news that the *Scoresby* would be sailing for Port Lockroy at the end of October. The ship would call at Deception Island en route, where she would pick up Flett, Howkins and Matheson. Marr would then accompany her back to Stanley, where he would consult with the governor regarding the coming season and make arrangements for the establishment of the new base at Hope Bay. Once this base had been built, the expedition's sphere of operations would expand enormously – a fact acknowledged in a message to the effect that two additional surveyors, Captain Victor Russell of the Royal Engineers and Sub-Lieutenant David James, MBE, DSC, would join the expedition at Hope Bay. In addition, Captain N.B. 'Freddy' Marshall of the Royal Electrical and Mechanical

Engineers would take charge of the dogs, which were to be shipped from Newfoundland, and Sub-Lieutenant Gordon 'Jock' Lockley, an acquaintance of Lamb from the British Museum, would assume command of Base 'A' when Marr moved to Hope Bay.

In the meantime, work carried on as normal. In the preceding weeks much of the snow on Goudier Island and at the penguin rookery had melted, exposing the underlying rocks and allowing more investigations in the fields of zoology, botany and geology. 'It is as though we went away in winter and returned in spring,' Lamb enthused.[2] Although Lamb had taken every opportunity to collect lichen samples throughout his stay at Port Lockroy, inevitably Marr had been preoccupied with other matters. Now, with the future of his expedition seemingly assured and its scope about to be significantly expanded, he too felt able to turn his attention to his own scientific specialism. Over the coming weeks, he took advantage of the unusually low tides to begin an ecological survey of the ice-worn and seemingly barren boulder beach of the island and very soon he had put together a surprisingly rich collection. Specimens included cunningly camouflaged fish which lay in the shallow water as still as stones; shrimp-like amphipods; giant jellyfish, 'their undersides no sight for a tender stomach';[3] sea urchins, sponges and worms; beautiful transparent ctenophores, which resembled swimming soap bubbles with iridescent colours flickering in their internal organs; and a bottom-dwelling diatom which grew in dense fist-sized tufts in the crevices between submerged boulders. As bucket after bucket of weird and wonderful creatures was brought to the hut for study and cataloguing, no one could cling to the preconceived notion of Antarctica as a lifeless desert. On the other hand, the conditions in which these organisms not only survive, but thrive, are the harshest on the face of the planet and, as he looked at his ever-growing collection, Marr acknowledged that perhaps the most interesting question of all was 'how such a community contrives to survive and maintain itself in spite of the severe grinding action by ice to which its habitat is annually subjected'.[4]

All those not fully engaged in their own duties or interests were press-ganged by Marr to assist in gathering specimens and though Taylor thought that 'collecting was not a very exciting task',[5] he and the others proved willing enough to undertake any function that would help pass the time before the arrival of the *Scoresby* and its cargo of mail. This outdoor work also gave them an opportunity to observe the changes that the new season had wrought and Farrington, whose job meant that he had spent the majority of his time indoors, wrote that:

It is the beginning of summer here now and, apart from occasional gales of seventy or eighty miles an hour, the weather is very lovely. The sea ice has all gone and the sun shines nearly all of the 24 hours. At midnight it is quite easy to read a book as you lie in bed with your head towards the window. During the day, especially when it is calm, it is quite warm enough to lie on the rocks and bask in the hot sun. One is tempted to bathe but the sea temperature is only about three or four degrees above freezing point.[6]

In these near perfect conditions, photography became a popular pursuit, and the explorers – singly and en masse – the scientific specimens and the natural environment were all recorded. 'The results of [Lamb's] developing and printing were interesting to all,' wrote Taylor, 'and a familiar sight was to see someone standing over the tub in which he washed the prints, fishing them out one at a time to examine the dripping pictures.'[7]

Another subject that proved irresistible was the penguin colony at Lécuyer Point. The rookery had been deserted since the end of April, but the birds had begun to return in large numbers during September and on 17 November Back and Blyth discovered the first eggs, returning to the hut with eighteen. Berry boiled them that evening, but their reddish yoke and tough, bluish albumen were not to everyone's taste: 'to see a pair of them peeled of their shell … translucent whites like a pair of octopus eyes, is not the most appetising sight.'[8] Those with less delicate stomachs were pleased to discover that there would be eggs aplenty for any who wanted them. Indeed, since some penguins lay three and even four eggs instead of the more usual one or two, some of the men even began to act as a benign *deus ex machina*, removing eggs from birds with a surfeit to give them to those less fortunate. With their squabbles, their courage, their thievery, their overt affection for their partners and their conscientious care of their eggs and chicks, the penguins very quickly endeared themselves to the explorers – but they were far from being the only bird life. Sheathbills, or paddies, blue-eyed shags and Dominican gulls (now known as the Kelp Gull) were also common, the paddies remaining resident year-round, feeding on the refuse from the hut. 'I'm not quite sure what happens to them if there isn't anybody there,' mused Back, 'they live on our excrement; a nice bit of stool is just the job for a paddy.'[9]

Seals, too, began to reappear. Weddells were by far the most numerous, and on one occasion a group of fifty or more was seen swimming in the outer reaches of the harbour. Two gave birth just a few hundred feet from the hut on the edge of the sea ice and a month later the pups took to sea, though Lamb noted that one 'did not take at all kindly to the water on the first occasion, and very soon climbed out again'.[10] These inoffensive creatures seemed to live quite contentedly with the neighbouring birds and though both had their predators, including leopard seals, killer whales and men, none of the hunters proved particularly voracious. Taylor once saw a leopard seal thrashing an unfortunate penguin to and fro', flinging it into the air to strip it of its skin and feathers, but neither leopard seals nor killer whales gathered in any numbers. As for the men, their overall satisfaction with their tinned foodstuffs, and their mixed feelings about slaughtering the seals, kept their depredations well within bounds. 'I was never frightfully enthusiastic about seal,' Back remarked. 'I'd rather have bully beef.'[11]

Hearing that the *Scoresby* had been forced to retreat by a belt of impenetrable pack ice to the north of Deception Island, on 18 November Lamb, Blyth and Ashton set out on a short sledging expedition to Wiencke Island to collect bird specimens for the British Museum. By 3 p.m. they had reached the tent and sledge that had been abandoned a month earlier, finding them 'just as we had left them, apart from being more drifted up with snow'.[12] The following morning the trio set out for Blyth Point, and soon discovered that the warmer spring temperatures had caused many of the crevasses to open up and the snow bridges spanning them to sag ominously. Crossing the crevasse zone without accident, they parked their skis at Blyth Point and began to examine the rocks exposed by the thaw. Although the expedition had been intended to gather bird specimens, Lamb's attention was almost immediately diverted by the fresh growths of lichen, which he thought 'very rich', and the party spent several hours making a collection and taking photographs before returning to their camp. The bird population remained just as secure the following day, when Lamb and his assistants explored the rock buttress on the northern side of Noble Peak: 'We arrived at the lower part of this buttress at 1100hrs. Much more rock was exposed than previously, and I found the piled rocks and stones constituting the base of the buttress to be profusely clothed with fruiting *Neuropogon*, forming stately tufts, with black shield-like *apothecia*.'[13] For more than two hours Lamb fossicked about among the rocks, as giddy as a schoolboy, scraping samples and taking photographs.

Perhaps sensing that his companions did not altogether share his enthusiasm, after a lunch of biscuits and tea he proposed an experiment in which all could participate and from which all might one day benefit: 'I had the idea of finding out if we could use dry *Neuropogon* as fuel.'[14] Though it would be impossible to harvest enough of the lichen for normal daily use, it might serve in an emergency. With this idea in mind, they set fire to a handful and found that it burnt well. Ashton then made a rough oven out of stones, kindled a *Neuropogon* fire inside it, and put a biscuit tin of snow on top of it to melt. 'In this way we got enough water for a drink, and filled two thermos flasks. I wonder if anyone else has ever made a fire out of lichens.'[15] As well as proving that the lichen could help sustain a sledging party running short of paraffin, the trial also gave Blyth and Ashton a new respect for a growth which, hitherto, no one had thought might possess a practical use.

In addition to making this discovery, during the day Blyth learned an important – and extremely painful – lesson about polar travel. Throughout the day the weather was beautiful, gloriously sunny, and the temperature rose so far above freezing that all three men quickly shed their jumpers and coats and rolled up their shirtsleeves. As they laboured up and down the slopes in search of vegetation, Blyth found that his goggles kept steaming over: 'I said to the man behind me, "I think I'll take these goggles off for a few minutes." "You make sure it is a few minutes," he said.'[16] According to Blyth, he heeded the advice and 'did only have them off for a matter of minutes', but it was long enough for him to develop the tell-tale symptoms of snow-blindness and as the party descended towards their camp he began to complain that he had grit in his eyes. That evening Lamb applied some boric acid solution, but the next morning Blyth 'felt as if I had a cartload of peat mould in my eyes … I could not bear light to get at them.'[17]

With Blyth now completely blind and in considerable pain, and with no real benefit to be obtained by staying out any longer, Lamb and Ashton agreed that they should place him on the sledge and make for the base. After an hour of hauling up the glacier, they reached the survey flag of 1 May, from where they could see the hut. They also saw that the sea ice linking Goudier Island with the Rookery had broken up, making it impossible for them to sledge back. However, the party had been seen from the base, where there were 'all sorts of conjectures of some calamity having occurred',[18] and by the time they reached the Knife Edge a dinghy had put out from the boat harbour. 'Blyth had to be guided along the crest with one of us on each side of him,' wrote Lamb, 'and altogether we slid down the slope to the bottom.'[19] Here they were met by Marr, Taylor and Back, who soon rowed them back to the island. 'On arrival at base,' Blyth recalled, 'Doc put drops in my eyes, and I was blindfolded for six days, and my sight restored to normal on the seventh day. I expected a few harsh words from Commander Marr, but all he said was "You learn by your mistakes, then you don't repeat them."'[20] Back remembered the incident somewhat differently: '"I never took me goggles off, Doc," [Blyth] said. Unfortunately there's a lovely picture … showing Johnny Blyth, up on the mountain above the Peltier Channel, looking out to sea and wearing no goggles!'[21]

Learning that the *Scoresby* would start again on 2 December and could be expected a week later, everyone concentrated on completing and typing diaries and reports, adding to the letters that they had been writing, on and off, for the last seven months, developing photos and labelling and packing specimens, ready for their transportation north. In response to a request from Marchesi for a report on local ice conditions, on 3 December Back and Blyth climbed up the Channel Glacier to make a survey. They found that the channels were virtually ice-free on all sides and optimism soared. In these conditions it should take the *Scoresby* no more than a day to sail from Deception Island to Goudier Island, and when news came through that the ship had departed from Base 'B' on 6 December, the anticipation became almost unbearable: 'People paced around restlessly about the house all the following morning, peering out the doorway every few minutes for a sight of the ship, but she did not arrive.'[22] That afternoon the wind began to pick up and Farrington received a message to the effect that Marchesi had been forced to heave-to in Dallmann Bay, about 30 miles to the north of Port Lockroy, until the storm abated. Gloom descended in the hut, but then lifted almost immediately when another signal arrived indicating that the *Scoresby* was once again under weigh. At 10 p.m. she appeared at last, rounding Damoy Point to anchor to the west of the island.

A few moments later Marr welcomed a landing party of nine, including Marchesi, Howkins, Flett and Matheson, the last two almost unrecognisable beneath their thick winter growth of whiskers. Of course, even more welcome than these new faces – the first to be seen at Port Lockroy since April – were the mailbags they carried and very soon the visitors were left to their own devices as their hosts devoured their letters in the privacy of their two-man cabins. The following morning three more visitors arrived, though two, an army dentist and his assistant, were perhaps greeted with more trepidation than enthusiasm. 'The house became a hive of activity; Tomlinson, who had brought with him a complete dental surgeon's outfit with chair, foot-driven drill, etc, examined the teeth of each of us in turn and did what repairs were necessary.'[23] The third visitor, John Bound of the Falkland Island Post Office, faced the unenviable task of stamping and cancelling the voluminous mail, a great deal of which was intended for philatelists and consisted of empty envelopes with complete sets of the Graham Land stamps affixed. These would later be sold by the Falkland Islands Company. Those not sitting in the dentist's chair spent most of the day locked away answering letters, but that evening Berry and Blyth cooked a meal for seventeen and everyone put their correspondence to one side so that they might fulfil their duties as hosts. Farrington wrote to his father that 'After so many months with only eight companions the house now seems packed with crowds of people and of course everybody is excited and there has been all sorts of high jinks going on.'[24] Dinner was followed by drinks, games and more drinks, the party culminating in the obligatory and increasingly discordant concert, at which all joined in singing 'probably the same songs that sailors would sing the world over under such bibulous circumstances'.[25]

Hangovers notwithstanding, Tomlinson and Bound completed their work the next day while the ship's company prepared to sail north. After dinner, just as Marr, Matheson and Howkins were taking their leave of the men remaining at the hut, Back suddenly decided that Blyth, too, should visit Stanley so that his hand, injured in a skiing accident, could be x-rayed. While Blyth dashed about gathering his chattels, Bound accepted the outgoing mail. Then, almost as an afterthought, Marr turned to Taylor 'and appointed me in charge of the base during his absence'.[26] Minutes later, the launch returned to the *Scoresby* and soon the passengers were clambering up her side. At 10 p.m., with a strong east wind whipping up the grey waters of the harbour, the ship turned in a wide arc, gave a valedictory blast on her horn and headed for the Neumayer Channel.

With Marr and Blyth gone, but with Flett remaining in order to undertake some geology, there were now eight men at Port Lockroy. They would have to wait until mid-January before being collected and taken to Hope Bay to begin the second year's work. However, this period of waiting would not be entirely devoid of novelty. During its brief visit, as well as supplies of fresh meat and fruit, the *Scoresby* had landed a basket of Falkland Island plants and lichens, together with 4 hundredweight of soil, for an experiment in transplantation. Lamb made a small raised bed against the steep north-facing slope to the east of the inner harbour, retaining the soil with boulders. Having planted the specimens, he then used wire mesh to prevent the paddies and other birds from damaging them. Next, he placed the imported lichens on rocks in front of the hut, protecting these in the same fashion. 'It reminded one of home to see the little border of flowering plants and ferns,' he wrote that evening.[27] This was not the first attempt to introduce plant life to the Antarctic. In 1905, R.N. Rudmose Brown, Bruce's second-in-command during the *Scotia* Expedition, had sent twenty-two Arctic phanerogams to Laurie Island. Some thirty years later, Rymill's British Graham Land Expedition had tried a casual sowing of grass seeds on the Argentine islands. Neither of these experiments had resulted in germination and Lamb's proved equally futile. By 7 January 1945, he could still describe seven of the nine vascular plants as 'apparently healthy', with two more 'somewhat healthy'. Realising that the extremely low humidity and lack of precipitation would cause the plants to dry out, he began to water them, but by 16 January 1946 all but two of the specimens were reported as 'dead or dying'. By January 1950 all had succumbed and, with no root systems to bind it, the imported soil was soon scattered by the prevailing winds.[28]

While Lamb wrestled with the problems of the imported flora, Davies became equally preoccupied with alien fauna, in the shape of a pig. Thinking that the men of Operation Tabarin would welcome a supply of fresh pork after their long winter, the governor had arranged for two pigs to be transported on the *Scoresby*, one for Deception Island and the other for Port Lockroy, 'and we were to fatten these up on our scraps and to enjoy a nice feed of pork.'[29] What the governor had not appreciated was the degree to which men starved of an object for their affections would welcome the pig into their society. Knowing that the sow's fate was pre-ordained, the explorers tried to stop themselves from humanising her and persisted in calling her simply 'The Pig', but the attempt proved futile and from the moment the animal landed, looking 'very pitiful, standing there on the shore, stark naked and shivering',[30] Davies, in particular, took her to his heart. 'It was my job to look after her,' he later wrote, 'and soon she became the tenth [*sic*] member of our little crowd down there ... The pig and I sometimes played "Chase-me-Charlie" around the rocks, back and fore ... We all got fond of the little creature, which had to put up with the cold, like we did.'[31]

At Port Lockroy, the pig could live fairly comfortably, sleeping in a shelter lined with wood shavings and sharing her mash with the paddies. At Hope Bay, however, where her neighbours would be half-savage huskies, it would be a very different story, a fact that was later proved when the huskies broke loose on Deception Island and tore that base's resident pig to pieces. Bowing to the inevitable, at last Davies decided to despatch the Port Lockroy animal himself, 'if only to save her from that fate':

> One day, when the pig was asleep in the sunshine, I shot her with a .45 revolver, point-blank in the head. It was all over in a second, and I hope that she felt neither pain nor fear. We all had mixed feelings about that, and missed her afterwards. That well-meant feast of pork was not relished by most of us. We were only a small crowd together in that vast and lonely place and the pig had become one of us ... I remember that little pig to this day, and her picture is on my mantelpiece, along with those of my family.[32]

'It just shows, you know, how attached you can get to these things,' he recalled wistfully more than forty years later. 'I suppose if a bluebottle had come down there, we would have made friends with that too.'[33] On one point all agreed: that the fresh mutton, which arrived in the form of ready butchered joints, was far preferable to 'pork on the hoof'.

In the weeks leading up to Christmas a number of short boat journeys were undertaken in order to search for geological and other specimens. Although they still experienced windy and overcast days, the weather continued to improve and, island-hopping around the harbour, the explorers became familiar with an Antarctic landscape far removed from the dominant picture of unremitting blizzards and bitter cold. Visiting Doumer Island, Lamb noted that:

The sea was glassily calm, the sun hot, and the scenery beautiful, with not a cloud in the sky. On the way out we took some photographs of Port Lockroy and the surrounding mountain ranges, and also of Mount Français, the base of which was now visible. Apart from two narrow lines of small brash, through which we were able to row easily, and a few widely scattered bergs, there was no ice … In the hot sun (the temperature reached 107° in the sun today!) the snow on the slope above was melting rapidly, and rivulets of water were running down channels among the rocks and making miniature waterfalls … Several times I drank from these cool clear rivulets of snow water.[34]

A few days later, on Casabianca Islet – a low rocky mound rising less than 20ft above the surface of Neumayer Channel – they discovered the remains of a stone cairn and a wooden post erected by Charcot in 1905. The cairn had contained a message for the Argentine vessel *Uruguay* – but the *Uruguay* had missed it and this had given rise to fears that the *Français* had been lost, possibly even before she had reached the Antarctic. This discovery provided an unexpected link with the Heroic Age and an impressed Taylor noted that 'The wooden pole marking the cairn in which [Charcot's] message had been left still stood when we arrived there that morning forty years later.'[35] The message once hidden in the cairn had long since gone, however, having been recovered by Charcot himself when he returned four years later on board the *Pourquoi-Pas?*

On Christmas Day it was inevitable that the men's thoughts should turn homewards. With their plentiful supplies of fresh meat and fruit delivered by the *Scoresby*, two bottles of champagne sent down by the manager of the Royal Bank of Canada and a gift of cakes from 'some of the good ladies of Port Stanley',[36] everyone recognised that their dinner was 'certainly much better than one would get at the present time in a restaurant at home. There were seven courses to it, and the company rose from the table in a state of repletion.'[37] But the quality of their fare did little to make up for their feelings of isolation – particularly for those men with young families like Taylor, Farrington and Lamb.

During the early days of January 1945 this isolation began to seem even more absolute when thick belts of pack ice began gradually to move north, threatening to cut off Port Lockroy completely from the outside world. On 7 January Farrington and Taylor rowed to Wiencke Island and climbed the Channel Glacier to gauge the seriousness of the situation. Scanning the surrounding channels through binoculars, Taylor noted anxiously that 'the sea to the south was one continual mass of thick and heavy pack ice, studded with tremendous icebergs'.[38] Three days later these bergs were rubbing shoulders in Neumayer Channel and very soon the waterways around Port Lockroy were becoming dangerously clogged with ice.

Fortunately, the high temperatures prevented the pack ice from coalescing and while the bergs – some of them up to 2 miles in length – sometimes grounded, the tides eventually freed them so that they could continue their inexorable drift northwards.

While the ice was still gathering in the channels, Farrington picked up a message from Marr advising that, following his discussions with the governor, the plans for 1945 had been expanded still further. It was while taking down this message that Farrington and Back, perhaps as an antidote to the growing tension over the ice conditions, decided to play a trick on their companions, as Taylor recalled:

> [Back] and Farrington did the decoding together, and we listened with bated breath as they read out the results of it to us: 'An advanced southerly base under Marr will be established,' they read, 'at Peter I Island, to which will be attached Lamb, Ashton, Berry, Davies, Farrington, Back' … Ashton almost overturned the table in his eagerness to examine the maps on the wall of the mess room in an effort to discover the locality of Peter I Island, and he was followed by all the others, knee deep in overturned chairs. 'Good Lord,' he cried, 'the bloody island's almost off the map!' And indeed it was, almost a thousand miles to the south west of Port Lockroy, hundreds of miles from any known coasts, and a blank space on the map to the south. Peter I Island stood out on the map, isolated and alone, and they all stood staring at this ominous solitude, babbling excitedly to each other. The consternation that ensued for the next few moments was almost mutinous![39]

Only when Back and Farrington could contain their mirth no longer did they reveal the genuine content of the message. An entirely new base, Base 'E', would indeed be established 'as far south as possible down the east [sic] coast of Graham Land'[40] – but this was likely to be on Stonington Island, one of the many islands hugging the coast of the peninsula and not Peter I Island, located some 280 miles from the Antarctic coast in the Bellingshausen Sea. Marr, Russell, James, Marshall and Matheson would man this new base while Taylor took charge at Hope Bay, with Flett as his second-in-command. The bases at Deception Island and Port Lockroy would also continue to be manned, though Port Lockroy would have a much smaller complement than in 1944. The sledge dogs would be divided between Hope Bay and the new Base 'E'. Fortunately, excitement over these genuine plans diverted the explorers from lynching Back and Farrington for what Taylor called 'the biggest hoax of the year'.[41] Interviewed more than forty years later, a solemn-faced Back admitted that 'It was really rather unkind – it wasn't funny!'[42] A second later he broke into unrepentant guffaws.

All efforts were now concentrated on packing specimens, equipment, clothing, supplies and personal belongings, and moving as much material as possible down to the beach to expedite loading. Time was also devoted to laundering personal kit – a task that had been so studiously avoided during the previous months that much of the clothing was now 'so dirty that it could be stood in a corner and would support itself'.[43] Given that melting just one bucketful of ice could take several hours, it also became essential to recycle the water as many times as possible, with the result that, even after washing, the men's clothes were 'thoroughly homogenised with the same drabness'.[44] Only Ashton and Berry seemed to retain any individuality in their dress, leading some to assume that their years of seafaring gave them the advantage. Those less charitable put it down to Berry's ready access to the galley's water supply.

On 20 January, Farrington learned that the Newfoundland sealer, SS *Eagle*, had arrived at Stanley and by the 25th she, the *Fitzroy* and an oil barge, which would meet the *Scoresby*'s fuelling needs, had sailed south to rendezvous with the *Scoresby* at Deception Island. On board were Marr and Blyth, accompanied by the new members of the expedition. Howkins, however, had been invalided home as a result of appendicitis. The next signal, on 31 October, revealed that, soon after leaving the Falklands, the convoy had run into heavy weather and during a night watch Captain Robert C. Sheppard of the *Eagle* had fallen down a companionway, breaking a number of ribs. Marr had strapped up the captain's ribcage, but by the time they reached Deception Island his pain had become so great that the *Scoresby* had been despatched to Port Lockroy to fetch the doctor. She arrived at 7.20 the following morning but stayed for only 20 minutes – just long enough for Back to climb aboard with his medical kit, for the mail to be delivered and for Marchesi to advise Taylor that he and the rest of the men would be collected and taken to Deception Island in the next couple of days. From there, they would be ferried to Hope Bay on board the *Eagle*.

Having delivered Back to Deception Island, the *Scoresby* immediately turned round and, in company with the *Fitzroy*, sailed again for Port Lockroy, arriving mid-afternoon on 3 February. 'We went aboard almost before the *Fitzroy* lost way,' Taylor reported, 'and were warmly greeted by all our visitors, including Marr and Blyth.'[45] Also on board were the new arrivals, Russell, James, Marshall and Lockley, plus Layther and a cook named Frank White. The last three would immediately take charge of Base 'A'. Finally, there was Sub-Lieutenant Alan Reece, who had taken over as base commander on Deception Island after Flett's appointment to the Hope Bay contingent.

Taking Taylor to his cabin, Marr explained in more detail the plans agreed with the governor. The stores and equipment destined for Hope

Bay would be taken north to Deception Island, where they would be loaded onto the *Eagle*. Once they arrived at Hope Bay, Marr and his men would assist Taylor in establishing his base before sailing south to identify a suitable spot for Base 'E'. The *Scoresby* and the *Fitzroy*, meanwhile, would seek to establish yet another base at Sandjefjord Bay on the western tip of Coronation Island in the South Orkneys, though this additional station would remain unmanned, at least for the present. The programme seemed highly ambitious but, as Taylor admitted, the 'prospect of having the two bases on east [*sic*] Graham Land had already created a refreshing spirit of competition of which one already could perceive the keenness.'[46]

The next morning, while the working parties loaded the materials to be taken north, Jock Lockley and his two companions explored Bransfield House. Of course, the numerous extensions that had done so much to make life comfortable for a party of nine now seemed excessive for a party of just three, as Lockley was quick to point out. 'This hut,' he observed in his first report, 'is of course overlarge for a party of four.[47] Spaciousness has been a great advantage but the heating and cleaning requirements are somewhat uneconomical for a small party.'[48] For their part, the departing explorers must have wondered just how Lockley and his companions would keep themselves fully occupied over the coming year. Extravagant though the dimensions of Bransfield House might now seem, its design, construction and furnishing had kept Marr and his men fully engaged for months. They had also explored and surveyed as much territory as the lack of stable sea ice permitted and had done much in the way of zoological, geological and botanical study. From being the seat of the most intense activity during the first year of Operation Tabarin, Port Lockroy would now be reduced to little more than a backwater, an outpost supplanted in importance by the new bases. For all their enthusiasm and commitment, therefore, the residents of Goudier Island might find themselves largely redundant and what work they did achieve little more than a footnote to that already completed. Fortunately, both parties were sufficiently diplomatic to keep their opinions and doubts to themselves and when they bade farewell on the evening of 4 February they did so very amicably.

As Marr and his companions prepared to descend to their cabins on the *Fitzroy*, they paused at the rail to admire the magnificent sunset, which painted the surrounding mountains with a pallet of red, amber and gold and set the waters of the harbour alight. The last year had been enormously frustrating in many respects but now, with new opportunities opening up before them, these historic obstacles faded into insignificance and the explorers 'took leave of Bransfield House with feelings heavily mixed with sentiment, and memories full of the happy incidents we had enjoyed within its rough walls'.[49] Only a few days previously the channels surrounding Wiencke Island had been choked with pack ice and tower-ing bergs, but as the ships rounded Damoy Point the following morning the Neumayer Channel was virtually ice-free. The clatter of the engines settled into a rhythmic hum, the brash ice slid almost noiselessly down the ships' sides and flocks of cape pigeons and dainty Wilson's petrels wheeled across the sky, borne on the omnipresent east wind. It seemed that the omens for the next phase of Operation Tabarin were all good. Moreover, whatever the difficulties overcome and still to be faced by the expedition, Marr could now rest easy in the knowledge that he and his team had fulfilled their most important objectives. Two permanent bases had been established and a mass of meteorological, scientific and survey data was being collated and transmitted to London. In his report on the expedi-tion's activities during its first full year, Marr wrote:

> After a break of five years forced upon us by war, the active interest dis-played by Great Britain since 1925 until the outbreak of war has once again been revived and there already appears to be a prospect of larger operations to come.[50]

What none of his companions realised as they bade farewell to Port Lockroy – and what Marr himself may not have known – was that he would play no part in those 'larger operations'. Very soon he would be leaving his beloved Antarctic forever.

1 Personnel of Operation Tabarin, 1944–45, photographed on the *Highland Monarch*, *en route* to the Falkland Islands in January 1944. Ship's officers are indicated with an (s). Back row, L to R: Berry, Layther, Blair, Farrington, Matheson, Taylor, Back and Ashton. Middle row: Graham (s), Marchesi (s), Marr, Fleck (s) and Howkins. Front row: Smith, Flett, Davies and Lamb. (Courtesy of Gerry Farrington)

2 The Falkland Islands Company ship *Fitzroy*. Commandeered after the expedition's original vessel had been declared unseaworthy, the *Fitzroy* was not ice-strengthened. As a result, Captain Keith Pitt refused to endanger her in the ice of Hope Bay, making it impossible to establish Base 'A' in the intended location. (Courtesy of Gerry Farrington)

3 The Neumayer Channel with Anvers Island in the background. Photographed from the *William Scoresby* on the expedition's first approach to Port Lockroy, 11 February 1944. (Courtesy of George James)

4 Goudier Island, Port Lockroy, from the north. Savoia Peak and the Fief Range in the background. (Courtesy of British Antarctic Survey Archives Service, ref. no. AD6/19/1/A78. © Natural Environment Research Council)

5 Unloading stores for Base 'A' on Goudier Island, February 1944. The steep incline above this landing point made it essential to find a better alternative in order to prevent needless damage to vital equipment. (Courtesy of British Antarctic Survey Archives Service, ref. no. AD6/19/1/A1/29. © Natural Environment Research Council)

6 Lieutenant-Commander James Marr, leader of Operation Tabarin from 1943 to 1945. A highly experienced marine zoologist who had served with both Shackleton and Mawson, Marr had only limited knowledge of shore bases. His inability to establish his base at Hope Bay weighed heavily on his conscience and contributed to his early retirement from the expedition. Dated 5 November 1944, this photograph was taken a month before he left Port Lockroy and the strain of the previous year is clearly etched on his features. (Courtesy of British Antarctic Survey Archives Service, ref. no. AD6/19/1/A55. © Natural Environment Research Council)

7 Bransfield House, Goudier Island, from the east side. (Courtesy of British Antarctic Survey Archives Service, ref. no. AD6/19/1/A5/41. © Natural Environment Research Council)

8 Personnel of Base 'A', Port Lockroy, 1944–45. L to R: James Marr, Gwion Davies, Lewis Ashton, Tom Berry, 'Fram' Farrington, Eric Back, Andrew Taylor, John Blyth. Photographed by Ivan Mackenzie Lamb. (Courtesy of British Antarctic Survey Archives Service, ref. no. AD6/19/1/A210/8. © Natural Environment Research Council)

9 Midwinter's Day, 21 June 1944. L to R: Taylor, Ashton, Back, Davies, Blyth, Berry, Farrington, Lamb, Marr. (Courtesy of British Antarctic Survey Archives Service, ref. no. AD6/19/1/A8/20. © Natural Environment Research Council)

10 Marr's sledge in a crevasse close to the Luigi Glacier, Wiencke Island, 22 September 1944. With the sledge firmly wedged and the snow bridge seriously weakened, Marr was forced to rope-up and unload the sledge one item at a time before it could be hauled free. (Courtesy of British Antarctic Survey Archives Service, ref. no. AD6/19/1/A40/23. © Natural Environment Research Council)

11 Camp 'A', Wiencke Island, September 1944. Appalling weather kept the four-man sledge party confined to their tents for a miserable fortnight, during which only very limited fieldwork was feasible. (Courtesy of British Antarctic Survey Archives Service, ref. no. AD6/19/1/A40/35. © Natural Environment Research Council)

12 A lunchtime halt at the base of the Wall Range during the survey of Wiencke Island, October 1944. (Courtesy of British Antarctic Survey Archives Service, ref. no. AD6/19/1/A42/1. © Natural Environment Research Council)

13 Taylor with the temperamental survey camera. He later wrote that it was 'an interesting journey to have partaken in, giving one an insight into the laborious methods and equipment which explorers had been forced to use in the early part of the century. But it is not a method which should be followed today.' (Courtesy of British Antarctic Survey Archives Service, ref. no. AD6/19/1/A46/7. © Natural Environment Research Council)

14 Dr Eric Back at Port Lockroy with probably the first pig ever to set trotter on the Antarctic continent. The animal was intended to provide the explorers with fresh meat. Instead, it became an accepted member of the expedition whose demise was deeply mourned. (Courtesy of British Antarctic Survey Archives Service, ref. no. AD6/19/1/A512/6. © Natural Environment Research Council)

15 Base 'B': the derelict whaling factory at Whaler's Bay, Deception Island. Formed from the sea-filled mouth of a still active volcano, the island consists of a ring of snow-capped basalt mountains which rise to nearly 2,000ft and enclose a deep lagoon, accessible only through a concealed passage in the cliff wall. (Courtesy of British Antarctic Survey Archives Service, ref. no. AD6/19/1/B118/2. © Natural Environment Research Council)

16 The personnel of Base 'B', Deception Island, 1944–45. L to R: Charlie Smith (cook), Norman Layther (radioman), 'Bill' Flett (leader and geologist), 'Jock' Matheson (handyman) and Gordon Howkins (meteorologist). Located in the South Shetlands, they knew that they faced the greatest risk of encountering an Argentine force, making Deception Island the most probable flashpoint. (Courtesy of British Antarctic Survey Archives Service, ref. no. AD6/19/1/B53/6. © Natural Environment Research Council)

17 Captain Andrew Taylor of the Royal Canadian Engineers at Port Lockroy. Originally appointed as senior surveyor and second-in-command of the main base party, Taylor assumed command of the expedition after Marr's unexpected retirement. (Courtesy of British Antarctic Survey Archives Service, ref. no. AD6/19/1/A50. © Natural Environment Research Council)

18 The veteran sealer, *Eagle*, photographed at Deception Island. Built in Norway in 1902, *Eagle* was the last of the ice-strengthened, wooden-walled steamers used for hunting in Arctic waters. During Operation Tabarin she would come closer than ever before to total destruction. (Courtesy of British Antarctic Survey Archives Service, ref. no. AD6/19/1/A220/3. © Natural Environment Research Council)

19 The reconnaissance party search for a suitable base site, Hope Bay, 12 February 1945. (Courtesy of Justin Marshall)

20 Eagle House under construction at Hope Bay, February 1945. To the left, a 4ft gap in the corrugated iron cladding of the Nissen hut has been filled with a tarpaulin – a temporary expedient which eventually became a permanent feature. To the right, 'Uncle Tom's Cabin' or the 'Tin Galley', which served as temporary accommodation for the explorers until the main hut was ready for occupation. (Courtesy of the Russell family)

21   Hope Bay in February 1945. (Courtesy of the Russell family)

22   Lewis 'Chippy' Ashton at his workbench in Eagle House. A popular and highly competent member of the expedition, Ashton was responsible for the construction of the expedition huts at Port Lockroy and Hope Bay. In his spare time he created wonderfully detailed 'ships in bottles' and presented them to his companions. (Courtesy of the Russell family)

23 Interior view of Eagle House. The loss of essential stores with the *Eagle* meant that the hut was far less comfortable than either Bransfield House at Port Lockroy or Bleak House on Deception Island. (Courtesy of Justin Marshall)

24 Eric Back fishing through the sea ice of Hope Bay. His catch is a rock cod. (Courtesy of the Russell family)

25 Eagle House buried in the winter snow. Drifts behind the hut reached a depth in excess of 10ft and it became necessary to dig tunnels to facilitate access. The loss of building materials when the expedition ship, *Eagle*, was driven from Hope Bay made the hut particularly prone to the incursion of drift snow. (Courtesy of Justin Marshall)

26 A dog team in action close to Eagle House. The photograph was probably taken during one of the trial runs, when supplies dumped at Eagle Cove were brought to the base site. Commenting on the sledgers' inexperience, Gwion 'Taff' Davies wrote that 'the dogs taught us'. (Courtesy of Justin Marshall)

27 'Freddy' Marshall at his scientific bench in Eagle House. (Courtesy of Justin Marshall)

28 Depot Glacier, Hope Bay. This glacier would form the main route for sledgers travelling from Base 'D' to Duse Bay and then down the Prince Gustav Channel on the eastern coast of the Graham Land Peninsula. Its traverse was complicated by a combination of deep, soft snow and high winds. (Courtesy of the Russell family)

29 The remains of Otto Nordenskjöld's winter quarters on Snow Hill Island. During the sledge journey of August to September 1945, Taylor hoped that he might find sufficient supplies at this Heroic Age base to enable him to extend his survey expedition. Instead, he found the hut derelict and devoid of any usable materials. (Courtesy of British Antarctic Survey Archives Service, ref. no. AD6/19/1/D1227/7. © Natural Environment Research Council)

30 Captain Victor Russell, RE, and Sub-Lieutenant David James, RNVR, photographed at the end of their first sledging expedition, 11 September 1945. The two men made an effective team – but badly frostbitten feet prevented James from taking part in the second major sledge journey between November and December. (Courtesy of British Antarctic Survey Archives Service, ref. no. AD6/19/1/D1237/1. © Natural Environment Research Council)

31 Taylor, Russell, Davies and Lamb reach Duse Bay at the beginning of the second major sledge journey from Hope Bay, 9 November 1945. (Courtesy of British Antarctic Survey Archives Service, ref. no. AD6/19/1/D183/13. © Natural Environment Research Council)

32 HMS *William Scoresby*, main expedition ship of Operation Tabarin. Originally built as a whale-marking vessel for the *Discovery* Investigations, she was commandeered by the Admiralty and commissioned as a warship in 1940. After the war she saw service with the National Institute of Oceanography and was scrapped in 1954. (Courtesy of George James)

The Rendezvous

Upon first setting eyes on the SS *Eagle*, David James, the expedition's new assistant surveyor, thought her 'a villainously dirty wood steamer with a clipper bow and a large barrel in her foretop. That impression was later modified by affection, but never abandoned in principle.'[1] And the 25-year-old sub-lieutenant knew what he was talking about. Aged just 17, this scion of the Scottish nobility had evidenced a precocious impatience with convention by leaving Eton to sign on as an apprentice, or trainee officer, on the four-masted merchant ship *Viking*. Four months before the mast, sailing some 30,000 miles from Sweden to South Africa, on to Australia, round Cape Horn and back to England, had been a vacation rather more gruelling than most upper-class schoolboys might have chosen for themselves, but in James' case, the whole experience had proved Nietzsche's contention that 'what doesn't kill us makes us stronger'. Certainly, it had done nothing to quench his thirst for adventure because, immediately before going up to Oxford to read geography, he chose to travel to Spain with his MP father to observe the Civil War at close quarters. Here his career was nearly curtailed by sniper bullets from one side and artillery shells from the other, but he survived to then fritter away a whole year partying and playing strip poker at Balliol with the likes of Leonard Cheshire. Germany's invasion of Poland on 1 September 1939 turned James' mind to more serious pursuits – and back to the sea. Within days of Britain's declaration of war he had volunteered for the RNVR and June 1940 found him serving as a midshipman on the destroyer HMS *Drake*, when she became the last British warship to leave occupied Europe. Patrol duty on an armed merchant cruiser in the Denmark Strait gave him his first experience of pack ice and this was followed, in December 1941, by his appointment as second-in-command of Motor Gunboat (MGB) No. 63 based at Felixstowe.

Designed to counter the threat of German E-boats in coastal waters, the 70ft wooden-hulled MGBs were powered by three Rolls Royce Merlin aeroplane engines, giving them a top speed of 40 knots. Their armament consisted of four .303 Vickers machine-guns mounted in a Boulton & Paul turret aft and a brace of twin Lewis guns amidships. On paper, this may have seemed an ideal combination of speed and firepower. The reality was very different. The Merlin's marine modifications, including saltwater pumps, gear boxes and propeller shaft couplings, caused an endless stream of problems; the boats were flat-bottomed and, at full speed in moderate seas, bounced so violently that they could quite literally break a man's back.[2] Moreover, the electrical systems used to drive the gun turrets malfunctioned constantly, causing them to jam at the most inopportune moments. Only when the Lewis guns and Boulton & Paul turrets were replaced with two .5 calibre guns and a single 20mm Oerlikon gun, and the boats equipped with self-sealing fuel tanks, did the confidence of the Admiralty and the crews increase.

Over the coming months the once despised MGBs, now under the inspired leadership of Lieutenant-Commander Robert Hichens, proved their worth by scattering, damaging and sinking a number of E-boats and other vessels. As part of their aggressive and wide-ranging new approach to coastal defence, on 27 February 1943, the flotilla of four MGBs engaged a small German convoy off the Hook of Holland. In the ensuing action, James won the Distinguished Service Cross 'for courage and skill during an action in light coastal craft',[3] but his boat was reduced to a blazing wreck and he and the rest of the crew were forced to abandon ship. Hichens managed to pick up six survivors while under heavy fire – but James was not one of them. Wounded in the head and shoulder by shrapnel, and accidentally run down by one of the retreating MGBs, he was eventually plucked from the water by the crew of an armed German trawler, patched up and sent to Tarmstedt, near Bremen, as a prisoner of war.

Even before he arrived at the Marlag und Milag Nord camp, James had become a committed escaper, intent on making the best use of any and every opportunity to win his freedom. An attempt to escape while still in transit was foiled by the watchfulness of his guard; another, involving the use of homemade wire cutters to snip his way through two high barbed wire fences, was rendered impracticable by unusually bright moonlight; and a third came to nothing when the Germans discovered his escape tunnel. Following these failures, in December 1943 he succeeded in escaping through the prison bathhouse and, dressed as an officer in the Bulgarian Navy, managed to reach Lübeck before being recaptured. Still undeterred, he made his next attempt almost immediately after being released from ten days of solitary confinement. This time, disguised as a badly wounded

Swedish sailor, with fresh burns simulated with a foul concoction of acri-flavine, cardboard, beeswax and surgical spirit, he again exited via the bathhouse and caught the local train from Tarmstedt to Bremen, followed by more trains, to Lübeck, Rostock, Stettin and, ultimately, Danzig. After five days in hiding, he boarded the Finnish ship *Canopus*, which sailed soon afterwards for neutral Stockholm. Although Finland was still at war with the USSR, Britain's ally, he succeeded in bribing a stoker to keep him hidden and, on 22 February 1944, he reached safety at last – almost exactly a year after being pulled from the black waters of the North Sea.

Successful escapees were seldom subjected to the risk of recapture and, adding an MBE for 'gallant and distinguished service' to his DSC, James spent the next few months in Naval Intelligence, lecturing his fellow officers on escape techniques. Reluctant to continue his lecture tour in the Far East, where the methods he had used in Germany would hardly be relevant, he had inquired whether there might be any opportunities to undertake survey work. Interviews with Mackintosh, Wordie and Debenham followed swiftly with the result that, on the evening of 24 January 1945, a red beard worthy of his Scottish forebears adorning his chin, he had found himself on the deck of the *Eagle* as she steamed south from Stanley, bound for Deception Island.

Whatever his views of the *Eagle*, James' assessment of the old sealer's captain, Robert C. Sheppard, was definitely positive: 'all took an instantaneous liking to him. Aged fifty but looking thirty-five, he had a soft voice and beautiful manners, which clearly cloaked a character of considerable determination.'[4] In the preceding weeks, that determination had been required in full. Built in Norway in 1902, the *Eagle* was the last of the ice-strengthened, wooden-walled steamers still used for hunting in Arctic waters, and she had completed more than forty voyages as a member of Newfoundland's sealing fleet, bringing home thousands of pelts. But since the beginning of the war she had spent much of her time tied up at Bowring's wharf on the south side of St John's harbour, used only occasionally to carry supplies to the US bases in Greenland. In spite of her increasingly decrepit old age, or even because of it, in the autumn of 1944 the Admiralty had chosen the *Eagle* to support Operation Tabarin. This role would require her to make by far the longest and most demanding voyage of her entire career and, with severely limited resources and time available, Sheppard and his crew of twenty-eight officers and men had been hard-pressed to make her ready in time to reach the Antarctic before the end of the austral summer.

The voyage south had been every bit as difficult as Sheppard had expected. Like many ships built for ice work, the *Eagle* rolled abominably in anything approaching heavy weather, making 'mad plunges into the sea, and then staggering like a drunken sailor'.⁵ During the early stages of her voyage, from St John's to Halifax, she kept up with her convoy only with the greatest difficulty, and all too often she had trailed behind, becoming just the kind of lame duck so beloved of marauding U-boat commanders. Fortunately, by the closing months of 1944, U-boat losses were such that even the most audacious commander would hardly risk his boat for so paltry a prize and the *Eagle* continued her voyage unmolested. From Halifax she sailed for Bermuda, but as she entered the tropics the crew was nearly asphyxiated by an all-pervading stench that proved impossible to eradicate: four decades' worth of seal blubber melting and bubbling up from the cracks and seams where it had lain frozen for so many years. She also proved to be seriously weakened amidships and repairs were necessary at every port she visited so that by the time she reached Rio de Janeiro on 28 December, she had fallen well behind schedule. The original plan had been for the *Eagle* to pick up the new expedition members and the huskies at Montevideo, but when she arrived there on 6 January 1945, Sheppard discovered that his impatient passengers had all transferred to the *Fitzroy* and sailed for the Falklands. The *Eagle* finally reached Stanley a week later and was immediately put into the hands of the local shipwrights, who not only recaulked her seams but also added steel ties athwart her bunkers in the hope of strengthening her sufficiently for the next, and most critical, stage of her long voyage. As Harold Squires, the ship's radio operator, recognised, 'It was now the turn of the last of the famous, old wooden-walled Newfoundland sealing steamers to show her mettle.'⁶

The *Eagle* sat dangerously low in the water when she sailed from Stanley. A hundred and fifty mutton carcasses hung from her rigging and spars, and canisters, crates and boxes of all sizes and descriptions crowded her decks, making it almost impossible for her crew to move from one side of the old ship to the other. Surmounting the whole precarious pile was a battered scow that would be used to ferry the cargo from ship to shore. Despite this burden, for two days she made excellent progress, calm seas and fair weather enabling Lewis, the octogenarian chief engineer, to maintain a steady 7 knots. But on 27 January the glass began to fall ominously and soon the heavily laden ship was wallowing in choppy seas and being buffeted by gale-force winds which threatened at every moment to overwhelm her. To make matters worse, even in these comparatively unfrequented sea lanes, the *Eagle* continued to adhere to Admiralty regulations concerning blackout, and Squires observed that 'in the darkness of the gathering storm you could hardly see the other members of the watch'.⁷ This combination of blackout and heavy seas almost proved fatal for Captain Sheppard.

As he made his way from the bridge to the main deck at the height of the storm, a sudden violent roll of the ship caused the captain to lose his footing and he fell headlong down the companionway. At precisely this moment, the door of the saloon swung open and he struck its sharp edge before landing heavily on a hatch. The howling wind had drowned his cry as he fell and some time elapsed before the drenched and semi-conscious captain was discovered and the alarm raised. It was this accident, and the subsequent deterioration in Sheppard's condition, despite Marr's ministrations, that had ultimately resulted in the *Scoresby* being dispatched from Deception Island to collect Back. On his arrival, on 2 February, the doctor recommended an immediate evacuation to the hospital at Stanley – but the captain refused on the grounds that, if he left, the *Eagle*'s part in the expedition must also come to an end as there was no other officer on board qualified to command her. The realisation that the loss of the *Eagle* would result in the abandonment of the Hope Bay plans for the second year running eventually led to Marr, Marchesi, Back and the captain agreeing a compromise. Sheppard would remain in command of the sealer until the vital work of establishing the Hope Bay base had been completed; a decision on whether he should remain thereafter could then be based upon Back's assessment of the state of his recovery. In the meantime, the crew sewed several eiderdown sleeping bags together so that the captain might at least rest more comfortably in his bunk.

Having picked up the rest of the Port Lockroy party, the *Scoresby* and the *Fitzroy* arrived back at Deception Island on 5 February, dropping anchor in Whaler's Bay at 8.40 p.m. after a trouble-free voyage through the Neumayer Channel and across Bransfield Strait. In the gathering darkness, only Reece rowed ashore that evening to check on the status of his new command, but early the next day Taylor, Farrington, Berry, Ashton, Lamb and Davies all had an opportunity to explore Base 'B' – and to be reunited with Blyth, who had returned on the *Fitzroy* after medical treatment at Stanley.

If the accommodation of Bransfield House had seemed generous to Jock Lockley, that of the old whaling station appeared little short of pala-tial to the newly arrived men of Base 'A'. Not only did each member of the station's five-man crew enjoy the privacy of his own room, each had a small combustion stove, salvaged from the debris strewn about the station and installed by Jock Matheson, the handyman. The large south-facing dormitory building that they had commandeered also provided them with a communal mess room, a combined library and workshop, and six additional rooms used as storerooms, workshops and 'repositories for useful salvaged material'.[8] Crucially, it also boasted an unrestricted view of the harbour entrance so that the arrival of what Flett euphemistically described as 'casual visitors' would be detected immediately. To ensure that these same visitors would be under no illusion regarding Britain's sover-eignty over the island, the base party had erected two signs at conspicuous

points, one a pre-painted Union flag on a metal panel, the other manufactured from a reclaimed white tabletop. On the latter they had stencilled
the British Imperial monogram and the words 'Port Foster Post Office' –
though Flett noted, rather ruefully, that the base's 'claim to be the farthest
South Post Office [*sic*] was quickly outmoded by the establishment of a
Post Office at Port Lockroy'.[9]

Despite the comparative luxury of its accommodation, Base 'B' was
not as well provisioned as Port Lockroy where rations were concerned.
According to Flett, as a consequence of 'some misunderstanding regarding the time limit before renewal of food … several articles of foodstuffs,
other than essential commodities, were in short supply'.[10] The temperature
during their first few months on the island had also proved too warm for
the preservation of the fresh meat, but too cold for the preservation of
the vegetables brought from the Falklands. The resulting shortages made it
impossible for 'Smitty', the cook, to achieve anything like the quality and
variety of the meals produced by Berry. Fortunately, unlike Port Lockroy,
Deception Island was never completely deserted by Weddell seals and seal
steaks and livers 'provided tasty meals', while 'the flesh of penguins and
shags also furnished palatable meat'.[11] The hot volcanic ash of the island
also allowed some opportunities for culinary novelty, Gordon Howkins,
the meteorologist, observing that 'we could cook a penguin egg quite well
by burying it'.[12]

Food was not the only resource in short supply. Howkins, who had
served on HMS *Rodney* during her victorious engagement with the
Bismarck in May 1941 and had trained as a meteorologist only after he
failed to qualify as a pilot with the Fleet Air Arm, thought himself 'lucky
to be able to set my own agenda'.[13] However, he had discovered that a
number of his delicate instruments had been damaged in transit, while his
only reference books were two American publications that he had picked
up in Buenos Aires. Moreover, in order to wake for his eight three-hourly
observations, he was forced to improvise his own alarm clock using a spare
drum clock for the barograph attached to the loudspeaker of Layther's
radio. Despite these problems, Howkins had soon managed to initiate
his onerous programme of observations, which were taken over by Flett
and Layther when he fell sick with suspected appendicitis, 'and, as acting
Doctor, failed to cure myself'.[14]

The difficulties of operating in a polar environment have left many scientists feeling thwarted, particularly when their ambitious plans, which
seemed eminently sensible in the comfort of a London office, prove
impossible in the field. As senior scientist as well as base leader, it was probably not surprising that Flett felt 'more frustrated than everyone else'.[15]
In the early weeks of the expedition the unusually fine weather had been

ideal for geological fieldtrips, but he had considered it essential that everyone should concentrate on preparing the base for the winter. Also, 'owing to certain political considerations in the earlier stages of our stay, it was deemed inexpedient for the Geologist, who was also Acting Magistrate, to absent himself from the Base for any considerable length of time.'[16] Together, these factors had obliged him to restrict his fieldtrips to areas accessible by foot during the course of a single day. Only when the base had been made ready and the likelihood of a visit by Argentine ships had receded with the closing of the season, could Matheson devote time to making the expedition's clumsy and unsuitable dinghy more seaworthy. He manufactured oars from salvaged timber and added a sail and mast. Then, in the manner of the ship-supported surveys dreamed of by Marr and Taylor, Flett could at last visit a number of sites without time-consuming and sometimes dangerous overland treks.

Just how perilous these excursions could be was demonstrated on the slopes of Mount Pond, to the east of Pendulum Cove, when Flett slipped on an ice slope and began to glissade uncontrollably. As he shot past, Matheson dived after him and managed to grab him by the head, but then both men continued to slide downhill until they crashed onto the rocks below. The outcome could have been disastrous, but they were lucky to escape with sprains and severe bruising. By the time they were once again fully mobile, winter had set in, reducing any further fieldwork to a bare minimum. Flett had hoped that the loss of daylight would be compensated, in part at least, by the freezing of the harbour, which would enable sledge trips directly across the ice, instead of round the rocky rim. But these plans, too, were foiled by the island's volcanic nature: 'the harbour ice though thick in places was either completely thawed or very thin in the littoral fringe owing to the flow of hot streams. This made movement over the harbour ice quite impracticable.'[17] With the ice too thin for sledging or skiing and too thick for boating, he and his companions had been reduced to fishing from the beaches and observing from afar 'the fantastic architecture of the small grounded bergs'.[18]

In spite of these constraints, by the time of their relief, the men of Base 'B' had achieved all of their political and many of their scientific objectives. Britain's sovereignty over the island had been reasserted; Howkins and Layther had compiled and transmitted detailed synoptic reports for the benefit of Allied shipping; daily observations had been made of ice conditions in the Bransfield Strait; and Flett had been able to collect representative geological specimens from the inland exposures, the glacial streams and the beaches. In addition, by using a series of rods driven into the ground, he had been able to measure the movement of the island's glaciers. Towards the end of these observations he noted that:

> From a survey of some of the glaciers, and from the frequent occurrence of
> huge transported boulders in areas remote from existing glaciers, it would
> appear that the local glaciers are now recessive in character.[19]

This was an observation that would resonate with climate change scientists
in the decades to come. These achievements were undoubtedly significant. Nonetheless, after twelve months on the barren, sulphurous ring of
Deception Island, the men of Base 'B' could be forgiven for viewing the
arrival of the ships at the end of January with very considerable relief.

On 6 February, after marvelling at the whaling station's luxurious
appointments, the men bound for Hope Bay had their first opportunity to
become acquainted with Tommy Donnachie, the red-haired Glaswegian
radio operator who had taken over from Norman Layther on the latter's appointment to Port Lockroy. Aged only 23, Donnachie had already
spent a number of years on armed merchant cruisers, and with his quiet,
unassuming manner he would soon become a popular member of the
expedition's personnel. Even more importantly, they also met the twenty-
five huskies brought from Labrador by Freddy Marshall, a 30-year-old
marine biologist of 'a somewhat cherubic appearance'[20] who had interrupted his honeymoon to join the expedition.

Much was expected of the dogs in the year ahead, and in the view of
Taylor, whose work would be particularly reliant upon them:

> They were full of life, and seemed very pleased to see us, but would prowl
> about in groups, and fall upon one of their own fellows every time he was
> unfortunate [enough] to be alone, in the course of which a terrific din
> ensued, though none of them seemed to be seriously hurt.[21]

As vivid testament to the huskies' savagery, penguin corpses could be seen
strung in a long line along the black beaches; indeed, there was not a living
penguin to be seen anywhere, those birds that had escaped to sea being
altogether too sensible to return while the dogs roamed free. 'It was impossible to prevent the dogs tackling them,' wrote Taylor, 'and they did it not
for food, for they were not hungry, but just because of their lust to kill.'[22]
And, of course, the indigenous inhabitants of the island were not their
only prey. The pig that had been delivered at the beginning of December
had soon become a victim, torn limb from limb in its sty within a month
of its arrival on the *Scoresby*. Yet the men themselves were fairly immune to
the huskies' ferocity, nips tending to be accidental rather than deliberate.
According to Surgeon-Commander Ted Bingham, who had handled the
dogs on Watkins' and Rymill's expeditions and had helped Marshall with
the selection for Operation Tabarin, 'huskies are in reality perfectly safe,

since they are brought up alongside Eskimo children, so that any biter is shot while still a pup.'[23]

While Taylor and his companions made their introductions, the *Fitzroy* drew closer to the *Eagle* and the backbreaking process of unloading, checking and reloading stores and building materials began. After the care that had been taken in packing and labelling the crates and boxes at Port Lockroy, Farrington, in particular, thought the task much more laborious than it needed to be, and attributed this to the rush at Stanley: 'I don't think the same care was taken about having the 'B' stuff in at the top of the cargo, and the 'A' stuff at the bottom.'[24] He also doubted that more could reasonably be expected of a ship's crew unfamiliar with handling anything other than seal carcasses and pelts. For his part, James, who had admired the efficiency and conscientiousness of the Stanley stevedores, believed that the stowing of stores and equipment was made 'a jigsaw puzzle by the *Eagle's* small cargo capacity'.[25] Originally, Marr had hoped that the *Eagle* might be able to carry all of the Base 'D' and Base 'E' stores in one trip, but it soon became clear that this would be quite impossible. Instead, all the stores for the more southerly base would have to be placed on the oil barge for easier transhipment once the *Eagle* returned from Hope Bay. Inevitably, this change in plan would make the available time all the more precious and place even more pressure on the men establishing the new bases.

Work continued the following day, which turned out to be cold and miserable, the men soaked by an unremitting drizzle as they trudged down to the beach with lengths of salvaged timber. On one of these trips, Taylor and Flett were intercepted by Marr and Kenneth Bradley, the Colonial Secretary, who had travelled down from the Falklands on the *Fitzroy*. Marr, who seemed exhausted and much older than his forty-two years, told them that they must talk, and together the four men made their way to Flett's old office in the dormitory building. With everyone working outside, no stoves other than the kitchen range had been lit and the room felt damp and cheerless as they sat down, the rainwater running in rivulets from their clothing. Taylor described their interview:

> We knew that Marr had not been in the best of health when he left [for] Port Stanley in the *Scoresby* two months previously, and he looked tired and haggard as he stood before us. After consultation with the Colonial Secretary, he had decided to relinquish his command of the expedition, and return to England. Several months before he had mentioned [to] Lamb and I his apprehensions of being able to continue this work for another year, on account of his failing health, as he felt very greatly the strain of his responsibilities during the establishment of the bases, for he had been engaged upon similar jobs almost throughout the war at Iceland and South Africa … We joined Bradley

in trying to have him reconsider his decision, but he was adamant, saying that he had considered it frequently over a long period of time before taking this action, on which his mind had now become definitely made up.[26]

Despite Marr's earlier intimations, Taylor claimed to be astonished at this sudden turn of events. He also insisted that his 'astonishment increased' when Marr asked whether he would accept command of the expedition in his place. Given that Taylor had acted as second-in-command of the party at Port Lockroy for a year, that he had been made leader of the Hope Bay party, that an appointment needed to be made urgently if the business of the expedition were to be prosecuted in the limited time available, and that there was no other suitable alternative candidate within a thousand miles of where they stood, his surprise seems rather improbable. Indeed, astonishment would have seemed a more reasonable reaction if anyone else had been appointed in his place. Whatever the truth of the matter, Taylor accepted the offer on the spot and his appointment was confirmed in a signal from the governor two days later.

His resignation accepted, in consultation with Taylor, Flett and Bradley, Marr agreed that he would remain with the expedition until the two new bases had been established. As soon as this work had been completed, he would return to Stanley on the last of the retreating ships. This agreement then gave rise to further debate regarding the wisdom of setting up and maintaining the Stonington Island base without the benefit of Marr's experience. After reviewing their options, the four men reluctantly accepted that it would be more sensible to postpone this element of the expedition and instead focus all efforts on Base 'D' at Hope Bay.

The following day Marr's condition suddenly deteriorated. On 7 February, when first told of his decision to retire, Back had noted in his diary that he had 'long thought he was overworking and while very sorry for him [I] am sure it is best for him to go home'.[27] On examining him again on the 8th, he went much further, admitting in a confidential report that he found it 'difficult and painful to write' that:

> Lt-Cdr Marr is suffering from mental and physical exhaustion associated with depression. He requires very careful observation and treatment since suicide is not unknown in such cases … He has a marked tremor, cannot sleep and worries a great deal. He is the type of man who will not give in but keeps on and on until he is exhausted. Under the circumstances I feel it is essential that he should leave the Antarctic at once.[28]

In his own report, Taylor confirmed that he, too, was 'extremely concerned with Marr's well-being'.[29] Up to this point no one had questioned

Marr's ability to stay until the next phase of the expedition was properly underway; indeed, according to Taylor, both he and Bradley had attempted to dissuade him from leaving. This sudden deterioration in Marr's condition was therefore unexpected. It may be that, with Base 'E' abandoned, and Taylor more than capable of establishing Base 'D' without his supervision, the adrenaline that had kept Marr going for so long simply drained away, leaving him even more depleted than before. Another factor may have been the painful realisation that, by staying on unnecessarily, he risked becoming an embarrassment to Taylor, who would naturally want to assume his new responsibilities with immediate effect – and without his predecessor and erstwhile commander looking over his shoulder. With Back and Taylor's agreement that Marr should be evacuated without delay – and with Marr offering no resistance – the *Scoresby*, which had sailed with the *Fitzroy* to set up the new unmanned base on Coronation Island in the South Orkneys, was immediately recalled. The decision clearly brought Marr some relief because, when he embarked on 9 February, Back observed that 'He seems better and more cheerful today'.[30] The *Scoresby* sailed that morning and Marchesi later reported that 'Once he got to Port Stanley his condition improved.'[31]

The reaction to Marr's departure was one of almost universal regret. Despite his constitutional dourness and occasional depression, he was generally popular with his men. In addition to fulfilling his responsibilities as leader, he had made it a matter of principle to share even the most unpleasant routine duties in equal measure and he had drawn no invidious distinction between officers and men. He and his mouth organ had also played active parts in all the festivities of Base 'A'. As always, the most vocal of his champions was Davies:

> I had a very great regard for Marr … It's only looking back on it I realise what a fantastic job he did; it would have driven me round the bend: I could never have done it … I think he did a miraculous job of work.[32]

Although he admitted that 'we all used to have a quiet jibe, on the side',[33] Davies firmly believed that these criticisms were just the expression of petty differences inseparable from such a life – not evidence of a strong undercurrent of dissatisfaction. Back, who generally took a balanced view and was certainly not prone to the kind of hero worship sometimes displayed by his colleague, stated that 'I admired Marr. I think he did very well … And he'd put his heart and soul into it.'[34] Farrington, too, considered it a 'privilege to have had the opportunity of serving under his leadership'.[35] Even James, who hardly knew Marr, thought the news of his departure 'very sad … During the six weeks that we had been together we had conceived a great liking for him, and I for one greatly regretted that we were not going to spend the year in company.'[36]

The only discordant note in this paean came from Taylor. Half a century after Marr's resignation, he wrote that 'I was told by someone (AC) who knew more than a little about Operation Tabarin, that the best thing Marr did in his first and only year with it was to appoint Andrew Taylor to succeed him.'[37] If Taylor's account of Sir Allan Cardinall's remarks is accurate, then the governor's analysis seems profoundly unfair. In spite of the extraordinarily limited amount of time he was granted to prepare the expedition, the difficulty of obtaining suitable equipment in the face of demands from more warlike units, and the conditions of absolute secrecy under which he worked, Marr had ensured that his team was very well prepared for its sojourn in the Antarctic. He had also taken responsibility for selecting personnel and, in almost every instance, he chose well. The refusal of Pitt and Roberts to risk the *Fitzroy* in February 1944 had forced him to abandon, temporarily at least, the plans for a base at Hope Bay – but no one regretted this decision more acutely than Marr himself, and he would continue to reproach himself bitterly for his failure to persuade the two captains – over whom he held no authority – to make the attempt. In fact, his inability to put this failure behind him may have been one of the most potent factors in the subsequent deterioration in his health – even if, as Taylor suggested, this breakdown was accelerated by alcohol (in his private memorandum, Taylor noted that Marr 'returned to England at his own request on medical grounds – *bottles*').[38] But Taylor's comments have to be placed in context, and there can be absolutely no doubt that his later experiences gave him a jaundiced view of the operation and of the parts that he and Marr played in it. Specifically, he felt that his own rewards, in comparison with those supposedly 'lavished' upon Marr, were wholly inadequate. In stark contrast, Marchesi, whose distance from the affairs of the base gave him a significant degree of objectivity, 'always felt that poor old Jimmy Marr really didn't get quite the recognition he deserved'.[39]

While Marr sailed north, the rest of the explorers continued to sort the stores and ferry them to the *Eagle*. Back had already stated his opinion that, as long as the seas were not too rough, Sheppard should be fit enough to resume command – so everything now depended on the meteorologists' weather report. 'About midnight, Reece had assembled all the information he required to make his forecast … it was to the effect that the morning would be overcast with patches of fog, clearing later in the day when visibility in excess of 30 miles would ensue.'[40] To Reece's immense relief, the morning of 11 February dawned foggy, but calm, just as he had predicted, and the final preparations for the expedition's departure began.

Filled to repletion with penguin flesh and fully exercised after their days on shore, the excited dogs were swung from the scow and lashed to convenient projections on deck. 'We looked more like a replica of Noah's Ark than a ship on a secret admiralty mission,' opined Squires, '… Between the dogs and our strange and varied cargo, there wasn't room to put your feet down properly, but somehow we made do and carried on.'[41] For his part, James thought that, in common with every other expedition ship, 'we looked like a Christmas tree':

> On the forecastle head were dogs. The deep well-deck forrard was flush with the poop, being filled with lumber, anthracite, beds, benches, ladders, and yet more dogs. On either side of the bridge a pound had been built round the fiddleys, which were heaped high with coal. Athwart the after hatch and far too big for convenience of passage was the scow, which had lumber piled high around it and dogs inside, while aft, tied round the emergency steering wheel, were more dogs still.[42]

The huskies secured, the explorers tossed their kitbags to the waiting sailors and clambered over the rail. Lamb photographed the proceedings and then, just before noon, he and his companions bade a cheerful farewell to the Deception Island shore party. Minutes later the *Eagle* began a slow, wide turn, hardly disturbing the thousands of decorative cape pigeons floating on the calm, clear waters of the harbour. The old ship was now so grossly overloaded that her Plimsoll line lay some 2ft below the surface, but she slipped through the narrow passage of Neptune's Bellows without incident and continued out into Bransfield Strait.

Besides a few isolated bergs, the waters of the strait were largely ice free and the old sealer made such good progress that soon the jagged outline of Deception Island had been lost to view. Exactly one year and five days earlier, the *Fitzroy* and the *Scoresby* had sailed from here, bound for Hope Bay. On that occasion, ice conditions and the caution of Pitt and Roberts had forced Marr to abandon his carefully laid plans and to accept a compromise that had severely limited the work that he and his team could complete. Now Marr was gone and Andrew Taylor stood in his place, confident in his own abilities, ambitious and highly motivated – but, ultimately, no more certain of success than Marr had been. Until his party and its stores had been landed on the rocky beach of Hope Bay, he would remain totally dependent upon Sheppard and his decrepit steamship, the former still swathed in bandages and the latter held together with a web of steel ties. In the coming weeks more would be expected of these battered veterans than ever before. And in rising to the challenge both would come within an ace of total destruction.

New Horizons

It was typical of the contrariness of life in the Antarctic that once Operation Tabarin had been equipped with a ship capable of forcing a passage through pack ice, the pack disappeared. Large flat-topped bergs studded Bransfield Strait, but these were easily avoided and the *Eagle* maintained a steady 7 knots throughout the afternoon of 11 February. Not long after Deception Island sank in her wake, the sun broke through the fog, illuminating the mountains of Graham Land some 50 miles away and providing the lookouts with superb visibility. The temperature rose swiftly and soon the tired explorers could lie down and drowse on the grimy decks, though their slumbers were disturbed in the middle of the afternoon by two whales breaching within a cable's length of the ship's side, 'flinging themselves vertically out of the water forty feet or more and then floundering back into it with a thunderous splash'.[1] All in all, the new members of the expedition could hardly have hoped for a better introduction to the Antarctic.

In the early hours of 12 February Ashton was called to the bridge to confirm the captain's landfall. A year earlier, he, along with Marr, Lamb and Back, had taken part in the *Scoresby*'s reconnaissance of Hope Bay. Lamb and Back were also on board the *Eagle*, but Ashton was by far the most seasoned mariner of the three and with the bergs increasing in frequency the captain wanted to benefit from his experience of these waters. Sheppard need not have worried: although the bergs were certainly more numerous in Antarctic Sound, the ship's path remained entirely free of pack ice and at 6 a.m. she entered the mile-wide mouth of Hope Bay unopposed. 'With luck on our side,' wrote Harold Squires, 'Captain Sheppard thought we would make Hope Bay in about twenty hours and he was dead on.'[2]

In the teeth of a strong cold breeze from the south-west, the members of the shore party immediately began to push their way to the ship's rail to obtain what, for the majority, would be their first view of their new home. Naturally, the excitement of the veterans was tinged with anxiety: would they be able to establish themselves this year, after failing in 1944? Or would their second attempt also end in dismal failure? But the enthusiasm of the novices was unalloyed. 'At first sight,' wrote James, 'the place charmed':

A deep bay about a mile wide and three miles deep was headed by a highly individualised valley glacier with two striking lateral moraines ... At the head of the bay on the north-west side was a high mountain mass with sheer cliffs rising some 3,000 feet, and a flat table top covered by a thick ice sheet. Below this were several sharp ridges followed by a heavily crevassed glacier, the rest of the northern side being composed of a 'Chinese wall' of the usual ice cliffs. The south-eastern side was as different as it was unexpected. It was headed by a very ice-free scree peak containing a snow-filled 'armchair' corry very suggestive of Scotland ... there were several acres of pleasant hilly ground which were entirely devoid of any ice or snow-cover. It was somewhere on this ground that it was proposed to erect the base.[3]

Most important of all, the waters of the bay were completely free of ice. The picture could hardly have been more different from that which had greeted Marr, Marchesi, Pitt and Roberts twelve months earlier, when the ice had jostled for entry to the bay.

As the wind began to abate, a boat was launched and an anchorage with 25 fathoms of clearance quickly located in a small inlet in the southern shore. Then, with the ship riding at anchor in this inlet, subsequently called 'Eagle Cove', the shore party landed and began to search for the best place to build the base. After examining and rejecting a number of potential sites, they eventually chose a spot to the south of a rocky promontory named Seal Point by Gunnar Andersson. Lying at the toe of the massive sheet of inland ice, some 25ft above sea level and three-quarters of a mile inland, it consisted of two level areas of moraine, each about 100ft sq. and divided during the summer months by a swiftly flowing glacial stream. The advantages were obvious: the site was located some distance from the noisome penguin colonies, it gave ready access to the glacier for sledgers, the glacial stream provided a source of fresh water and, at the shore, a 7ft-high ice foot would serve as a natural jetty for offloading. In fact, this 'jetty' and the approaches to 'Hut Cove' would prove to be the only real disadvantages of the location. In his interim report on the establishment of the base, Flett noted that 'Unfortunately, the ship could not lie off this site, as the sea, in its immediate neighbourhood, is dotted with sea-stacks, reefs, and submarine pressure ridges due possibly to the movement of the sea ice.'[4] These obstacles meant that heavily laden boats could only reach the jetty at high tide, so deliveries had to be timed very carefully. In addition, the underpowered motorboat, which Flett described as 'fantastically and dangerously inadequate', struggled to pull the scow into the cove in the face of the strong south-westerlies. Together, these defects would eventually result in an alternative landing point being identified opposite the ship's anchorage in Eagle Cove. The distance of this landing point from the building site made it necessary to form a temporary depot and to sledge the stores much further, but at least it could be reached when the weather or tides rendered Hut Cove inaccessible.

While the other members of the party conducted their survey and selected the base site, Lamb photographed the remains of the low stone hut built in 1903 by the three men of Nordenskjöld's Swedish Antarctic Expedition, Andersson, Toralf Grunden and Lieutenant Samuel Duse. Rising to a height of 5½ft and built of loose stones enclosing a space about 12ft sq., the walls tapered from a width of 4ft at the base, to 2ft at the top, the gaps between the stones stuffed with seaweed and moss, much of which Lamb found to be still dry and crisp despite the passage of some forty years. Over the coming days the explorers would discover a wealth of artefacts, either buried in the penguin guano which filled the hut or scattered across the ground outside, each item bearing testimony to the appalling conditions in which the hut's inhabitants had lived for eight long months: the broken handle of a hammer, used to stir the penguin soup; the homemade 'smoker' stove, still half full of rancid seal blubber and, most poignant of all, the wooden signal which they had erected in the hope of attracting the attention of any passing vessel.

By the time the party regained the ship late in the afternoon, Sheppard had retired to his bunk, exhausted and in some pain after an unbroken stint of sixteen hours on the bridge. Bob Whitten, the acting first mate,[5] had been left in charge of the offloading, but he considered it too late to begin the work that night despite the beautiful weather; besides, a number of his men had left the ship in order to hunt seals for dog meat. 'I believe,' wrote Taylor, 'there were a number of subsequent occasions on which he must have regretfully thought back upon this missed opportunity.'[6] With time unexpectedly on their hands, the explorers lingered on deck, laughing at the antics of the thousands of Adélie penguins as they darted through the calm waters of the bay, propelled themselves vertically onto the ice edge and waddled back to their nests and their impatient chicks. Dazzled by the benign aspect of the scene, James wrote that it 'was all so utterly unlike any conceptions we had of the Antarctic even at its best that we all thought Hope Bay to be a land flowing with milk and honey. Yet it must be savage enough in winter, as the Swedish stone hut bears mute witness.'[7]

A delay expected to last only a few hours eventually extended to cover a full twenty-four, as the next morning the strong south-west wind was once again blowing down the glacier, preventing a landing. The scow had been lowered over the side, but it shipped so much water that it had to be unloaded and baled out. In addition, one of the ship's dories broke loose and floated away before it could be recovered and the *Eagle* herself dragged her anchor for several hundred feet before it caught again and halted her drift. The wind eventually dropped around noon, but the low tide meant that it was 4 p.m. before the first boatload of building materials reached the base site. Ashton then began the erection of a 'tin galley' which he had prefabricated at Port Lockroy and which, measuring 16ft x 20ft, was large enough to serve as a temporary dormitory as well as a place for Berry to prepare hot meals for the construction gangs. The dogs were also put ashore, though, as Squires observed, their landing was rather less disciplined. 'We put the twenty-five excited animals in the scow and carried them very close to the nearest point of land, then threw them overboard.'[8] Fortunately, all the dogs proved to be excellent swimmers and they soon scrambled up onto the beach none the worse for their dip. With appetites sharpened by their swim, they then made for the nearby penguin colony, though Back later claimed that 'the number of penguins they actually killed was … not very many'.[9]

Ashton completed the tin galley the next day and towards evening the large timbers for the main hut, the sections for one of two Nissen huts, and crates of stores all began to be offloaded by scow and dories, with Victor Russell supervising the loading on board the *Eagle* and Back acting as beachmaster. The doctor proved particularly adept in this role, noting: 'we did a lot of planning in Lockroy about the loading of the stores and how we were going to do things. As a result of that we got off to a very good start in Hope Bay.'[10] In particular, he erected six homemade signs on which he had printed the words 'Main hut timbers', 'Nissen', 'Hardware', 'Scientific stores', 'Food' and 'Radio', and then ensured that each consignment was sorted immediately after being landed. 'It is thus easy,' wrote an appreciative James, 'to lay one's hands on almost anything.'[11] Only Farrington uttered any words of criticism, observing that:

> there was something like a week before we were able to get out even what was called 'portable' [radio] equipment so that we could keep in touch with the *Eagle* from the base. It was much longer than that before we got the main wireless equipment out from the *Eagle*.[12]

The only other item mistakenly placed too deep in the hold was Berry's box of cooking utensils. This mischance meant that he had to cook meals for ten to fifteen men using only a single pot, 'though fortunately, it was a large one'.[13] That night, Berry, Lamb, Blyth, Flett and Charlie Smith, who had accompanied the expedition from Deception Island, elected to sleep ashore in the temporary galley. In so doing they enjoyed what Flett described as 'the distinguished privilege of being probably the first Britishers to sleep ashore in this area'.[14] The following morning they raised a 20ft pole that they had found near the Swedish hut and unfurled the Union flag.

Work on the first of the Nissen huts, which would serve as a storeroom, began on 15 February, but three days later a violent gust of wind brought the first section crashing down, bending the frame and shearing the securing bolts. 'That didn't help,' remarked Davies tersely,[15] and it took two days to repair the damage. This destructive gust was just one example of the savagery that James had predicted, and a few days at Hope Bay effectively destroyed any lingering illusions regarding the conditions the expedition would face. Violent gales, rain, overcast skies, heavy snow and blizzards succeeded one another with bewildering swiftness and the unloading quickly became 'one continual fight against the winds, weather, tides, ice and darkness'.[16] Worst of all were the gale-force south-westerlies, which could spring up with hardly any warning, funnelling down the glacier and driving the boats like frightened ducklings back to the shelter of the ship.

In spite of these conditions, the stores continued to flow from the *Eagle* under Whitten's watchful eye and on 24 February Davies and Matheson began to transfer them into the finished Nissen hut, doing their best to ignore a 4ft gap in the building's cladding that they had been obliged to plug with a tarpaulin. By this point the men had been living in the tin galley for over a week and, as Back recorded in his diary, conditions were miserable:

> Nothing ever dries and one has to put on wet socks and boots in the morning. Snow comes in all over the place, frost condenses on the roof and drips down at breakfast time. It is alright if temperature is fairly high but not in the low temperatures.[17]

It came as a considerable relief, therefore, when Taylor chose this moment to share the blueprints for the expedition's main building, later named 'Eagle House'. While Bransfield House had 'evolved' over time, Taylor wanted to follow a preordained plan for the new building; he also wanted his men to comment upon the design and to make their own suggestions for possible improvements – a democratic approach which James considered 'a sound psychological move'.[18]

In design and construction the building closely resembled the core elements of Bransfield House. Two prefabricated huts, each 16ft x 38ft, stood side-by-side to provide mess room, dormitory and workroom. However,

just as he had done at Port Lockroy, Ashton then added a number of sizeable extensions, which housed the galley, storerooms, an engine room
for the radio generator, toilets, a laboratory and a carpenter's workshop.
According to Flett, 'Ashton made surprisingly good progress under dis-
heartening conditions,'[19] and by the end of February the main structure
of this 'hodge podge of buildings'[20] was very well advanced. Although the
explorers would continue to live in what they called 'Uncle Tom's Cabin'
until the main building was nearly complete, the expedition now seemed
secure and the *Eagle* could be released to return to Deception Island
for a second load of stores. More important still, she would be able to
ascertain why Base 'B' had maintained an unscheduled radio silence since
21 February – a silence that James thought 'rather worrying, for down
here one rather tends to think of the worst that can happen'.[21]

When Layther reported from Port Lockroy that, shortly before going
off air, Tommy Donnachie had told him of a fire in Deception Island's
engine room, it began to seem likely that this might be the cause of the
interruption. Accidents happen and machinery fails, but the incident
inevitably raised concerns regarding Donnachie's competence, particularly as Layther had recorded, on leaving Deception, that the 'equipment
is in good repair and giving good service'.[22] Conferring with Farrington,
Taylor decided that the older and more experienced operator should now
exchange places with the younger man, who, they agreed, 'appeared to be
the weaker link in the radio side of things'.[23] So far as Farrington was concerned, the swap would mean a transfer to a comparative backwater and,
while he supported Taylor's decision, he also admitted to feeling:

> very disappointed at having to leave the centre of main activity … I expected
> it to be an uninteresting ten months or a year sitting in a hut looking out at
> the uninteresting hills round about and the ash-ridden snow-covered areas
> and an old, ruined, derelict factory – with very, very little to do.[24]

On the evening of 28 February a final load of stores and personal gear
was sent ashore and at noon on 1 March the *Eagle* sailed. In addition to
Farrington, she carried Smith, who would now return to his usual duties;
Russell, who hoped to gather more useful building materials; and Flett,
who, as Taylor's second-in-command, would be able to provide an official
report should the radio silence prove to be the result of a more significant
disaster. Already anxious about the party on Deception Island, Taylor was
horrified to learn that, in weighing anchor, the *Eagle*'s windlass had been
damaged, with three teeth stripped from its gear. He knew only too well
that this accident could have a profound effect on the future course of
the expedition. Although the plans for a base at Stonington Island had

been put on hold, he had agreed with Sheppard that the *Eagle* would lay a number of depots down the eastern edge of the Graham Land coast. These depots would then be used to support the sledging parties sent out from Hope Bay. Sites provisionally identified included Snow Hill Island, where Nordenskjöld had over-wintered, and Robertson Island further to the south. Additional emergency depots would be placed at Joinville Island and Dundee Island in case a small boat party was blown across Antarctic Sound by one of the south-westerlies. Taylor had hoped that the *Scoresby* would be able to assist in this depot laying, but the delays caused by Marr's retirement and the need to complete the establishment of the base at Coronation Island had been further compounded by trouble with the *Scoresby*'s boiler. In addition, as he later admitted, Marchesi was extremely reluctant to undertake the mission: 'I didn't really think it was a very wise thing to do, to go down the Weddell Sea at that particular time of the year … just to drop stores off and return, especially as it was in that vicinity, or not far off, that the *Endurance* got crushed.'[25] With the *Scoresby* unavailable and the *Eagle*'s machinery damaged, the expedition's plans hung in the balance once again.

The news from Deception Island proved rather more positive than feared. Although James, who was acting as temporary wireless operator, could not make direct contact with the *Eagle*, on 2 March he overheard a radio telephone conversation between Farrington at Base 'B' and Squires on board the ship. This at least confirmed that the *Eagle* had arrived safely. Then, on the 4th, he picked up another message transmitted direct from Base 'B' to Hope Bay: 'OK here, *Scoresby* not arrived yet.'[26] On arrival at Deception Island, Flett and his companions had found everybody fit and well, but they learned that the previously reported fire in the engine room had completely destroyed one generator and partly damaged the second. The failure of the second generator, which Donnachie had since repaired, had led to the worrying silence first noticed on 21 February. The cause of the fire was uncertain, but Farrington thought it likely that a spark from a loose connection had ignited petrol vapour in the engine room. Although he generously acknowledged that it was 'an accident that might have happened to anybody', he also fully appreciated that 'it was unfortunate that it should have happened to Donnachie so soon after his arrival in Antarctica'.[27]

Concerned at the possibility of a similar incident occurring when the base was cut off during the winter months, Flett decided to adhere to the plan agreed by Taylor: Farrington would stay at Base 'B' and Donnachie would transfer to Hope Bay, where he would have the support of the larger team. Of course, whatever gloss Flett and Farrington tried to put on the matter, Donnachie could only view the decision as an adverse judgement on his abilities. 'I don't really know whether he minded,' Farrington mused, 'but I would think he was very disappointed at what happened.'[28] As for Farrington himself, he told his wife that 'there are other spots in Antarctica where I would prefer to live',[29] but he also recognised that being stationed at the expedition's most northerly base would bring distinct advantages: 'there is absolutely no doubt about our being relieved at the beginning of 1946 and then it's "Home James and don't spare the horses."'[30]

On 5 March the *Scoresby* arrived at Deception Island. After carrying Marr to Stanley, on 20 February the ship had continued to Coronation Island, where a working party spent three days erecting a small hut as part of the expedition's overall objective of reinforcing British claims over the region. Marchesi had then proceeded to Laurie Island, intent on 'showing the flag' to the resident Argentine meteorologists. In future years the conflicting claims of Argentina and the United Kingdom would occasionally lead to tension and even to armed confrontation, but these incidents were exceptional; by and large, the men on the ground were willing to treat their opposite numbers with courtesy and even affability, leaving their respective governments to rattle diplomatic sabres. At Scotia Bay Marchesi reported that the Argentine meteorologists:

> ... were pleased to see us, as they had not seen anybody for fourteen months. I gave them a thousand cigarettes, and half a sheep, as they had no cigarettes for four months, or any fresh meat for a considerably longer period. I was then informed that their relief ship, the Argentine Naval Transport *Chaco* was due there about the 27th or 28th February. The following day I was shown over the Station; it appeared to be well fitted out, but the living quarters were rather old and appeared to be in need of repairing. The Senior Officer had dinner aboard HM Ship that night.[31]

When the *Chaco* arrived during the morning of 28 February, relations became rather more frosty. Marchesi sent a signal, asking the captain to call upon him, but the Argentine officer clearly understood that, in answering, he might inadvertently recognise British jurisdiction and he made no reply. The following day Marchesi sent an officer ashore, where the *Chaco*'s First Lieutenant informed him that the Argentine ship would be sailing shortly. When the wind freshened in the afternoon Marchesi followed suit and weighed anchor. Years later he laughed at the posturing: 'they sailed about ... and so did I.'[32] Operation Tabarin's first and only meeting with the forces of Argentina had ended in a cordial stalemate.

With Base 'B' now fully operational once again, Flett and Donnachie sailed for Hope Bay on the *Scoresby*, arriving at 3 p.m. on 6 March. 'She did not stay long,' wrote James. 'A boat came ashore with Flett and Tommy. Marchesi stayed chatting with Taylor for about ten minutes and then they were off.'[33] The *Scoresby*'s next port of call would be Port Lockroy, where she would augment the Base 'A' personnel with a Falkland Island handyman named John Biggs; thereafter, she would retreat to Stanley. Six days later the *Eagle* returned to Hope Bay, carrying Russell and a bulky load of stores, coal and timber from the whaling station's seemingly inexhaustible stockpile. The weather at Base 'D' had deteriorated significantly during her absence and Squires observed that 'it was clear that the winter season was coming to Antarctica, and we would be wise to complete our work if we wanted to get back to Port Stanley before the ice trapped us at Hope Bay.'[34]

Snow had proved to be the dominant climatic phenomenon of early March at Hope Bay, the falls sometimes so thick and fast that the men were driven indoors. In addition, the temperature had dropped 20 degrees lower than at the same time in Port Lockroy the previous year and Lamb wrote that:

> To go outside in one of these blizzards is like plunging into cold water; the drift assails one's eyes, mouth and nostrils with such force that it is difficult to get one's breath, and in a few moments one is white from head to foot. Coming into the shelter of the house, one realises to the full the danger of getting lost in such weather; one would not remain alive much over half an hour, perhaps less.[35]

Completion of the roof on 7 March was to have been a holiday, but with the house now so nearly finished and the men increasingly tired of living in the cold, damp and draughty galley, no one felt inclined to take advantage of the fact. Instead they laboured on, installing a stove in the east end of the hut and adding partitions. Between 8 and 11 March, the temporary building was finally abandoned, with a jubilant James noting that 'after four weeks living in "Uncle Tom's Cabin", alias the tin galley, I moved into the house proper – and had a bath!'[36]

Time was also spent offloading timber and other supplies from the *Eagle*, laying the foundations of the annexe to the main hut, and hunting and gutting seals and penguins to feed the dogs, which were now tethered in two long lines close to the shore. James admitted in his diary that he found the killing of penguins:

> a loathsome business as they are as tough as an indiarubber ball. My weapon is an iron blubber hook, yet a blow as hard as I can swing it will not knock one out unless it hits him right on the head, and even with their skulls split wide open they are often still very much alive.[37]

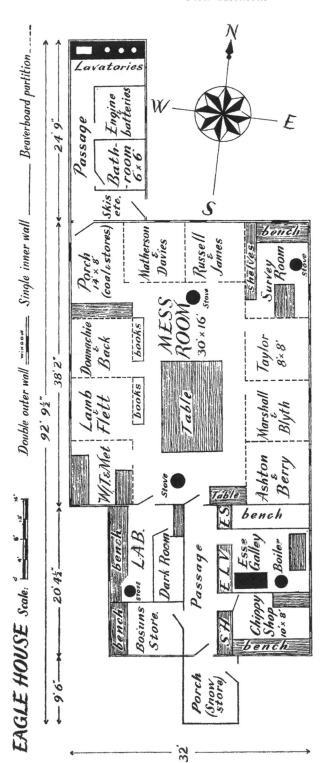

Plan of Eagle House,
Hope Bay

A few weeks earlier, the explorers had been amazed by the skill of the *Eagle*'s third mate, the octogenarian 'Skipper' Tom Carroll, when he had flensed a seal, removing the heavy jacket of skin and fur and blubber over an inch thick in just ten minutes of highly skilled butchery. Now they discovered that it took two inexperienced men an hour to complete the same bloody task, though their slowness was explained in part by their difficult working conditions. In particular, they found themselves fighting constant battles with another of Hope Bay's denizens, the ubiquitous paddy: 'These little devils are as bold as they are hungry. While you are cutting up one bit of meat, they will be eating that already done behind your back, and no barrage of stones or abuse will deter them in the slightest.'[38] With these distractions, James calculated that, by mid-March, the expedition had succeeded in stockpiling enough dog food to last only until the end of May. The slaughter continued.

Life was also becoming much more difficult for those on board the *Eagle*. Although brash ice had been only very light in the bay, from the moment of her first arrival on 12 February the ship had been threatened by icebergs calving from Depot Glacier, and on more than one occasion she had avoided a collision by only the narrowest of margins. Now the glacier was calving with ever-increasing frequency and a constant watch had to be maintained. Inevitably, these conditions reminded the old hands among the crew of past adventures in Arctic waters, and Squires recalled that 'When the day's work was finished there would be stories of bumper voyages, and the many narrow escapes from death that were part and parcel of the seal hunt.'[39] Little did these veterans realise that they and their ship were about to face the narrowest escape of their entire careers.

The glass had begun a slow, steady fall on 16 March and on the morning of the 17th Squires woke to gale-force winds and thick driving snow that reduced visibility to just 20yd. Shortly after daylight he heard the bridge telegraphing the engine room demanding full speed ahead. Then his cabin began to vibrate noisily as the steering chains running beneath the deck rattled through their pulleys. Moments later the young radio man was called to the bridge by an anxious-looking Captain Sheppard:

> He told me that even with the *Eagle*'s engine at full speed, the wind had forced her to drag her anchors and they had snapped under the strain, so that we were now drifting at the mercy of the elements. He told me to try and contact the shore base to let them know what was happening … The storm was growing stronger by the moment and visibility in the driving snow was nil. I quickly made my way back to my cabin and set about contacting the shore base. (At first, I had no luck, for the 'Walkie-Talkie' radio was off at the shore base.) As I was trying to contact the shore, without warning, all hell broke loose.[40]

The *Eagle* lurched so violently that Squires was practically thrown through his cabin door. From this vantage point he witnessed the horrifying spectacle of a colossal iceberg floating by almost within arm's length. Worse still, the 'iceberg had our bowsprit and part of our bow sticking out of it. Some of the rigging and a portion of the rail from the forecastle deck were also embedded in the ice'.[41] Seconds later, the ship suffered another collision, though the second berg gave her only a glancing blow, causing little additional damage.

The storm made it impossible for Sheppard to obtain a proper damage report, but it was abundantly clear that the old sealer had been struck with such force that, despite a 22in-thick hull and sturdy bracing, a large section of her bows had been torn out. The *Eagle* now had a gaping hole approximately 4ft above the waterline and every time she dipped her head, freezing cold seawater flooded into the forecastle; in addition, the chief engineer reported that the water level was rising so swiftly in the engine room that the pumps could not keep pace with it. Finally, the blizzard made it absolutely impossible for the captain to determine his exact position, or to know where the surrounding obstacles lay until they were too close to avoid. With the storm showing no signs of abating, the *Eagle* taking in water and her responsiveness likely to diminish rapidly as she filled, and with all her anchors lost and her windlass inoperable, Sheppard was forced to adopt a desperate tactic: he would make for Eagle Cove and attempt to beach his crippled ship.

'My hopes for survival fell,' wrote Squires when he heard the captain's decision. 'Eagle Cove was a rocky beach strewn with boulders and the huge seas sweeping over our ship would tear her bottom out long before she was beached.'[42] Despite his horror, he returned to his radio room and transmitted what he thought would be his last signal:

> We have carried away our other cable, we have carried away our other cable, and almost given up hope of saving the ship, and almost given up hope of saving the ship. The skipper is thinking of beaching her rather than take her to sea in her present damaged condition. Will you go to 'Handy Cove' [not a gazetted place name] with ropes and stand by please, will you go to 'Handy Cove' with ropes and stand by please.[43]

The men on shore were no less appalled by what they heard. 'It was but the work of minutes to pull [on] our anoraks and load the sledges with all necessary equipment, but what a desperate expedient!'[44] It seemed to everyone concerned that the ship and her crew were doomed, that there was practically no chance of anyone being pulled alive from the raging seas. The grim-faced sledgers had just set out along the coast, when a breathless James caught up with them with another message from Sheppard.

Lewis, the chief engineer, had reported that the pumps had begun to take effect and the water in the engine room was receding. This vital news gave Sheppard a choice, where none had existed before: he could either attempt to beach the ship, as originally planned, or he could make for Stanley, hoping that the pumps continued to keep the water at bay and that the great Southern Ocean was not too violent in its handling of his battered ship. He called his crew together and presented the options to them. All agreed that beaching on such a shore and in such conditions meant almost certain death for every man on board. Making for the Falklands would be a desperate gamble – but it offered some chance of success, however small. Their decision was unanimous: they would fly before the storm and trust their fate to Sheppard and the *Eagle*.

Hearing this news, Taylor and his men abandoned their sledge and its cargo of ropes and tools, and ran down to Seal Point to catch a last glimpse of the ship as she headed out to sea. As they reached the rocky knoll, the *Eagle*'s two tall masts came into view and then 'the ship was silhouetted against her background of drift and haze'.[45] Ice encrusted her sides and all on shore could see how her bow had been torn away, giving her a strangely truncated appearance. Taylor wrote:

> She was making for the open sea, in iceberg ridden waters and in the midst of a gale; her bow was gaping open, and part of her foredeck was swept away; she had neither anchors nor windlass, and was none too well supplied with either water or fuel … She had fought the wind and the sea and the ice and still found time to land our cargo; she had made a proud voyage, for all her grimy rough appearance. As she sailed away, with all their anxieties occupying so much of the crew's attention, they would not likely have seen the little knot of four men, who stood, braced against the wind, waving them 'Bon Voyage!'[46]

The last transmission they received from the ship before she disappeared was a message from Squires regretting that the *Eagle* had been forced to depart before discharging all her cargo, and expressing the hope that the shore party would not be too inconvenienced by this necessity. 'That Sparks has got guts wishing us luck,' Back scribbled in his diary that night. '… May God preserve the *Eagle* and her brave crew. At 2130 the gale still raging.'[47] As they retired that night, few entertained much hope for Sheppard and his men, Davies admitting that 'we never thought we'd see her again or hear of her again'.[48]

The Witches' Cauldron

The wind continued to beat at the walls of Eagle House throughout the night of 17 March, causing the unfinished building to creak and groan with each gust and generating, in Lamb's opinion, 'a curiously distressing psychological effect, like that produced by a person shrieking demented threats and abuse at one unceasingly at the top of his voice.'[1] On 6 May 1915, during Shackleton's Imperial Trans-Antarctic Expedition, the steam yacht *Aurora* had been torn from her berth in McMurdo Sound in circumstances markedly similar to those now being experienced by the personnel of Operation Tabarin. Then, the ship's acting captain, Joseph Russell Stenhouse, had been tortured by thoughts of the fate of the shore party, marooned at Cape Evans with only a fraction of the supplies and equipment deemed necessary for their survival through an Antarctic winter. Now, the roles were reversed: though their base hut was incomplete, the personnel of Base 'D' could feel reasonably secure and, crucially, their whereabouts were known to the outside world. The *Eagle*, on the other hand, had been forced to sea in a severely damaged condition and with only limited fuel and water. 'Listening to the thunderous roar of the wind,' wrote Taylor, '… we lay there sleeplessly, and could not keep our thoughts free of our friends aboard the *Eagle*, fighting for their lives on so wild a night.'[2]

At noon the following day Donnachie picked up a reassuring message advising that the *Eagle*, the hole in her bows covered with a tarpaulin, had weathered the storm and was now in radio contact with both Deception Island and Stanley. 'It was most inspiring news to us all,' admitted a relieved Taylor, 'and coupled with a moderation of the wind producing a bright and calm day by noon, we tackled our construction problems with renewed energy.'[3] Chief among those problems was the fact that the *Eagle* had been blown out to sea with her holds still two-thirds full of materials intended for Base 'D'. These included the whole of the second Nissen hut, intended as an emergency shelter, and the corrugated iron sheets needed to complete the first; lumber for the construction of the annexes; stoves and heaters; about 25 tons of coal; some of the radio equipment; the battery acid for the radio and lighting plant; spare boots; all of the boats; and a miscellaneous assortment of food and scientific gear. 'Still,' wrote James, 'we could not complain; on checking through the stores we found that we had just enough timber to complete our building and were not in critically short supply of any one commodity.'[4] Moreover, while it would not be as comfortable as it had been at Port Lockroy – particularly if the winter conditions at Hope Bay lived up to expectations – the expedition possessed enough clothing and equipment to undertake the majority of its planned survey and scientific work.

The weather at Hope Bay now took an unexpected turn for the better, with the recent blizzards giving way to calm and sunshine so warm that the men could actually sunbathe. 'It really is a pleasure to work on a nice day compared with the drudgery on the bad ones,' Back observed in his diary. '… This Indian summer is truly amazing and very much appreciated.'[5] These sunlit days also provided Lamb with an opportunity to take a series of photographs, including some of his companions in their 'Sunday best'. Blyth, however, noted that it was fortunate that the photos were in black and white: 'my best was a pair of grey boots, grey flannel trousers, a khaki army shirt, a tartan tie and a light brown jacket, so I would have looked no good in colour.'[6] The lull lasted for ten full days and the construction work progressed rapidly. By the end of 20 March, the building had been fully enclosed and seven days later Berry cooked his first meal in his permanent galley. This last event had been delayed by the need to construct the large Esse stove by a process of trial and error, as Taylor and Berry discovered that they had been provided with an instruction manual for an entirely different model. 'Smoke poured from almost every orifice the stove possessed,' the former complained after their first trial, '… we emerged from the galley at the end of our two-hour-long bout with the new stove, both of us smelling like a couple of smoked hams.'[7]

James, who had taken over the care of the dogs from Marshall, faced an even more intractable problem. Initially, the dogs had been fed 'by the simple expedient of knocking off a penguin per dog, per day',[8] but by the end of February the entire Adélie penguin population had migrated and a month later all but a handful of the Gentoos had followed them. Worse still, seals, which would form the dogs' staple food during the winter months, were also becoming extremely scarce and could be expected to disappear altogether when the bay froze over at the beginning of April. The problem was compounded by the premature departure of the *Eagle*, which otherwise would have added to the larder during her depot laying cruises. By the time the gales blew her from the bay, she had added a mere twelve carcasses to the fifteen that James and Russell had so far collected during their daily hunting expeditions – a total far short of the hundred that James had thought necessary. To eke out this meagre supply, occasionally he would prepare a meal of mixed pemmican and dog biscuits, which, to the dismay of his companions, he cooked on the heater in the hut's mess room, 'smelling the place to high heaven in the process.'[9] Although the dogs seemed happy enough on the available rations, feeding them would remain an ever-present anxiety until the onset of spring.

Having heard with immense relief that the *Eagle* had limped into Stanley after a gruelling voyage of seven days instead of the usual three, concern over her fate had given way to another topic on the minds of the men at Hope Bay: would the *Scoresby* be able to reach them again before the onset of winter? If she did, then they might hope to make good the shortfalls in their equipment and supplies. Of even greater consequence to most was the thought of being able to receive and dispatch one more mail before the long months of isolation – an opportunity rendered especially important as there had been no chance to send mail with the *Eagle*. Throughout the first two weeks of April, the explorers were tortured by alternating freeze-ups and thaws of the bay, with hopes reaching their zenith on the 12th, when Back announced: 'There's a heatwave on today, boys.'[10] The temperature soared to 45°F, or 13 degrees above freezing, and, with the bay and Bransfield Strait both appearing to be completely ice free, the *Scoresby*'s arrival seemed guaranteed. Taylor declared a holiday, 'and some intensive pen pushing resulted, the messroom table being lined with bearded figures bending over the lines on which they were pouring out their hearts.'[11]

In his letter, which he added to whenever his other duties allowed, Freddy Marshall described conditions at Hope Bay for his wife, Olga:

Now we are settling in at our base and the major part of the building has been completed. I have tried my hand at foundation laying, cement mixing, brick laying, joinery and carpentry, and I am not too bad at these activities. Shall I try to give you a picture of what is going on at present? I am sitting down at our mess room table writing this letter to you (in pencil as I can't find any ink at present). It is eight o'clock by our time here (midnight by GMT) and it is pretty dark outside. Inside our Tilley lamps are hissing away and the hut is very spacious and warm … Generally the temperature is something like 6°F which is surprisingly comfortable, provided there is no wind (and what a proviso that is, as this place is a witches' cauldron for winds). However, it is still quite bearable with strong winds provided one is wearing suitable wind proof clothes. In fact I can quite honestly say that I don't object to this

spot at all, except for the time you and I are missing away from each other
… I am wearing a beard (recently trimmed), thick studded boots, white sea
boot stockings, which I have pulled over a pair of battle dress bags, my thick
blue sweater and of course pretty thick underclothes.[12]

Like all the other letters on which Marshall and his companions expended
so much labour, this message would not reach its destination until the
middle of 1946. On 14 April, Donnachie picked up a signal advising that
the *Scoresby* had met heavy pack ice in Bransfield Strait and that she had
returned to Deception Island. After another unsuccessful attempt to break
through the next day, she retreated to Stanley for the winter. 'Needless to
say we are all disappointed,' wrote James, 'and there is some disposition to
make a whipping boy of Marchesi.'[13] Back was more blunt: 'no mail until
December, no more lino, no fresh food. The most unsatisfactory thing of
all is that she cannot even have tried … In evening we drowned our sor-
rows in rum punch and I got very tight.'[14] The plight of the men's loved
ones was no less pitiable: 'There was just silence,'[15] complained a disconso-
late Olga Marshall, who had not even completed her honeymoon when
her husband went south.

Despite the helter-skelter of emotions, the loss of three fine days spent
in futile letter-writing and the rapid reduction in the number of daylight
hours, by the middle of April, Ashton and his helpers could begin adding
the finishing touches to the hut – though Marshall noted wryly that 'the
touches never quite seem finished'.[16] Indoors, one of the most critical
tasks was to find a substitute for the linoleum the *Eagle* had been unable
to offload. 'The lack of linoleum,' wrote Taylor, 'was a much more serious problem than it would perhaps appear at first glance, for the floor
of the house consisted of nothing but bare unjointed boards.'[17] Although
deep insulating snowdrifts had begun to form around the hut, the gaps
between the boards still served as an avenue for every gust of wind and
every particle of drift snow and they would make the hut a chill habitation indeed in the fast approaching winter. After some consideration, the
expedient decided upon consisted of four layers: heat-reflecting insulation
paper, tightly stretched tarpaulin, three-ply boarding and, finally, canvas.
With a temperature of −3°F at Hope Bay on 17 April, and Port Lockroy
and Deception Island both experiencing 22 degrees below freezing (10°F),
the work could not be completed too quickly.

Throughout this period, the explorers listened regularly to the BBC's
updates on the death throes of the Third Reich and on 1 May Back
noted that they had 'heard announcement of Hitler's death, wise fellow'.[18]
When they learned of the surrender to Montgomery of German forces
in the west 'a rowdy party was held with lots of beer and punch … Good

singsong until midnight.'[19] Three days later, on VE Day, Winston Churchill and King George VI broadcast to the Empire and Taylor responded with a message to the governor:

> In these lonely outposts, His Majesty's loyal subjects from England, Scotland, Wales, Ireland, Falkland Islands, New Zealand and Canada, join with the Empire to celebrate this historic day.[20]

Douglas Mawson's Australasian Antarctic Expedition of 1911–14 had been the first Antarctic expedition equipped with wireless telegraphy,[21] and from the moment that its primitive Telefunken equipment had burst into erratic life, polar explorers had learned that wireless could be a double-edged sword. At its best, it enabled them to exchange messages with their loved ones at home and to learn something of events in the civilised world; at its worst, it served to remind them just how far removed they were from the concerns of that world. Listening to a BBC broadcast, which described at great length the scenes of jubilation in London, Taylor admitted that their own party fell rather flat, despite liberal libations of a punch concocted for the occasion by Berry: 'the wanton spirit of celebration which should have been present among us was noticeably absent. Perhaps our thoughts turned too readily to other places and other people with whom we would have given so much to have spent this of all days.'[22]

On 7 May they began the process of moving the stores from the landing point at Eagle Cove, where they had been hastily dumped, to the Nissen hut about a mile away. Although a few boxes still poked through the snowdrifts, most were deeply buried and excavating them from the hard-packed snow proved an exhausting task, requiring shovels, picks and crowbars. The occasional warm spells had also rendered the task more difficult as the dark colour of the boxes had caused them to absorb the heat of the sun so that the snow around them melted. When the temperature dropped, the melted snow froze again, encasing the boxes in rock-hard ice. The sacks of coal were particularly difficult as they were frozen solidly to the rock on which they had been landed two months earlier and any attempt to dislodge them almost invariably resulted in the sacks being torn and the coal cascading out onto the snow.

Despite these difficulties, the movement of the stores provided a welcome opportunity to test both the dog teams and their drivers. So far as the latter were concerned, trial and error would again be the order of the day as none had any real experience. Even Marshall, who had selected the dogs in Labrador with Ted Bingham and had benefited from conversations with both Bingham and the Inuit, had never enjoyed an opportunity to put their lessons into practice. As Davies remarked:

I think the dogs taught us, for they'd been trained by the Eskimos, you see, and … they knew the orders: 'Irrr' for left and 'Yook' for right and 'Aah' for stop, and "Now boys, Huit now," that was when we wanted them to get up, to start off after breaking the sledge out.[23]

On the first attempt, four dogs known collectively as the 'Big Boys' were harnessed together, but they managed to pull only 40lb per dog, owing to a combination of gradient, snow surface and novice drivers. Things improved when they reached a level surface and the dogs demonstrated that they could pull loads of up to 120lb each. Back observed that it was 'Very satisfactory to see that dogs remember how to pull and seem to enjoy it'.[24] Soon they were careering down the steep snow slope towards the base, one man lying flat on top of the loaded sledge while the driver clung onto the handlebars at the rear, his clothes and whip flying in the breeze. They moved over a ton of stores on the first day; more importantly, they had 'learned the fundamental lesson of all dog-sledging – that loads depend entirely upon gradient and surface, that soft, deep snow is worst, and hard, wind-packed névé the best.'[25] The sledging became much easier towards the end of May, when the bay ice reached a thickness of 18in, making it possible for a team of seven dogs to haul loads of up to 800lb across the even surface. This meant that, with two teams each completing two round trips, they could move 1½ tons every day before the light failed shortly after lunchtime.

Unfortunately, although it provided a much better surface for sledging, the bay ice could still be treacherous this early in the season – as the second dog team, the 'Drinks', discovered to their cost on 28 May. With no experienced drivers to advise him, James was still in the habit of letting the dogs off their wire spans to hunt or simply to find shelter in the worst of the blizzards, and on the night of the 28th the dogs named 'Punch', 'Whisky', 'Gin' and 'Bitters' set out towards the ice edge in search of seals. Their expedition coincided with a 30-degree rise in temperature and a flood tide which caused the ice to disintegrate up to a distance of 300yd from its seaward edge. All four dogs were lost. 'I for one bitterly blamed myself for the occurrence,' James admitted:

Yet in retrospect I am not so censorious. More experienced men than I have lost dogs in the same manner and with the best care in the world a certain casualty rate of these impulsive, high-spirited animals must be expected. One is between two fires, for loose animals fight and wander, while if they are permanently tethered it is only a matter of time till one of the dogs succeeds in throttling himself with his chain; this despite swivels at either end.[26]

As James acknowledged, the solution was 'to have so many dogs that the death of one or two will not affect the plans of the expedition'. But this was certainly not the position of Operation Tabarin: it had started with just twenty-five dogs, and a handful of these had since died as a result of illness, old age or fights. On the credit side, a number of pups had been born – but it would take them a year or so to grow into 75lb adults with the stamina to undertake lengthy sledge journeys. The situation would worsen still further by the time the sledging season began, with the loss of another two dogs – one old animal, the popular 'Rover', expiring of a heart attack in the middle of a fight and another, 'Ginger', having to be destroyed after breaking its leg. A third, also wounded in a fight, limped heavily and could not be expected to make journeys of any duration. This reduced the number of fit dogs to just fourteen – or two teams of seven dogs each.

The expedition was now physically prepared for the winter ahead; how-ever, mental preparedness was proving rather more difficult to achieve. Inevitably, the exhaustion resulting from weeks of hard physical labour, minimal privacy and the prospect of weeks of semi-darkness had begun to prey on the men, and at times incompatibilities in personality and outlook were becoming difficult to reconcile. Taylor's style of leadership also did little to smooth ruffled feathers. Whatever his failings as a commander, during the first year Marr had shown a willingness to give his men the benefit of the doubt and to overlook their peccadilloes, no matter how irritating. The only exception to this rule was his decision to repatriate the handyman, Kenneth Blair, in March 1944. Although Marr's approach had won him the respect and loyalty of most of his men, Taylor ascribed his tolerance to 'scruples about airing dirty linen in public'[27] and his own attitude was very different. During the first year he had made a number of observations regarding his companions, but while he asserted that his purpose was 'to record all the credit that each one has earned, and at the same time also record such discredit as I feel in some instances some mem-bers have also earned,' few would have felt flattered by the vignettes that he now committed to paper. Of the ex-Lockroy men, he thought Lamb and Ashton exceptional and Blyth excellent. Of the new intake, he found James to be 'bursting with energy and enthusiasm, prepared to tackle any job'[28] and Russell 'one of the best men we have here, having plenty of verve and energy'.[29] Donnachie, too, despite the doubts arising from the fire at Deception Island, he considered competent and 'most likeable and respectful … very popular with all of us'.[30]

His opinions regarding Back and Flett were more equivocal, but positive overall. In particular, he thought that the doctor had improved significantly over the course of the last twelve months, 'applying himself willingly and assiduously … His main fault is his garrulousness, which is not altogether free of a certain element of mischief making.'[31] Flett, his second-in-command, he found reliable and likeable, but also, at times, pedantic, too quick to offer opinions on subjects about which he knew nothing and 'somewhat of a moody disposition … nor yet has he either much of a grasp of the practical aspects of the work, nor the ability to make men follow his lead'.[32] He also admitted that the geologist, 'At one time … felt so low that he wanted to resign his position as 2/i/c, due to some inadvertent remark I had made which hurt his rather sensitive feelings.'[33]

Of the remaining four men he had very little good to say. Davies, though essentially harmless, had done little to alter Taylor's negative perceptions of the previous year; Jock Matheson, who attracted nothing but praise from the other members of the expedition both at Deception Island and at Hope Bay, he considered dishonest and incompetent; and Marshall he thought a 'typical "yes man" who would "yes" one to death, and join the radical elements immediately one's back is turned … and totally lacking in energy or initiative.'[34] Taylor's *bête noire*, however, continued to be Tom Berry: 'His addiction to liquor is such that he cannot be trusted with its charge … His inquisitiveness knows no bounds, and his knowledge of manners stops at the table.'[35] Previously, Berry's cooking had compensated, in part at least, for these faults, but even the food had declined in quality since the move to Hope Bay, probably as a result of the loss of stores with the *Eagle*. Worst of all, he thought Berry a barrack room lawyer – and as expedition leader he was no longer prepared to bite his tongue. On 24 May, he and Flett interviewed Berry in the galley, advising the cook that, henceforth, all alcohol would be removed from his control, that he would be denied access to the radio cabin in order to prevent his reading confidential messages, and that any further instances of indiscipline would be considered 'tantamount to mutinous behaviour'. Finally, Taylor informed him that any further lapses would be reported to the governor, whose intervention 'might delay his return to England for some time'.[36]

Although talk of 'radical elements', mutiny and jail constituted an extreme manifestation, the breakdown of relations during a polar expedition was not quite as exceptional as it might at first appear. In 1908, disagreement between Shackleton and the captain of the *Nimrod*, Robert England, had resulted in a permanent breach between the two men and in 1912 Mawson had become involved in a furious and public altercation with his expedition surgeon, Dr Leslie Whetter. Most notorious of all, at the end of his Imperial Trans-Antarctic Expedition, Shackleton had refused to recommend Harry McNish for the Polar Medal because of the latter's insubordination following the loss of the *Endurance*. However, the possible effects of such a breakdown on the morale of an expedition cannot be overstated – particularly at the very commencement of the polar winter, when the explorers were preparing to embark upon months of unavoidable intimacy and relative inactivity.

Perhaps the most extraordinary feature of this confrontation is not so much that it took place, but that it occurred within weeks of Taylor himself dissuading Berry from resigning his post after a heated argument with Ashton. Blyth had long ago demonstrated his ability to step into Berry's shoes, so what stopped Taylor from jumping at the opportunity to rid himself of a man he both loathed personally and thought capable of causing widespread disruption? In his notes of the interview, Taylor attributed his decision to 'a reluctance to believe of anyone the opinions I now have formed of him'.[37] But his dislike of Berry was long established, so this explanation seems disingenuous. It is far more likely that Taylor was concerned about the impressions others, most notably the governor, might form of his leadership if one of its first consequences was the resignation of a long-serving member of the expedition. Moreover, by allowing Berry to return in advance of the rest of the expedition, he would be presenting him with a golden opportunity to spread his own version of events unchallenged. Taylor also knew that Berry was popular with at least some of the other explorers, including Matheson, Davies and Marshall. If he chose to leave, they might follow – and that could have extremely serious consequences for his leadership of the expedition. In other words, while the departure of one undesirable element might be extremely welcome to Taylor, he may well have feared that a more general break up would prompt the governor to sacrifice him rather than let the expedition fall apart – a possibility rendered more probable by the fact that Taylor had been forced upon the governor by circumstance. Flett's intended resignation in March had the potential to be equally damaging, but as Flett was definitely not numbered among the cook's cronies, it is less difficult to believe Taylor's assertion that he dissuaded Flett on the grounds that 'he would long afterwards regret … leaving this interesting geological field.'[38]

Perhaps the individual who suffered most as a result of this conflict was Taylor himself, as he made clear in the autobiographical element of his Private Report on Personnel:

When I took on this job, I thought it would be an easy one as long as one treated the men fairly: but as someone has remarked, 'There are some horses to whom you cannot feed oats' – and there are some people who look upon fairness and decency as weakness. I had not run against any of that particular stripe before, and it is obvious that my tactics with them must alter … Moods of depression seem to be settling over me with increasing frequency, and though largely due to my physical condition being not quite what it should be, they are also due to the sense of frustration I feel in having pleased neither party concerned. However, one can but do one's best.[39]

In the same passage, Taylor asserted that 'In order to stand by the expedition members, I have not hesitated in the past to make known to the Governor my firm convictions regarding matters concerning the men.'[40] This frankness, he believed, had led him to tread 'upon official toes' and he felt sure that this was a transgression for which he would 'later have to pay'.[41] Depressed and disillusioned, and apparently blind to the irony of proclaiming his willingness to 'stand by the expedition members' in a document devoted to recording their every fault, he may have found in this episode sufficient justification for his later belief that the government deliberately ignored his meritorious service while it rewarded Marr's.

Throughout this period Taylor spent long hours at the typewriter, working on the expedition's official diary during the day and on his personal journal in the evenings, 'by way of recreation'.[42] 'His style is very readable,' James noted 'and this *magnum opus* is now beginning to assume the dimensions of *Gone with the Wind*.'[43] But Back believed that Taylor's commitment to recording the expedition's activities resulted from something more complex than a simple love of writing:

> he was known as 'Quadruplicate Andy' … his doctrine was, 'If you put it down in writing and in quadruplicate, nobody can lose it' and, therefore, that if you've done anything, you'll get the credit for it. If you don't write it down, somebody else will get the credit for it.[44]

It may be that, over time, the stress of Taylor's responsibilities, his feelings of insecurity regarding his own position and the strain of a divided command festered to become something akin to a mild persecution complex. This diagnosis is supported by the fact that the only examples of neglect that he cited in later years were the tardy notification of the award of the Polar Medal and the failure of the British Army to advise the Canadian Army of his promotion from captain to major.

For the time being, the best possible antidote to such introspection and depression was work. From the days of Captain John Ross, trapped by Arctic ice for four winters between 1829 and 1833, previous Arctic and Antarctic explorers had learned the importance of keeping their crews active, usually by a combination of routine maintenance, scientific observations and structured leisure. The ability of the men of Operation Tabarin to occupy themselves varied from individual to individual. Blyth, for instance, though generally cheerful, admitted to finding the weeks of semi-darkness and intense cold 'very boring'.[45] James, on the other hand, brimming with enthusiasm for all aspects of his new life, discovered that 'the main worry was not to find occupation so much as to get everything done':

> With no shops, and thrown entirely on our own resources, there were endless jobs of repair, improvisation and maintenance on sledging equipment; there were domestic chores, cabin furnishings to be made, photos to develop and print, diaries and notes to be written up and scientific observations to be taken.[46]

Of course, his chief occupation was the care of the dogs – an onerous duty at the best of times and particularly so when gales of force 10 or 12 on the Beaufort scale made it impossible to move about outside except on all fours, and when the driving snow could so disorientate a man that he might become totally lost within 30yd of the hut's door. Despite these trials, he was far from being unique in thinking that the dogs provided 'the chief charm of polar life',[47] and many of the men found in the dogs an uncritical companionship that was very welcome.

Back, too, experienced no difficulty in keeping busy. In part, this was due to the fact that the worsening weather made his job as meteorologist far more arduous and time consuming than it had been at Port Lockroy, though an admiring Blyth remarked that 'he never complained, just said "it's cold outside"'.[48] But the climate was not the only factor that made the completion of his scientific work problematic. The dogs also introduced some novel challenges, as the doctor explained:

> One of the more unpleasant habits of the dogs [was] that they had a sunshine recorder the second year … This was put up on the roof of the hut but unfortunately, this was the nearest approach to a lamppost that the dogs could see for miles around, and it's not very pleasant to try and get out a sunshine card, which has been frozen into the recorder with a lot of dog's urine … finally, we constructed an anti-Rover device, with bits of upright nails skilfully placed around the sunshine recorder so the dog, if it [lifted] his leg, would find himself on the nails.[49]

Back also found another occupation to wile away the winter: production of the base's magazine, the *Hope Bay Howler*. 'Everybody knows about Scott's *South Polar Times*,' he recalled, 'and we felt that we ought to do something.'[50] James, who produced the first issue, timed its publication to coincide with Midwinter's Day, and though one or two of the humorous sketches cut a little too close to the bone for some tastes, overall the magazine proved a great success – not least because Berry's thirteen-course

celebration dinner left the explorers too gorged for more vigorous activity.
Thereafter, Back assumed the role of editor-in-chief, with Lamb taking
responsibility for the illustrations and cartoons. According to Taylor, 'None
of us would claim the six to ten page sheet to have much literary merit, but
its production was always looked forward to by all hands with considerable interest and perhaps did something toward broadening our horizons
beyond the small circle in which we moved.'[51]

Although his indifference to his companions' minor ailments remained
as uncompromising as ever, there was one medical case that the doctor
could not ignore. In early March, the personnel at Deception Island had
been augmented by a Falkland Island handyman named Samuel Bonner.
Almost 60 years old and obviously unfit, Bonner had been an odd choice
for such a posting, but his application had been strongly supported by
J.E. Hamilton, the Naval Officer in Charge at Port Stanley.[52] According
to Farrington, 'Within a month of his being selected in Stanley and sent
down to strengthen the 3-man team at Deception it became apparent that
he was a sick man.'[53] Bonner's condition deteriorated so rapidly that Alan
Reece, Flett's replacement as base leader, had decided to relieve him of
all physical work until such time as one of the ships could collect him
from Base 'B'. Then, on the morning of 23 June, Charlie Smith discovered
Bonner in a comatose condition in his room. A hurried radio consultation
with Back ensued and the doctor quickly diagnosed a cerebral haem-
orrhage. Although Bonner recovered consciousness a few days later, his
condition remained a cause for serious concern among his three companions and they would require constant guidance and reassurance from Back.

As well as marking the publication of the first *Hope Bay Howler*,
Midwinter's Day saw the completion of what Taylor called the 'Eagle
Cove transport contract' and, as a result, more time could be devoted
to scientific work which, so far, had been limited to the meteorological
programme and occasional observations of sea ice and sea temperatures.
There had been little time, or energy, for glaciology, botany, geology or
tidal observations. Since landing in February, Taylor and Flett had made a
number of minor fossil discoveries, but it was not until 8 July that more
systematic collecting could begin, focused on a bed of shale below the
summit of Mount Flora. Here, in 1903, Gunnar Andersson had discovered an astonishing number of fossils dating from the Jurassic and Triassic
periods, which he had described in the scientific reports of the Swedish
expedition. As Back told his mother, these fossils revealed that the peninsula had not always been a desert of snow and ice:

Apparently millions of years ago this icy wilderness was a tropical swamp
full of trees and ferns. All these have been fossilised and on cracking a rock

you can see the imprints of leaves as clearly as if they were growing. Even the little veins of brackeny looking plants are plain. There are all sorts of different kinds of leaf as well as stems and trunks. These fossils are being packed in boxes by the hundredweight for the British Museum.[54]

With such a wealth of finds available to even the most amateurish and poorly equipped collectors, fossil hunting became so popular a sport that Flett, packing and cataloguing from morning till night, soon found himself hard-pressed to keep pace with the discoveries. Lamb, too, was inundated with specimens of lichen picked up by his companions. But, with a fine catalogue already to his credit, few of the new discoveries added to his knowledge. As a result, while he always accepted donations with courtesy, he subsequently discarded the majority and an amused Taylor noted that 'on more than one occasion, on passing the back of the house shortly afterwards ... I have almost been struck by the specimen in question being tossed through the window.'[55]

Another form of specimen collecting that proved more immediately satisfying to all concerned was fishing. Fish had proved extremely scarce at Port Lockroy during 1944, but the explorers had still benefited from a fairly varied diet. At Hope Bay, the loss of so many stores had severely reduced the range of Berry's cooking and, as Back observed, 'there is a limit to what even our cook can do with spam and corned beef.'[56] As a result, any fresh ingredient was welcomed with real enthusiasm. Initially, fish had proved elusive, but then, on 14 June, Marshall had tried baiting his line with seal meat and in less than an hour he had pulled twenty-three through the hole dug in the 4ft-thick sea ice, 'pulling them in almost as fast as he could replace the bait'.[57] All of the same species, and weighing a little under a pound each, Berry fried them, 'and they made a meal that was truly delectable.' To everyone's relief, the fish continued to bite and by the end of July 800 had been caught and cooked, the thousandth being consumed as part of the celebration held on 15 August to mark the surrender of Japan.

Absorbing, and occasionally mouth-watering, as these pursuits could be, so far as Taylor was concerned, the expedition's overriding concern must be to plan and prepare for the sledging season – a season he hoped would more than compensate for the frustrations of 1944. Although he would later complain that no instructions of any kind were given to him when he assumed command of Operation Tabarin,[58] in reality, he can have had very little doubt regarding his objectives. He had been appointed as Marr's second-in-command during the earliest days of the expedition and he had been heavily engaged in every element of the operation from that point onwards. Most importantly, he had been a prime mover in determining

the provisional sledging programme for 1944 and, when a lack of navigable sea ice and the absence of a ship suitable for coastal survey work and
depot laying had curtailed this programme, he had played a key role in
modifying and updating the plans to suit circumstances. It is also true that,
in the absence of explicit instructions from the Governor of the Falkland
Islands, he was granted a free hand in determining his sledging programme
for 1945 – a latitude which most survey leaders would have expected as
their right, as no authority remote from the scene could expect to have
any clear understanding of the constraints and opportunities governing
the movements of the men on the ground.

According to his own account, the planning for the 1945 season
'remained in a very fluid condition for many months',[59] but on 22 July, at
a conference 'well lubricated by the consumption of a couple of bottles of
... port',[60] Taylor finalised the details of the programme with Lamb, Russell
and James. There would be three main journeys, all timed to avoid the
worst of the equinoctial gales that had caused so much disruption during
the Wiencke Island journey the previous year. First, at the beginning of
August, a trial trip would be made towards Snow Hill Island following
the route blazed by Andersson, Duse and Grunden in September 1903.
The party would then return to Hope Bay via the Crown Prince Gustav
Channel, leaving a depot at a point named Cape Longing by the Swedes.
The second journey would follow a route due south, pushing as far as possible down the Larsen Ice Shelf in an attempt to identify a viable sledging
route connecting the ice shelf with the Graham Land Plateau. Finally, in
October, a trek would be made into the interior of Graham Land, with
the objective of locating the top portion of the sledging route that they
hoped to find during the second journey.

All four sledgers would be equipped to undertake a compass survey of
the area through which they passed and all would keep diaries in order to
maintain as comprehensive a record as possible of the journey. In addition,
Taylor would be responsible for the survey instruments and for the preparation of charts; Lamb would assemble the camping equipment and take
charge of botanical and geological collecting and observations; Russell's
duties would include the packaging of sledging rations, glaciology and
obtaining time signals to maintain the accuracy of the chronometers;
and James would take overall charge of the dogs. That the three surveyors, Taylor, James and Russell, should take part in at least some of these
journeys was obvious, while Lamb, though not a surveyor, was one of the
party's most experienced sledgers. The limited number of dogs also made
it impossible to send out a number of teams in different directions at the
same time. However, selecting the same four men, no matter how well
qualified, for all of the planned journeys meant that nine of the thirteen

stationed at Hope Bay would never enjoy the opportunity to escape from the immediate environs of the hut in which they had been trapped for months. Indeed, of the nine men now serving their second year in the Antarctic, six would never experience a sledging journey exceeding a few hours. On 1 April Back had written to his mother that 'I have not been a hundred yards from the house since we landed,'[61] but while such limited movement might have been expected during the establishment of the base and during the winter, few would have expected it to continue through the Antarctic spring and summer months.

As with practically every sledging expedition made over the last forty years, preparations involved a considerable degree of 'make do and mend'. One of the first jobs was to devise and manufacture an accurate and robust sledge meter. Those sent south by the 'wretched authorities at home'[62] at the beginning of 1945 turned out to be simple cyclometers 'such as are used on the bicycles which wheel around the English country roads'[63] and, on average, they survived just two hours in the more demanding conditions of Antarctica. The task of replacing them with something more suitable fell to Ashton and, after some consideration, he succeeded in introducing a number of improvements to the design he had developed in 1944. An admiring Taylor later noted that the perfected device 'gave extremely accurate and satisfactory results … we would certainly have found ourselves at a very decided loss had we not had this improvisation to use as a sledge meter.'[64]

Another ingenious contrivance was a 'sledge boat' designed by Matheson and intended for use in the event of the sledgers finding themselves in the midst of very thin sea ice. Consisting of a combination of a waterproof tarpaulin that could be tied round a sledge, boxes for buoyancy and skis for oars, a similar boat had been developed and used with great success by Sandy Glen's Oxford University Arctic Expedition of 1935–36. Davies, meanwhile, stitched sixty canvas shoes to protect the dogs' paws against sharp, salt-encrusted sea ice and James overhauled the two sledges to be taken. One of these, a 12ft Nansen sledge, had given sterling service during the Wiencke Island survey and was still in fair condition. The second, a 9ft model, needed considerable refurbishment after the rough and tumble of the Eagle Cove hauls. James also took responsibility for manufacturing the dog harnesses, using a combination of cod line and lamp wick, and carefully measuring each of the dogs for its own harness, ensuring a snug fit to minimise the chances of the animals slipping to their deaths should they fall into a crevasse. Finally, he packed sufficient tools and spare parts to repair sledges and harnesses in the field.

Activity during the last days of July was frenetic, the work greatly aided by the increasingly long daylight hours coupled with a spell of particularly fine, calm weather. On 23 July, James was able to work on the sledges outside and without gloves while Russell turned the survey room into something resembling a grocer's shop as he poured sugar and pea flour into small bags to be added to the 50lb ration boxes. It was a process that he found distinctly disillusioning:

> Looking at the various lists of ration scales, used by various expeditions, giving daily quantities to 0.1 of an ounce, we had always imagined nutrition experts poring over test tubes and saying, 'Let's cut down 0.2 ounces on the pemmican and give a bit more biscuit and pea-flour, it will give a better balance between fats and carbohydrates'. On closer inspection, however, it seems that if you multiply the daily quantity by twenty (ration boxes for two men, ten days) the answer is the amount that the manufacturers sell in their tins![65]

The rations eventually decided upon were based very closely on those of Rymill's British Graham Land Expedition, though additional quantities of coffee, tea, dried onions and dried apples pushed daily weights up from 25.9oz to 27.6oz per man.

By 28 July the expedition was ready; then, with a contrariness all of its own, the weather turned. The calm and sunshine of the last few days gave way to a dull, overcast one, with clouds of snow driven by a south-west wind and temperatures dropping to −7°F. Although the sledgers were able to complete the last of a series of journeys to Nobby Nunatak, where a forward depot had been laid at an altitude of 950ft above sea level, conditions were unsuitable for pushing further afield. Instead, they could only wait. For Taylor and Lamb, the forthcoming expedition constituted their last-ditch attempt to undertake a sledging journey of any real duration, and they discovered that the long months of construction work and base routine had done nothing to dampen their ardour. Indeed, if anything, their enthusiasm had reached a new pitch – spurred on, perhaps, by the news of Labour's victory in the July parliamentary election and their suspicions that this change in government would result in the expedition 'being pulled out next season'.[66] The new men, James and Russell, were also 'on tenterhooks to be off'[67] and Back noted that the longer the weather forced them to wait, 'the more fertile plans are evolved'.[68] Frustrated and impotent, for more than a week the four men watched the snow swirling past the hut's windows. But at last, on 8 August, they woke to a better day. It was dull and gloomy still, with a temperature of 0°F and a thick layer of snow covering everything – but the glass was rising and the wind had died away. It was, Taylor knew, a case of 'now or never'.

10

The White Warfare of the South

The two seven-dog sledge teams, the 'Big Boys' driven by James and Russell, and the 'Odds and Sods' driven by Taylor and Lamb, left Eagle House mid-morning, heading for the 1,130ft snow-covered saddle of land which separates Hope Bay from Duse Bay. In order to reduce the weights to be hauled up Depot Glacier, a cache of stores had been dumped at Nobby Nunatak, but deep soft snow still made the going very heavy and it was only with Davies, Marshall, Back and Matheson acting as 'extra dogs' that the two teams managed to reach the *nunatak* (rock outcrop) by lunchtime. Here, they selected additional supplies from the depot and adjusted their loads before completing their ascent. The round trip to Snow Hill Island was expected to last no more than a month, but with twenty-eight days' worth of dog food and thirty days' worth for the men, plus tents and other equipment, the sledges were heavily laden. The slightly built James joked that his 9ft Nansen 'looked exactly like a Carter Peterson van … and I could only just see over it'.[1] After a pull up the glacier that had been arduous despite the benefit of fresh dogs, extra men and lighter loads, the four sledgers could be forgiven for facing the onward journey with some trepidation. Everything would depend on the surface quality of the sea ice and the performance of the dogs.

At Summit Pass, the highest point on the glacier some 5 miles from Eagle House, Taylor and his companions bade farewell to the four men returning to the base and then made camp. By the time they had pitched the two tents, the cloud had lifted and the barometer was steady, so they had some hope of a good travelling day the next day. But it was not to be. The next morning the south-west wind had risen once again, whipping up dense clouds of drift that reduced visibility to much less than half a mile. By the middle of the afternoon, with the wind speed reaching 40mph and the barometer rising sharply, Taylor was forced to accept that there was no realistic prospect of their making any further progress that day: 'We did not move, but lay in our sleeping bags all day long, with the Primus stoves burning more perhaps than they should have burned, for we were feeling the cold, five below in the tent towards evening.'[2] James and Russell, meanwhile, managed to pass the time quite pleasantly playing patience for lumps of sugar. 'When this palled, we slept.'[3]

After this somewhat inauspicious start, the weather underwent a dramatic improvement over the next few days and the party began to make reasonable headway. 'Heaven's own day,' James declared on 10 August, '– glass up to 1027 and not a cloud in the sky.'[4] With each of the men taking his turn to break the trail on skis, they rapidly descended the gradient from Summit Pass to the sea ice, heading towards the southern end of Duse Bay and picking their way through the tangled mass of frozen-in bergs that had prompted Andersson to call it the 'Bay of a Thousand Icebergs'. Occasionally they crossed patches of soft snow, which slowed them down, but these proved mercifully few and far between and overall the surface remained good. The two dog teams, however, were proving to be ill matched. The 'Big Boys' were large, powerful animals that worked effectively together as a cohesive group, governed absolutely by a fine, brown-coated animal named Captain. The 'Odds and Sods' on the other hand, as their collective name implied, were a varied collection of misfits led by a scrawny black and white dog called Mutt, who, according to Taylor, achieved only 'a rather shaky supremacy over the others'.[5] The weakness of the 'Odds and Sods' often made it necessary for two men to push in an attempt to keep the 12ft sledge moving, and when they camped on the evening of 11 August, Taylor agreed to adopt a new arrangement. From this point onwards, the 'Big Boys' would haul the larger and heavier of the two sledges while the 'Odds and Sods' followed with the lighter but less robust 9-footer. This approach would have a number of advantages: in particular, it would mean that the greater load would fall to the stronger team while the smaller, top-heavy sledge would be less prone to becoming bogged down and capsizing if it followed a trail blazed by the larger Nansen.

On 12 August, still enjoying excellent weather and travelling with the dark scarred face of the Trinity Peninsula to their right, they broke free of Duse Bay by relaying their loads over the middle of a dogleg-shaped island that stood directly in their path. Once across this small island they could head towards the north-western tip of Vega Island, roughly 12 miles to the south. At a point about halfway to Vega Island, they would round Cape Corry in a westerly direction and then swing south to make their way down the broad Crown Prince Gustav Channel, which runs between the mainland and James Ross Island. 'As we ate our lunch,' wrote James, 'I remember thinking "Now all our troubles – bad going and difficult country – are over, and there is nothing to stop us making decent progress down the channel" – poor mutt.'[6]

Leaving the dogleg island to rejoin the sea ice, they observed a tell-tale streamer of snow blowing off the cliffs of Cape Corry, and soon they were enveloped in a cloud of drift that reduced visibility to just 100yd. They struggled on, but by 2.15 p.m. the wind had increased to force 7, and with the dogs growing increasingly reluctant to face into the south-wester and the thickness of the drift making it difficult for the two teams to remain in touch, Taylor decided to make camp after a day's run of just 5.2 miles. In these conditions there could be none of the usual distinctions between the duties of 'inside' and 'outside' man, and instead all four had to use their bodyweight to prevent the tents from opening up and blowing away like a pair of wayward umbrellas. Most frustrating of all, when they crawled inside after two hours of violent struggle with the flapping canvas, their faces covered with masks of snow and frozen mucus, they discovered that their accommodation was unusually cramped. 'We found ours to be four and a half feet square,' groaned Taylor, 'and Lamb and I, both being over six feet in height, suffered some inconvenience in folding ourselves into suitable shapes in which to try to sleep for the night.'[7]

Fortunately, the gale died away as suddenly as it had blown up and the following day dawned bright and clear, with a temperature of $-8°F$. It took more than an hour to dig the sledges free of the accumulated drift snow, but by 9.45 a.m. Russell and James were ready to start towards Vega Island. After an exasperating delay, caused by the 9ft sledge becoming so bogged down that the first team had to return to help dig it out, they maintained a good pace over a surface which improved with every mile travelled. At lunchtime they rounded Cape Corry – which they discovered to be a high, steep-walled island rather than a promontory – and then, as planned, swung west to join Crown Prince Gustav Channel. By sunset they had made a reasonably satisfactory 11.2 miles and had reached a small island where they planned to leave a depot for their return journey in a few weeks' time.

The weather again closed in during the night and the four men woke to a temperature of $-14°F$ and vicious 'whirlies' of force 3 to 6, which made it impossible to travel. Twisting counter-clockwise and roughly 20in in diameter at sea level, these fast-moving spirals of wind and drift could make life uncomfortable even in camp and, as James recorded, 'It was anxious work watching these "whirlies" if one's business took one outside the tent and at least one of us was caught none too metaphorically with his pants down.'[8] To occupy their time, Russell and Taylor plotted their survey notes while Lamb and James constructed the depot against a prominent boulder on a scree slope of the newly named 'Vortex Island'.

The depot consisted of two and a half days' worth of food for the sledgers; three and a half days' worth of dog pemmican; a gallon of paraffin (seven primus-fills); one of the sledge repair boxes; the rifle; the tarpaulin boat conversion; and three pairs of skis, which had so far proved redundant on the wind-polished sea ice. 'We have not used these since leaving the mainland,' noted Russell, 'and it does not look as if we would want them again. We have kept one pair of skis and one pair of snowshoes, however, just in case.'[9] Taylor later wrote that, when travelling in the Canadian Arctic in the 1930s, 'it had been drilled into me, never go anywhere without your snow shoes,'[10] but he failed to impress the importance of this lesson on his companions and within a very short time they would all come to regret deeply their decision to abandon their skis. Indeed, the somewhat naïve assumption that surface conditions would remain consistent throughout the remainder of their journey would imperil the lives of all four.

Between 15 and 20 August they covered 54½ miles down Crown Prince Gustav Channel. The party benefited from a combination of reduced sledge loads, generally fine but cold weather and surface conditions which remained good as long as they avoided the lee of the peninsula, where the hard ice gave way to soft snow. Except for a dull overcast day on the 16th, visibility continued to be excellent, enabling them to admire the contrasting scenery of the western and eastern flanks of the channel. To the west, the peninsula presented a sheer rock face, slashed with glaciers and rising vertiginously to 1,000ft before a gentler snow slope glided up towards the 4,500ft ice-capped Graham Land Plateau. In the foreground, the piedmont was indented by a series of seemingly indistinguishable ice embayments, ravine-like crevasses and occasional black pyramidal *nunataks*, all of which served to make it varied and interesting, if also austere and lifeless. In contrast, to the east, much of the north-west side of James Ross Island was ice-free – a result, James surmised, of its contours, which forced the glaciers into a limited number of channels, and of the prevailing winds, which prevented snow accumulation. The coastline consisted of high red and brown basalt cliffs with flat tabletops intersected by dry snow-free valleys, while the few glaciers that they could see pushing their way down from the blue-white ice cap were 'of a sad, dirty and truncated description like the snout of an alpine glacier rather than the usual virile Antarctic type'.[11] As they proceeded further south, ice became more prevalent along the island's coast, the ice cap descending to join large crescent-shaped bays of brown and red cliffs, 'for all the world like a huge iced Christmas cake out of which a giant has been taking bites.'[12]

Finally, to the south stretched mile upon mile of bay and fast ice, studded with frozen-in bergs but revealing few of the tell-tale signs of pressure. On 18 August James discovered a pair of Weddell seals basking behind one of these bergs and he immediately shot both. Having removed the liver and rump steak from one of the animals, he allowed the dogs to feast on the carcass. The other he left as an emergency depot in case they should run short of food on their return journey. Although the decision was a sensible one, providing the party with some contingency in case they were delayed by adverse weather, he still admitted to suffering 'a pang of conscience driving the dogs back and leaving the seal there dead and ungutted'.[13] Whatever James' reservations, the fresh meat was welcome to both men and dogs, though the latter expressed their satisfaction by keeping the men awake through much of the night with their antics and by delaying the party's departure the next morning as they indulged in a joyful scrap. Once they started moving, their new-found energy was put to better use and they made excellent progress towards the entrance to Sjögren Fjord (now Sjögren Glacier), which they would have reached had it not been for a great rift 200ft across and 80ft deep, which blocked their path and forced them to alter course to the south-east down the sea ice.

Although the weather had been surprisingly good, the temperatures experienced by the sledging party throughout the journey had been significantly lower than those at Hope Bay and, during the night of 19/20 August, it plummeted to −28°F. The four sledgers woke to find the insides of their tents thick with rime – frozen condensation from their breath and the heat of their bodies – which the slightest movement sent cascading down onto bags, clothes and equipment. James wrote:

> They say that if one sleeps with one's head under the sleeping bag, one gets condensation inside as well as outside the bag. Preferring to avoid certain present discomfort to hypothetical future, I have slept with my head underneath throughout and so far my inner bag is as dry as a bone … I have tried, and do not like, sleeping in my heavy duffle inner annarak [*sic*] with head outside the bag. This system makes any movement impossible and one wakes up with a heavy coating of rime on the face. Ugh. Better by far is it to take off as much clothing as possible and then, after leaving one very small airhole, to snuggle right down inside the bag – a warm chrysalis in a cosy cocoon.[14]

The only disadvantage to the policy was that, after a particularly cold night, the warm chrysalis might find itself having to climb into clothes as solid and unyielding as a suit of rusty armour.

Aiming for the southern tip of a large ice-covered promontory to the south-south-west – named Cape Longing by Nordenskjöld – on the morning of 20 August the party found itself in what Russell described as 'a most bewildering area'[15] of pressure ridges and hummocks caused by the impact of the Sjögren Glacier with the sea ice. Eventually, the surface became so bad that Taylor decided they had no option but to divert to the south-east. Disappointing as this was, it did lead them onto a smoother surface and they remained on the same course for the rest of the day.

Despite numerous attempts, so far James had been unable to make radio contact with Donnachie back at Hope Bay, a failure he attributed to a combination of climatic conditions, local topography and the vagaries of the Army No. 18 walkie-talkie set. However, after yet another failed attempt that evening, he did manage to tune into the BBC news at 6.45 p.m.:

> Not having heard anything for a fortnight, it was a wonderful surprise to learn that the Japanese war was just ending. Down here in this remote and silent land, one's own little problems assume such importance that there is hardly time to think of the outside world and, until this moment, we had not given the news a thought.[16]

To celebrate, he and Russell ate an extra bar of chocolate and smoked a cigar each.

The next morning they encountered another obstacle in the form of gigantic and fantastically shaped blocks of pressure ice, which reminded Lamb of 'the concrete "dragon's teeth" of anti-tank emplacements'.[17] However, at last, during the mid-morning, they felt able to resume a south-westerly course over an undulating windswept surface, darkened by morainic deposits and scored by occasional narrow rifts, but devoid of bergs. They covered more than 14 miles – the best daily total of the journey so far – but Taylor was becoming worried:

> By this time we had finished three of the five tins of paraffin with which we had started out thirteen days previously; this included the one which was still cached for our use at Vortex Island. With half of our ration period behind us, we found ourselves in a position to perhaps make some geographical discoveries of more than passing interest, without having adequate supplies to pursue them with safety. Had we but another two weeks stores in hand, there would have been no question of our turning back at Cape Longing, but though there was still the possibility we might continue as far as Cape Sobral, we could not hope to go farther.[18]

These anxieties were further exacerbated by a poor day's travelling on 22 August, when high winds and drift reduced the distance covered to a mere 4.5 miles. They camped at 1.30 p.m., just 3 miles from Cape Longing and with Snow Hill Island, site of Nordenskjöld's winter quarters, visible as a looming mass of ice on the horizon to the east.

After a gusty night, the 23rd dawned clear, bright and windless and, perhaps to compensate his companions for their disappointment at having to head for home so soon, Taylor decided that the day would be devoted to detailed exploration of the area in which they now found themselves. Leaving their camp standing, the party would split into two: Taylor and Russell travelling westwards with the 'Big Boys' to investigate a deep channel between Cape Longing and the Sjögren Glacier that they had observed the previous day, while James and Lamb pushed on to Cape Longing with the 'Odds and Sods'. Each team would take some emergency rations, their bedrolls and a shovel, in case circumstances prevented them from returning to their tents for the night. Within minutes of starting, Taylor and Russell encountered a 100ft-wide rift in the ice ahead of them. They crossed it with relative ease, but when they encountered a second and a third, each wider and deeper than the last, they decided to leave the sea ice and instead climb up onto a snow slope to their left. Heading almost due south and stopping to take aneroid readings every thirty minutes, they climbed towards the 1,300ft summit over an excellent surface of firm, wind-packed snow. They reached the top at 2 p.m. and were rewarded with a spectacular view. Some 60 miles to the south lay Robertson Island, Lindenberg Island and the Seal Nunataks; to the west and south-west, the almost unbroken face of the Nordenskjöld Coast, with the great white mass of the ice cap hanging suspended over precipitous rock faces; to the east rose Lockyer and Snow Hill islands, and beyond them the frozen Weddell Sea; finally, to the north, the disturbed and undulating sea ice over which they had been travelling. 'Altogether,' Taylor enthused, 'on so beautiful a day, it was an inspiring view, none the less so from the knowledge that it was one which no one else had ever enjoyed since time began.'[19]

For their part, James and Lamb reached the stratified cliffs just north of Cape Longing in ninety minutes, both men riding on the sledge. About 300yd from the cliffs they anchored the sledge and, leaving the dogs to curl up on the ice, they set off to work their way on foot through a confused mass of ice blocks. As they drew closer, Lamb, in particular, was thrilled to discover that the cape was sedimentary, consisting of sandstone, mudstone and shale – the latter bearing the clear imprints of fossils. With the exception of Mount Flora, whose shale they had examined with such enthusiasm in July, the entire coastline of Graham Land that they had explored appeared to be volcanic in origin, so this discovery was significant. While Lamb continued to fossick about among the rock debris on the sea ice, James pushed on towards the foot of the cliffs themselves. Like Taylor a few miles to the north, he found that the remoteness of the site affected him profoundly:

It was a strange feeling on such a warm and sunny day to approach this cliff so remote and yet so like any cliff at home, to reflect that its peace had never been broken before … it was those defences of smooth, timeworn ice, like the dead and frozen ruins of some bombed out city that invested the place with such atmosphere and made me want to talk with hushed voice as though in some medieval cathedral.[20]

By 5 p.m. both parties had returned to the camp well satisfied with their discoveries, which included a type of lichen not previously seen south of Deception Island and clear evidence that Cape Longing, like Cape Corry before it, was not a cape but an island. However, both also admitted that they had found their tents only through a combination of guesswork and luck. Unlike those used on Wiencke Island in 1944, the tents provided for the expedition's second year possessed white outer skins – possibly as a result of their having been deliberately camouflaged for use in operations against enemy troops in the Arctic – and against the background of the sea ice they had been all but invisible. 'In poor visibility, or had a blizzard sprung up, we would never have found them this night,'[21] admitted Taylor. Another important lesson had been learned.

After two nights spent in the shadow of Cape Longing, or 'Longing Island' as Taylor now believed it to be, on 24 August the party altered its course to head almost due east – towards Snow Hill Island. The discoveries of the 23rd and the opportunities for more productive work if they could prolong their excursion had convinced Taylor of the plan they should now pursue. All four would immediately head for Nordenskjöld's winter quarters in the hope of finding a stockpile of useable supplies, including fuel and food. With their rations replenished, they would then retrace their steps in the hope of continuing their investigations to the south and west of Longing Island. If the Swedes had left no stockpile, but their 40-year-old hut was still habitable, two men would stay there while their companions dashed back to Hope Bay for more food and fuel. In order to achieve these objectives, it was essential to reach the Swedish base in the shortest time possible. 'On such days,' wrote James, '… the only interest is the eating up of mileage.'[22] With superb weather and an excellent surface, they covered 10 miles between 9 a.m. and noon – an unheard of rate of progress. As they approached Cape Foster, the most southerly tip of James Ross Island, the surface began to deteriorate and to be scored by a series of weakly bridged fissures, caused by the grinding of the sea ice against the rock of the island. Luckily the surface crust was thick enough to support the sledge, but the men often sank to their knees, and while they managed to cover a total of 18.2 miles during the day, Russell asserted that 'Never again will I go sledging without a pair of skis or snowshoes per

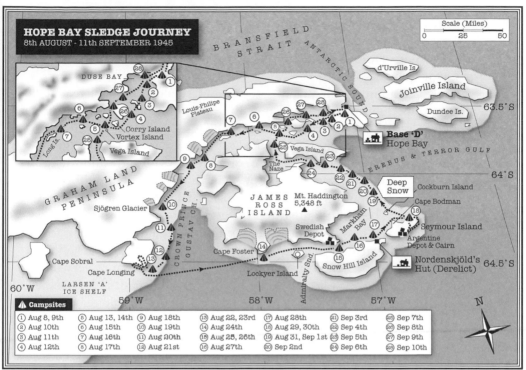

HOPE BAY SLEDGE JOURNEY
8th AUGUST - 11th SEPTEMBER 1945

Campsites				
① Aug 8, 9th	⑤ Aug 13, 14th	⑨ Aug 18th	⑬ Aug 22, 23rd	⑰ Aug 28th	㉑ Sep 3rd	㉕ Sep 7th
② Aug 10th	⑥ Aug 15th	⑩ Aug 19th	⑭ Aug 24th	⑱ Aug 29, 30th	㉒ Sep 4th	㉖ Sep 8th
③ Aug 11th	⑦ Aug 16th	⑪ Aug 20th	⑮ Aug 25, 26th	⑲ Aug 31, Sep 1st	㉓ Sep 5th	㉗ Sep 9th
④ Aug 12th	⑧ Aug 17th	⑫ Aug 21st	⑯ Aug 27th	⑳ Sep 2nd	㉔ Sep 6th	㉘ Sep 10th

Map created by Andrew Stevenson

man.'[23] Surface conditions improved when they rounded Cape Foster the next morning and headed up Admiralty Sound, which divides James Ross Island from Snow Hill Island.

Passing close under the cape, James had been struck by the deep sigh, 'as of someone in great distress', made by the downward slide of great masses of snow somewhere inland. Now the party encountered another, equally startling phenomenon: mirage. To the east, and over an arc of some 20 degrees, a complete double horizon could be seen, with every feature of the landscape, including myriad icebergs, perfectly duplicated. The effect was extraordinarily disorienting, but they pushed on regardless and made another good run of 16.9 miles by the time they camped at 5 p.m.

The glorious weather of the last three days could not be expected to last and during the night the wind began to rise. By breakfast time, great swathes of swirling drift snow were reducing visibility to 50yd, making further travel impossible and forcing the frustrated sledgers to spend a day writing up notes, reading and sleeping. Although a moderate breeze was still blowing the next day, the drift had largely subsided and Taylor decided that conditions would allow them to break camp. The party would now divide: while he and Lamb pushed on for Nordenskjöld's hut, Russell would try to locate a depot laid by the Swedes at the south-eastern tip of James Ross Island a mile from the campsite. Staying at the camp during the morning, James would attempt to keep a radio schedule with Donnachie before he and Russell followed in the tracks of Taylor's party.

These plans met with varying degrees of success. Russell reached 'Depot Cape' without incident and, after about an hour's search, succeeded in locating the Swedes' cairn, now all but buried in the deep snow that had accumulated since the depot was laid in March 1903. Digging down, he unearthed a tin chest: 'I opened it eagerly, and found it full of food.'[24] In total, it contained about 50lb of supplies, including forty-eight large tins of butter, sardines, pemmican, dried fruit and vegetables, tea and sugar. The chest had rusted through, but most of the contents were still in excellent condition, despite the passage of more than four decades. Having made a selection of items to carry back, he reached the camp at 12.30 p.m. to discover that, as usual, James had enjoyed very limited success with the radio: while he had been able to hear Donnachie for the first time since they had left Hope Bay, he had been unable to make himself heard in reply. After a lunch which they varied with some of Russell's newly discovered treasure, the two men broke camp at 2 p.m., but travelled only a short distance before signs of worsening weather forced them to stop just one day's march from Nordenskjöld's base. Recent experience had taught them just how difficult it could be for even four men to erect one of their tents in a blizzard, and they had no intention of fighting the same battle with reduced numbers if they could possibly avoid it.

Ahead of them, Taylor and Lamb had made good time, despite the low drift, which enveloped their feet like a clinging marsh mist. As they pushed their way up Admiralty Sound, the wind increased to 40mph and James Ross Island, on their left, disappeared in the blizzard. To compensate for the poor visibility, the prevailing wind had swept the sound free of loose snow, leaving an excellent travelling surface of hard glazed snow, only occasionally interrupted by small bergs, pressure ridges and drifts in places where the wind was deflected by the topography. Steering on a compass bearing and benefiting from occasional glimpses of surrounding landmarks such as Station Nunatak and the austere Basalt Peak, in the twilight of the late afternoon the two men rounded the base of some low ice cliffs and found themselves in a small cove, its ice discoloured by a smear of rock dust. Above them, 'on a little terrace with slopes as clean and uniform as a railroad grade'[25] stood Nordenskjöld's Snow Hill Station.

Taylor later admitted that during the march he had regaled himself with daydreams of 'a good coal fire to be built in the house, round which we could sit pulling at our pipes with a glass of "hollands" in our hands while the damp sleeping bags hung suspended from the rafters to dry and warm.'[26] As he and Lamb ascended the slope to the base site, these visions fled before the stark realities of the scene and his heart fell. Instead of the cosy time capsule they had envisaged, doors and windows sealed against the elements and shelves well stocked, they found a gaunt skeleton through which the wind blew eerily. At some point the glass in the hut's windows had been smashed, presumably by the violence of the wind, and the building's floor was covered in 3ft of hard compacted snow and ice. Inside the mess room, the communal table had buckled under the weight of snow, while the mounds on the bunks in the two-man cabins resembled nothing so closely as bodies draped in sheets. 'The whole place,' wrote a depressed Taylor, 'had an air of the utter desolation that had been in sole possession of it for nearly half a century.'[27]

Instead of enjoying a feast in the warm and windproof shelter of their imaginings, Taylor and Lamb now had to find a suitable spot to erect their tent and prepare their basic sledging rations. They trudged wearily back down to where they had left the dogs and lashed the reluctant animals into pulling the sledge up a steep slope of wind-polished snow to an area level enough to serve as a campsite. Here they discovered that at some point during the day a small bag of medical supplies and their tent pegs had fallen from their sledge, but walking back down to the hut Taylor succeeded in finding a few rusty iron pegs scattered on the ground. The ancient pegs were unusually strong, but even these proved 'hard to knock into the icy surface that formed our "feather mattress"'.[28]

After a cold and cheerless night, they returned to the hut on the morning of 28 August to make a closer inspection. The wind had dropped and the sun shone from a cloudless sky, but the scene had lost little of its grimness. Forcing their way into the building they found the same story repeated in every room: furniture and discarded possessions encased in ice and the whole sorry shambles painting a picture of a hurried and seemingly chaotic departure. On one bed they discovered a trussed up trunk, evidently packed in order to be taken by its owner but then forgotten in the rush of the final evacuation. From it, Taylor extracted a sheaf of papers which he hoped might be valuable – a diary, perhaps, or some other record of the life of the base – but when he carefully separated the brittle pages they contained nothing more revealing than a series of Edwardian advertisements for acetylene stoves and lamps. Further searches produced a jar of fossil shells, a couple of penguin skins, a few items of well-preserved clothing, a box of candles and some tins of assorted foodstuffs – none of it edible. There was no sign of any paraffin or fuel oil. Overall, it seemed that Commodore Irízar of the *Uruguay* had given the Swedes just enough time to strip their hut of everything that might be of interest or value to later visitors. So far as the building itself was concerned, Taylor thought it structurally sound, but it was leaking so badly that it 'would be almost less trouble to build a new building than to try to repair this one'.[29]

As an archaeological site, the Snow Hill Station had been disappointing; as a depot from which to replenish the survey party's supplies, it had proved catastrophically inadequate. Besides the tent pegs, the only useful item that Taylor had discovered was the box of candles and to this he and Lamb added a small collection of discarded tools that they found outside, the latter being gathered as souvenirs rather than as useable pieces of equipment. Finally, they removed part of a window frame so that new windows could be manufactured should they decide to put the hut in order at some point in the future. Looking at this pitiful haul, Taylor knew that he must now make radical changes to his plans:

> There being neither food, fuel nor shelter, all of our projected plans became impractical immediately. We had to abandon any ideas we had had of continuing our survey any farther south, the state of our supplies at this time precluding the entertainment of any idea we might have had of leaving a couple of men here to work out the scientific results of our travels up to this point, while the other pair returned to the base to bring out additional loads of supplies.[30]

James and Russell arrived that afternoon, but news of the 50lb of supplies located at Depot Cape made no material difference to the situation or to Taylor's conclusions. With their food and fuel now seriously depleted and the Swedish hut uninhabitable, all four men would head for home at the earliest opportunity.

Glad to turn their backs on the melancholy ruins — James likened his own disappointment to that of a man who had 'been invited to a wedding and gone to a funeral by mistake'[31] — they began their journey north at 10 a.m. the following day. For the first mile or so the surface consisted of glare ice, on which their sealskin boots obtained so little grip that Russell thought it 'just like an ice rink'.[32] However, this soon gave way to hard windblown snow and their pace increased as they made their way north-westwards towards the heavily weathered sandstone cliffs of Seymour Island's southern headland. From there, they proceeded up the island's west coast, past a series of knolls and snow-filled valleys sloping gently down towards the shore. As they struck eastwards into a wide bay between Cape Bodman and the northern tip of the island, they crossed patches of sea ice stained brown by rock dust blown from the cliff faces, but this grit did little to retard their progress and the dogs continued to pull well. Intending to make a survey of the island and, if possible, to locate a large depot left by the *Uruguay* at Penguin Bay after the rescue of Nordenskjöld, they hauled the two sledges across the tidal zone and then erected their tents on a patch of hard windblown snow just inshore. At this point, wrote Lamb:

> I made the pleasing discovery that there were several holes in the fabric of ours, due to friction on the sledge against the edges of a metal bound box, and there was nothing for it but to get out needle and thread and sew a couple of patches over them.[33]

It was difficult work for freezing fingers at −18°F, but later they lit the candles salvaged from Snow Hill Island for the first time and found them 'a great success. Soon the heat of the candles rendered all the wax down while a cheerful blaze giving off quite good heat continued to emanate from the floating wicks.'[34]

When Lamb and Taylor woke the next morning the thermometer between their bedrolls showed a temperature of −28°F. Undeterred, at 7.30 a.m. they set off inland, followed by James half an hour later. Russell, who was suffering from slightly frostbitten feet, remained at camp with the dogs. Having made their way down a valley running east–west through a series of sandstone hillocks, Lamb and Taylor separated: the former climbed northwards towards the island's 700ft plateau, while the latter continued eastwards in search of the depot.

The snow-filled valley soon led Taylor into the centre of Penguin Bay but, unable to find the depot cairn, he decided that he would follow the coastline round the island's northerly tip and then down its western coast back to the camp. He wrote a message 'in large letters in the snow beside my tracks to inform Lamb or James, whomever might see it, that I intended to follow the coast northward',[35] and then set off along the sea ice at the base of the steep sandstone cliffs bordering the edge of the bay. After several miles the cliffs gave way to sloping hills and valleys of crumbling khaki-coloured stone and at the top of one of these hills, about 150ft above sea level, he spotted a wooden pole sticking up from a pile of stones. Digging at the base of the 7ft pole, he quickly unearthed a rusty tin containing a handwritten note on which he could just discern the word *Uruguay*. Beneath this, he found a small and well-preserved wooden pillbox containing another note written on the page of a notebook. This note, which he managed to unfold that evening, was dated 7 November 1903 and bore the signatures of the *Uruguay*'s doctor and lieutenant. Evidently this was not the food depot left after the relief of Nordenskjöld's party, as Taylor had originally surmised, but a cairn erected by Irízar's crew the day before they located the Swedish base on Snow Hill Island. Taylor photographed his finds *in situ*, carefully replaced the stones that he had dislodged and continued on his way.

He reached the campsite at 2 p.m., having walked some 12 miles in six and a half hours. Lamb was waiting for him, but James and Russell, anxious at his late return and fearing that he might have been injured in a fall, had taken one of the dog teams and gone in search of him. They returned a little after 4 p.m. and any frustration they might have felt at having undertaken an unnecessary 'rescue mission' was soon forgotten in their relief at finding Taylor safe, and in their excitement at having discovered the supply depot left by the crew of the *Uruguay* on 10 November 1903. Following Taylor's route down the valley to Penguin Bay, they had missed his tracks heading north and his message written in the snow, so, instead of following him, they had searched as far as the southern end of the bay. It was here that they had found the depot, marked by a cairn and a wooden cross embedded in penguin guano. The depot lay in two piles, the first containing a Primus similar to their own and some tools, the second containing food. According to James, 'At first it seemed that we were going to find nothing left in fit condition to eat, as the boxes we unearthed contained rusted tins, whose contents were unrecognisable.'[36] But then, as they dug deeper, they managed to salvage a number of items that appeared largely unspoiled, including cases of corned beef, rice, beans, sugar and a bottle of alcohol that they later discovered to be 'orange bitters'. All the tins were on the point of rusting through, but it seemed likely that at least 50 per cent of the contents might still be edible. Certainly the sugar seemed to have survived well, because Russell noted that it was 'an extraordinary sensation hacking lumps off and gnawing away furiously at them'.[37] All of these supplies they had brought back to the camp.

All in all, the day had been enormously satisfying; indeed, James considered it 'one of the high spots of the whole trip'.[38] They had achieved everything they had set out to do: they had explored much of the island; located one message cairn and one depot left by the *Uruguay*; and Lamb had confirmed the sedimentary nature of the island's composition, as well as making a fine collection of shells, some coral and a tooth belonging to a zeuglodon. They had also augmented their rations and 'to cap it all we were able to recline in tents made gloriously warm by "candle smokers" puffing at a cigar and drinking orange bitters. Was ever such comfort heard of sledging before?'[39]

On the morning of 31 August, they left the shores of Seymour Island in a fog that produced near whiteout conditions. With the sun obscured, the landscape lost all traces of contrast, making it impossible to determine distances or even to recognise inequalities in the snow surface immediately in front of them. One Heroic Age explorer memorably described white-out as 'like living in a spherical tent made of sheets, except for the wind'.[40] Forty years later, the men of Operation Tabarin found the assault on their senses equally outrageous. 'Light conditions became very puzzling by a diffusion through which one lost almost all sense of perspective, and one couldn't even intelligently guess whether the next step would take one up or down from the elevation of the one which preceded it.'[41] Travelling blind could be extremely dangerous, and was certainly mentally and physically exhausting, but, keen to eke out their remaining supplies for as long as possible and to avoid wasting them by sitting idly in their tents, they trudged on by compass bearing.

The sea ice continued to provide a good travelling surface for most of the morning and Taylor's navigation proved accurate because, a little after noon, he and his companions saw the high rounded summit of Cockburn Island looming out of the fog. Like so many of the sites that they had visited in recent days, Cockburn Island was steeped in the early history of Antarctic exploration. In January 1843, Britain's premier polar explorer of the early Victorian period, James Clark Ross, had landed here and claimed it on behalf of the Queen. Ross had been accompanied by the naturalist, Joseph Hooker, and for many years the lichens collected here by Hooker had constituted the most southerly examples of vegetation discovered by man. These associations made Lamb very keen to undertake at least a cursory examination of the area. Ignoring the freezing fog that had again enveloped them, he set out to explore the lower slopes. Despite his oft-demonstrated enthusiasm for his subject, the conditions proved too much even for him and he returned to the sledges after only an hour. Taylor recorded that 'Had the weather been better, he might have spent a longer time at his work, but it was a most uncomfortable and dispiriting task on such a day, and we were all pleased to see him return.'[42]

In spite of the delay at Cockburn Island, poor visibility and a surface made increasingly difficult by a thickening layer of snow, by the time they camped at 4.30 p.m., they had covered 11½ miles. Weather conditions remained much the same the next day, 1 September, and Taylor decided to stay put. In particular, he hoped that the fog would lift, allowing him to make a new survey of the coastal area in order to correct Nordenskjöld's charts. While waiting they breakfasted on 40-year-old corned beef and Taylor and Russell turned their attention to updating their survey notes. As Taylor later acknowledged, he and Lamb 'had not a particularly happy day'.[43] Not only did the fog not clear, the beans they had eaten with the corned beef had been rather hard, probably as a result of the conditions in which they had been kept rather than because of any defect in the cooking, and the two men suffered from severe indigestion during the day. In addition, a strong north-west wind blew into the mouth of their tent's ventilator, preventing the release of the fumes from the candle 'smoker'. As a result they quickly developed terrible headaches. There was, however, one benefit to an otherwise wasted and uncomfortable day: 'between our indigestions and our headaches … we both lost our appetites, so saving almost one full day's rations.'[44]

James and Russell encountered none of these problems. They suffered no ill effects from their consumption of the antique foodstuffs and, as he settled down with his copy of *Anna Karenina*, James noted contentedly that it was 'quite warm enough to read in the tent with pleasure, which is all I ask of a lie-up day'.[45] The dogs fared less well, as depleted stocks of pemmican made it necessary to leave them without a meal on days when travel was impossible. 'One feels sorry for the hungry animals,' Lamb wrote that night, 'when we break camp in the mornings and harness them up to the sledge, they immediately make for the tent site and greedily devour any scraps of refuse that have been left lying about. Human excrement they look on as a delicacy.'[46]

They woke to slightly improved conditions on 2 September but, with visibility still only half a mile and paraffin reserves down to a quart for the two tents, Taylor decided that they must abandon any hope of completing the survey and instead press on towards Hope Bay. Initially, the day was calm and windless and the surface good, so he felt optimistic that they would make good progress, but when they passed through a belt of small icebergs to the north of Cockburn Island, the sledges ran into thick, sticky snow and soon the hungry dogs began to struggle with their loads. The position would improve once they reached the depot at Vortex Island some 35 miles distant; until then, any increase in the dogs' rations would be dependant upon their finding and killing a seal.

A shortage of dog food was not the only problem facing the expedition. The decision to depot all but one pair of skis and one pair of snowshoes at Vortex Island also came back to haunt them as two of the four sledgers floundered through the thickening snow, their feet continually breaking through the light surface crust so that they sank to their knees with every step. The 9ft sledge, always the weak link in their equipment, was also prone to ploughing the surface, sinking first one runner and then the next at every inequality in the surface. 'Trying to intercept its tantrums in such snow proved exhausting work,' groaned James, 'the more it bogged, the more the dogs lost interest and, of course, the more the dogs lost interest, the more the sledge bogged.'[47] As the distance between the sledges increased, eventually James and Russell decided that they would have to relay their load, but, with the barometer falling and the weather looking increasingly threatening, they felt very nervous about leaving any portion of their equipment behind. To their immense relief the weather held and, after an hour's steady pulling with the lightened sledge, they managed to catch up with Lamb and Taylor. They dumped their first load and then returned for the rest, finally making camp at 3.30 p.m., having covered just 4 miles. But their worries were not over for the day. Sounding the jerry can, Taylor discovered that there were only four more fills of paraffin left, including their ration for that night. 'A decent surface and a run of fifteen miles would alter the whole complexion of things but until this occurs we have got to go canny.'[48] In practice, that would mean cutting their use of paraffin by restricting themselves to two hot meals a day, foregoing their evening brew of cocoa and wasting no more fuel on warming the tent or drying their clothes.

The following day they set off at 9 a.m., continuing their journey in the direction of Vega Island. The temperature of −28°F seemed to have produced no material effect on the soft powdery snow surface and the dogs sank to their bellies with every step, making progress agonisingly slow, despite the huge amount of labour expended. At the end of a long tow line Taylor broke trail wearing his Canadian snowshoes, but he found it 'very heavy going, and the dogs soon lost interest in the work owing to the frequent stops, so that we were largely moving the heavily loaded sledge under our own power ... the stops becoming more and more fre-quent as the snow continued to deepen.'[49] These conditions were almost certainly caused by the fact that the massive bulk of James Ross Island was deflecting the winds from the surface, allowing the snow to collect in ever thickening drifts. Worse still, the colossal weight of the snow was pushing the sea ice down into the underlying water, with the result that, all too often, the men found that they were pushing their legs and feet down through the snow and into a foot or more of slush.

Once again, James and Russell were forced to relay their loads and by the time the party camped they had crawled a pitiful 3 miles. That night they fed each of the dogs their last ½lb of pemmican and, as he watched the hungry animals wolf down their last proper meal, Taylor accepted that the situation now risked becoming desperate:

> ... it was becoming increasingly evident that with our dwindling supplies of food, dog food and fuel, that any prolonged delay, such as a long storm extending over several days, might quite possibly have disastrous conse-quences ... With the heavy pulling and on their reduced rations, the dogs were beginning to show signs of weakening. The reduction in the loads they were hauling became an immediate necessity.[50]

In practice, this meant leaving a depot of all non-essential equipment and, after a night during which the temperature fell to a staggering −45°F, the

party rose at 5.30 a.m. to sort through their sledge loads, discarding everything that they could do without, including the radio, the theodolite,
empty jerry cans and ration boxes, the various mementoes from Snow
Hill Island and as much of their personal gear as they could spare. In total,
these items reduced the sledge loads by a very welcome 300–400lb and
with luck all would be recovered during a later sledge journey. The only
non-essential items that they chose to retain were the 150lb of geological
and botanical specimens.

The 4th of September dawned bright and calm and Taylor felt fairly
confident that they might now be able to make better headway with the
reduced sledge loads. This confidence received a serious blow when James
announced that both he and Russell had detected the tell-tale symptoms of
frostbite in their feet. During the cold, wet march of the previous day, James
had felt the burning sensation which presages frostbite, 'but there was nothing to be done about it'.[51] When he removed his boots that night he had
been shocked by what he found: 'The big toe of my right foot … was hard
and white without any trace of feeling nor did prolonged thawing seem to
produce any life. I could but smear it in resinol [sic], cover it up and pray
for a return of sensation.'[52] If the condition worsened – and there seemed
to be very little likelihood of it improving – then any gains resulting from
the lighter loads could be nullified and, in order to reduce the risks, Taylor
reluctantly agreed that they should delay their start until it grew warmer.

By the time they left their campsite at 11.15 a.m., the temperature had
risen from −40°F to −25°F, but the surface conditions remained appalling,
and even with Taylor helping James and Russell with the sledge in front
they made considerably less than a mile an hour during the first two hours
of laborious hauling. The lead sledge sank to the full depth of its runners,
'making the load we were moving act more like a plough than anything
else',[53] but Lamb's weaker team still fell behind and eventually Taylor went
back to help him. When they again caught up, they found that James and
Russell had become completely bogged down, as Taylor described:

> The snow seemed to have become deeper still, and one sank into it, without
> skis or snowshoes, almost to the waist. In handling the sledges from the rear,
> it was easier to move along behind it on one's knees, being dragged along
> by hanging onto the handlebars, than it was to attempt to walk. When one's
> foot did find bottom through the deep snow, it was to plunge itself into
> a foot of slush ice, which froze immediately the foot was exposed to the
> ambient temperature of thirty below zero into a solid cast of ice.[54]

The dogs, too, were obviously suffering. A growing number walked before
the sledges with slack traces, doing little or nothing to pull their weight,

and none exhibited the slightest inclination to fight among themselves – a clear indication that their spirits and energy were waning. Their rations now consisted of just one tin of corned beef divided between the seven dogs of each team once a day, and even this pitiful ration would last for only another day or so. Depressed, exhausted and bitterly cold, the party made camp at 4 p.m. having covered 3.5 miles.

That night they filled their Primus stoves with the last of their paraffin, meaning that they had enough for two hot meals a day for two days or one hot meal a day for four days. After that, they would be wholly reliant upon the remnants of their solid fuel and Nordenskjöld's candles to melt snow to drink – there would certainly not be enough heat to thaw their boots, increasing the risk of frostbite enormously. With their depot at Vortex Island still well over 20 miles away, Taylor noted that 'it was becoming a matter of some importance that we reach our little cache'.[55]

Naturally, he was not the only one feeling anxious. In particular, James was becoming increasingly worried about Russell, noting that:

> twice in the cold and fuel-short last 24 hours, I have seen that glazed look come into his eye, which I have only seen before on a chap clinging to a Carley float in very cold water. It is caused, I suppose, by cold penetrating to the higher nerve centres.[56]

Their calorific intake substantially exceeded that of the Heroic Age sledgers and they still had a week's supply of man food, but fuel was running short and in such circumstances the fate of Captain Scott's party in March 1912, just 11 miles from One Ton Depot, cannot have been far from their thoughts.

At a 'council of war' convened that night at the request of James and Russell, different opinions regarding the best course to pursue were hotly debated. James, in particular, suggested that if a limited reconnaissance proved that the deep snow continued for some miles, they should retrace their steps to Snow Hill Island. Here, he argued, they could repair portions of the hut with the materials available and, using redundant sections of the building as fuel, live off dog meat until such time as seals and penguins became available again. Taylor admitted to finding this proposal both startling and fundamentally impractical. Chief among its disadvantages, he believed, were: their depot at Vortex Island was considerably closer than Nordenskjöld's hut; killing the dogs would negate any plans for further sledging; and their inability to report their decision to the men at Hope Bay would almost certainly give rise to an unnecessary rescue mission, 'with all the attendant publicity which goes with an adventurous failure'.[57] Having listened to their suggestions, he told them that they would continue north – but he also admitted that the 'only immediate result of this discussion in the heatless tent … was a noticeable seed of despond-ency'.[58] James certainly felt dissatisfied with the rejection of his proposal and believed that, in public at least, Taylor tended to take too sanguine a view of their predicament: 'I suppose it is a matter of temperament but I find it no help to clear thought to cloak these situations in ambiguous terms, nor merit not to call them by their true name.'[59] Taylor, meanwhile, clearly resented James' willingness to challenge his views; in his official report he even asserted that he had made a mistake in including him in the party and that it would have been 'much more efficient, homogenous and harmonious' without him.[60]

Before turning in that evening, Taylor and Russell donned their skis and snowshoes and plodded on in the direction of Vega Island, hoping that the compacted snow would freeze solid during the night and provide the two sledge teams with a better surface on which to travel the next morning. The plan worked well and for the first 2 miles on 5 September they made good headway, but conditions rapidly deteriorated when they reached the end of the beaten path and soon they were floundering once more. When they stopped for an early lunch, Taylor again went on ahead on his snowshoes to break the trail and to see if he could find any indications of a better surface. Intending to swing south-west of Vega Island before resuming a more northerly course up Sydney Herbert Sound, he headed towards what appeared to be a tiny island hanging like a dewdrop from the most southerly tip of Vega Island. As he approached the island, almost imperceptibly, the surface began to improve. With growing excitement, he noticed that the snow had begun to show slight indications of the effect of the wind, then occasional patches of hard snow became visible. Unless these features were a freakish localised phenomenon, it seemed that at last he was coming to the end of the windless zone through which the party had been struggling for so long.

Rejoining his companions, who had started to follow in his wake, Taylor told them of his discovery. Having just stumbled through perhaps the worst 100yd of the entire journey, they received his report with obvious and deflating scepticism, 'for so often had someone made this same observation previously, and been proven wrong.'[61] But they were soon converted. Each of the men had been wading through the snow rather than walking on it, with the sledges grinding to a halt every few feet, but now 'thanks to the infinite mercy of God – the drift became less deep, five yard spurts became ten, ten became fifty and by the end of half-an-hour we were keeping the sledge moving.'[62] They began to detect faint lines and ripples in the surface and then a crust began to form, the effect of the burnishing action of the wind. Initially, this crust proved too weak to support their weight, but gradually the sledges began to skate across it instead of sinking and soon even their boots found purchase. Finally, the hard patches became the norm rather than the exception and by the time they camped at 5 p.m. they had completed a run of almost 5 miles. It was the greatest distance they had covered in a day since passing Cockburn Island and James admitted that 'we all felt as pleased as if we had run twenty. If we are really out of the bad surface, the distance remaining to our depot is of small account.'[63]

They soon discovered that they had indeed returned to a zone where the wind held sway. By 6 a.m. a south-westerly was blowing with considerable force, bringing with it dense clouds of freezing fog. Taylor observed that it 'was a day on which normally, we would not likely have travelled, but it had been several days previously that things had last been normal'.[64] They broke camp at 9 a.m. and, steering by compass, very soon climbed a spit of land which linked the small 'island' to Vega Island, making the first a cape. Once they had crossed this isthmus, they found themselves once again on good, hard sea ice and they maintained an excellent speed despite the appalling visibility. Gradually the wind increased in velocity and the banks of fog gave way to drifting snow so opaque that at times the sledges became separated. 'Normally,' wrote James, 'I dislike marching into a blizzard but this was the exception':

> Both Vic [Russell] and I mentioned afterwards that we were filled with exultation by the firm snow underfoot, by the sudden freedom of movement, even by forcing our way forward in the teeth of the wind and drift. It was the same with the dogs. Usually if given half a chance, they curl up in a blizzard at once but today they were full of dash and fire.[65]

That night the exhausted men climbed into their sleeping bags 'after having extracted from them with a spoon as much as possible of the snow which the blizzard had forced into them.'[66] They had covered 9 miles – but it was also clear that, for all the enthusiasm they had exhibited during the day, the dogs were now far too weak to maintain such a pace.

On 7 September they reached a huge, brown, rocky knoll called the Naze, on the northern coast of James Ross Island. Here they turned north up Sydney Herbert Sound. To their immense disappointment, shortly after changing direction, they again ran into deep snow and the dogs' spirit quickly buckled in the face of this unexpected obstacle. The 9ft sledge was now in the vanguard, with Lamb pushing and Taylor and Russell hauling alongside the seven dogs. However, in reality the men were doing nearly all the work, with three of the dogs walking with slack traces and only two exhibiting the will and the strength to really pull. James' team was performing slightly better, but even his sledge halted as soon as he stopped pushing. By lunchtime he had placed one of his dogs, Jimmy, on the sledge, as he was evidently too weak to keep walking, and a few hours later he was joined by Mutt from the 'Odds and Sods'. Subject to surface conditions, they now estimated that they were within a day's journey of the all-important depot but, with the dogs deteriorating rapidly, James felt that he had no option but to shoot one animal in order to give the others sufficient strength to keep going. That night, as they camped just off Cape Scott Keltie on the north-western tip of Vega Island, he shot and butchered Mutt. 'I can tell you it went against the grain for us to do it,' wrote Lamb, 'but it was absolutely necessary to save the other dogs.'[67] They had run 9 miles.

As if to reinforce the men's feelings of guilt at having first starved the dogs and then killed one of their companions, the next morning, visibility was so good that they could easily see Vortex Island, a mere 6 miles to the north. Although the dogs seemed very little improved by the 2lb of meat that each had consumed the night before, once again the surface consisted of an excellent windblown crust and they made very good time. At 11.30 a.m., the two teams separated in order to maximise their chances of finding a seal, one heading round the island to the west while the other proceeded along the eastern shore. James and Russell reached the depot first, but only just, and soon James, Lamb and Taylor were clawing at the base of the cairn, extracting skis, ration boxes and the remaining paraffin. Russell, meanwhile, set off in search of seals. By the time he returned, empty handed, the two sledges had been loaded with the precious supplies and, rather than camp so early in the day, they continued their journey. They kept going for some hours, crossing surfaces that ranged from glare ice to windblown snow to *sastrugi* and hummocks, to cover a distance of 13 miles. Finally, at 5.15 p.m. they stopped to camp among the string of islands which runs from the bottom of Duse Bay down towards Crown Prince Gustav Channel – a scene they had last visited during the middle of August.

'I can hardly convey what pleasure it was for us to give the dogs a double feed of pemmican tonight,' wrote a delighted James. 'One picture that almost brings tears to the eyes is of little Dainty, the gamest and most cheerful little bitch that ever wore harness, standing between her two lumps unable to make up her mind which to eat first.'[68] As for the men, they measured their luxury not in food, of which they had never run dangerously short, but in heat. For many days they had hoarded their remaining paraffin so jealously that even now they had a little remaining; on this evening they threw caution to the winds, topping up the stoves and keeping them at full blast until they were obliged to open the tent flaps to let in some cool air: 'It seemed like the transcendence of pure luxury.'[69]

Travelling conditions were ideal early on the morning of 9 September, but, as Taylor admitted, all sense of urgency seemed to have evaporated once they reached their depot: 'We all enjoyed a feeling of utter relaxation and restfulness, as though the anxious part of the journey being over with our regaining our paraffin, there now seemed all the time in the world to cover the last twenty miles or so to the base.'[70] As if to punish them for their complacency, the weather turned almost as soon as they set off at 10.15 a.m., with a west wind driving banks of black cloud across the sun and setting wisps of drift dancing and twisting over the snow. The dogs were still very weak, but this was to be expected. Rather more worrying was the fact that James and Russell were finding it increasingly difficult to pull, as both felt faint and weak at the knees – a product, they decided, of the 40-year-old meat paste that they had consumed with such gusto the night before. 'The tin had seemed particularly good,' groaned James, 'and we had both taken a fairly substantial taste out of it … it tasted very good paté!'[71]

With the wind steadily rising to force 8 and James and Russell clearly suffering, they camped at lunchtime having covered just 4 miles – and it was now that they discovered that their tent's ventilator had come adrift, so their grogginess was almost certainly the result of fumes from the Primus. Despite the early halt, the day was not a total loss. Shortly before stopping, both dog teams had seemed to scent a seal and they had seen birds circling close to a large berg to their left. Pitching their tents at the base of the berg, Russell and James walked around its northern edge and found three seals, which they immediately dispatched with the revolver and ice axe. The dogs were then taken, one team at a time, to gorge themselves on the steaming carcasses and Russell observed that 'After eating their fill, several had quite noticeably changed in size.'[72] The men, too, cut steaks for their supper – their first fresh meat for weeks. The wind continued to blow remorselessly, but with the wind came much higher temperatures, rising to 34°F (2 degrees above freezing) by 6 p.m.

The unaccustomed warmth served not only to suppress the drift; it also produced some remarkable and quite stunning changes in the landscape, which James, for one, found hugely uplifting:

I would that I could describe the grandeur of the scenery under these conditions. One of the speediest effects of a high temperature is to melt the film
of frost and fine snow that shrouds even the sheerest of rock exposures. One
has to see the change wrought to appreciate the enhancement of colour
when the reds and browns of the volcanic tuff and the delicate strata of
the sedimentary stand forth in bold and generous splashes, a transformation
from pastel to flamboyant. Overhead, the colour scheme was on as generous a scale – ragged low clouds chasing each other across a background of

iridescent cirrus, framed by flaming reds, golds and silvers to the west and a delicate light blue merging into deep purple to the east. Words cannot convey the intoxication of so wild a scene.[73]

James had frequently demonstrated his sensitivity to and appreciation of his environment, often finding points of comparison between the Antarctic and the hills and mountains of his native Scotland. Now it seemed to him that Graham Land had finally relented and had decided to display itself in all its glory to mark the end of his gruelling trek. With these thoughts passing through his mind, he bent his head low to enter the funnel of his tent, ready to turn his mind to the more prosaic but equally pleasurable matter of seal steak fried with onions.

With gulls and petrels wheeling across a cloudless sky and with the Depot Glacier, Mount Flora and The Pyramid now in clear view and looking 'as dear as any home',[74] the next day they travelled in a straight line towards the head of Duse Bay. The smooth surface was interrupted only occasionally by pressure ridges, and with the dogs 'pulling almost as well as they did normally on this improved surface',[75] that night they camped at the foot of the glacier, barely 8 miles from their base. After a comparatively warm and comfortable night they pressed on, crossing without difficulty the belt of disturbed ice where the glacier meets the sea ice to attack the steep lower portions of the long slope up towards Summit Pass. During the middle of the morning they noticed streamers of snow flying from the surrounding peaks and by 1 p.m. sledges, men and dogs were being buffeted by a gale-force wind – but they had no intention of stopping so close to home. From Summit Pass they could see the open water of Antarctic Sound reflecting the blue sky; they paused to take a few photographs in the shadow of The Pyramid and then began their descent towards Hope Bay.

Thus began what James described as 'one of the most trying hours of the whole trip'.[76] In early August the north-facing slopes of Depot Glacier had been covered in thick snow, making its ascent time consuming and laborious. Now they found that the south-west gales had swept the slopes clean so that the deep snow had been replaced by slippery, wind-polished ice that they found nearly as difficult to traverse. The sledges proved almost uncontrollable with the strong wind blowing them sideways and upsets became frequent. On one occasion Lamb turned a complete somersault, but when his companions tried to help him they could hardly maintain their own footing. During another capsize, the handlebars of Taylor's sledge became completely detached and he was forced to halt and make a temporary repair before continuing his erratic descent. With the dogs beginning to show the benefits of their improved diet and the sledges seeming almost weightless, the last portion of the journey became a helter-skelter race. James, Russell and the 'Big Boys' finally tore past their companions to skid to a halt a few yards from the door of Eagle House at 3 p.m. They had been spotted during their downhill rush and were immediately surrounded by a welcoming party:

> Greetings and handshaking all round, and many willing hands to help us unload the sledges and chain up the dogs. Into the house, everybody talking at the same time, a most welcome cup of tea from the galley, and we were at last back from our 5 weeks' journey, happy, healthy, and hungry.[77]

After stripping themselves of their filthy and 'very fruity' sledging garments, Taylor and his companions enjoyed a much needed bath and then sat down to a gala dinner prepared by Berry. Designed to celebrate both the expedition's safe return and Lamb's birthday the day before, the party was soon in full swing. At times, however, the heartiness of the welcome proved almost too much for the sledgers: the remorseless barrage of news and questions became a bewildering hubbub and, as course after course appeared and the bottles circulated round the mess table, they soon found themselves 'more celebrated against than celebrating'.[78] Nonetheless, Taylor thought it 'a very pleasant homecoming for the four of us'[79] and he admitted that 'I don't think I ever appreciated Berry's cooking quite so much as I did at his supper table that night.'[80]

Later, when the celebrations had died down and they had time to look back calmly on the events of recent weeks, the four men could feel well satisfied with their achievements: they had sledged some 300 miles, much of it over previously unexplored territory; they had made substantial collections of geological and botanical specimens; they had visited a number of important Heroic Age sites, most importantly at Snow Hill Island; and they had added substantially to Nordenskjöld's surveys of the area. And all of this had been achieved for the loss of just one dog. In retrospect, even the worst of their trials and tribulations – the blizzards, the plunging temperatures and the appalling travelling surfaces – possessed a real value because they brought with them a wealth of experience. Lying in his bunk that night, unable to sleep because of the adrenaline still pumping through his veins, James admitted that he found it 'satisfactory to have seen not only the best but also the seamy sides of sledging life (but no part of the dose in a fatal prescription), and many of our experiences were object lessons, should it be my fortune to go sledging again.'[81] The degree to which those lessons had been learned would only be proven when they harnessed the dogs and again headed south.

The Long Retreat

Little had changed at Hope Bay during the sledgers' absence. The gale that had blown them down Depot Glacier had swept much of the ice out of Hut Cove, and Eagle House was now so deeply buried that Blyth need only open a window to collect snow for melting; otherwise, life had continued in much the same vein. Now, while their companions continued with the programme of routine observations, radio schedules and domestic chores, the primary focus for Taylor, Lamb, Russell and James would be to write up the results of their journey before the next began. Assuming that the second journey would not commence until after the predicted equinoctial storms of September and October, this gave them roughly eight weeks to complete the task.

They agreed the division of work at a conference after breakfast on 12 September. Lamb would describe his lichen finds and preserve them in readiness for the long voyage to England, while Flett undertook the rather unenviable job of translating the sledgers' 'necessarily brief and scribbly'[1] geological field notes before packing their rock samples. He and Lamb would also work together on developing and printing the photographs taken during the recent expedition – an invaluable record, even though many turned out to be over-exposed. James would prepare his reports on the condition of the sea ice and on the meteorology. 'The former was a rather dull subject on which to write,' opined Taylor, remembering the deep snow which obscured so much of the ice during their trek, '… But the latter subject had many points of general interest.'[2] Chief among these was the clear evidence that the temperatures experienced in East Graham Land fell far below those encountered at the expedition's three bases: an average of $-5.7°F$ for the period of the journey compared with $19°F$ at Port Lockroy, $17.5°F$ at Deception Island and $15.5°F$ at Hope Bay. For his part, as well as writing his general report on the journey, Taylor would plot his survey notes in order to compile a detailed map of the area traversed. The complementary task of computing the astronomical reductions for positioning fell to Russell, as did the glaciology report. Finally, the four sledgers would type up their diaries.

Aside from completing this work, for the first week after their return the sledgers' main interest was food. Although they had no scales to record their weights before and after the journey, Taylor reckoned that he had lost between 15 and 20lb in the last five weeks and all four ate ravenously, effortlessly consuming double helpings at mealtimes and then munching chocolate, bread and jam or biscuits throughout the intervening periods and often during the night. 'And the strange thing,' remembered James, 'was that the psychological hunger was far harder to appease then the physical. Often we ate until we bulged and were quite incapable of swallowing another crumb, but that did not stop us still craving for more.'[3]

When not plotting his survey notes or feasting, Taylor began to draw up plans for the next journey. The sledging programme drafted in July had included two more trips – one over the Larsen Ice Shelf and another into the interior of the Graham Land Peninsula – but now he decided that he must curb his ambition. The key factor influencing this decision was his ongoing uncertainty regarding the government's plans for the expedition. Despite the explorers' earlier concerns that the change in administration would result in their being pulled out and their work abandoned, enough information had filtered through to convince them that the British occupation of Graham Land would be maintained, at least in the short term. However, they had received no news regarding their own fate. As well as being a cause for very considerable irritation among the men, this enforced ignorance regarding the details of their relief made it impossible to plan an extended journey which might result in the sledgers missing the ship and being left in the Antarctic for another season. According to Taylor, 'No one yet has spent three consecutive winters there, and the possibility of our being the first to do so held little appeal.'[4] And, of course, their concern was heightened still further by recollections of the often brief, even panicky, visitations of the *Scoresby* to Port Lockroy. In the face of encroaching pack ice, few captains would willingly endanger their vessels to wait for men whom they knew to be well provisioned and securely housed. Given these considerations, Taylor decided that the two journeys would be replaced by a second trip to the area already visited, with the sledgers exploring the eastern and western coasts of the northern portion of James Ross Island and the smaller islands in its vicinity.

As well as amending his programme, it had become apparent to Taylor that he would have to make a change to the personnel of the sledging party. James' frostbitten big toe had obstinately refused to heal and by

19 September Back was reporting that it looked inflamed and gangrenous. If amputation were to be avoided there could be no question of James undertaking any part in further sledging. Given their clash during the earlier journey, there is little doubt that Taylor welcomed his withdrawal. Back would dearly have loved to take his place, but, with the team at Deception Island still needing regular advice on Bonner's condition, and James' feet requiring careful observation, he could not be spared. Instead, Davies would join the sledgers.

Conditions during the next few weeks proved that the drift-laden winds encountered at Port Lockroy at the same time the previous year were not a local phenomenon and that the decision to delay the second sledging journey had been a wise one. In the Antarctic calendar October supposedly heralds the onset of spring, but at Hope Bay the sun became conspicuous by its absence, appearing for an average of less than two hours per day out of a possible twelve. Furthermore, the gales rose to a screaming force 9 and heavy snowfalls became commonplace, regularly blocking the windows and doors of Eagle House. As far as possible, everyone concentrated on indoor tasks, but some outside work could not be avoided. Back, in particular, conscientiously maintained his observations, his tortuous expeditions to the meteorological screen prompting him to remark that venturing out into the deep drifts was 'undoubtedly the way to get the maximum amount of exercise for the minimum amount of progress'.[5] By the 31st the hut had all but disappeared, the roof covered in a layer 4 or 5ft thick, while the snow immediately behind the building reached a depth of 12ft.

With recent events in Japan very much at the forefront of his imagination, in mid-August the doctor had remarked that 'all the atom bombs in existence could not release us from Nature's icy grip before November'[6] – but in the first week of November that grip seemed as tight as ever. On the 1st Russell dug out the windows of the survey room twice, but on both occasions they drifted up again within half an hour. Worse still, the intermittent gales became one continuous roar which lasted all week, the wind speed seldom dropping below 30mph and peaking at 69mph. However, the new month did bring one compensation: fresh eggs. The first penguins and shags had been spotted on the ice on 10 September, and on 4 November Donnachie collected fifty eggs from their nests: 'A fortnight earlier than last year and most welcome … it makes one feel that summer can't be far away in spite of the gale and cold.'[7] The next day they collected 200.

As well as making a very timely addition to their increasingly Spartan larder, the eggs provided the explorers with an important psychological fillip. With the long-anticipated spring made memorable by some of the worst weather they had encountered and the official silence regarding the relief of the expedition still unbroken, tensions in the hut were rising – as Taylor acknowledged:

> We were starving … for news of the plans which were being made for our relief. We longed to see other faces than those with which we were daily thrown into such close contact, at times all too intimately. It would be point-less to deny that some ill-feeling did not develop between some individuals, but it is well to assert that these feelings which often simmered beneath the surface were sufficiently controlled that they seldom bubbled up to break it. Like catalytic agents, the gentle kindliness of Lamb, the friendly helpfulness of Davies and the bantering good nature of our youthful doctor did much to ameliorate and assuage the ruffled tempers of others, making those of us who fell short of their own good behaviour contemplate our faults with shame.[8]

If Back successfully concealed his true feelings from his companions, he made no attempt to disguise them in his diary and letters, peppering both with increasingly vitriolic remarks on the deliberate neglect of the expe-dition by the authorities. Others found release through speculation: 'the slightest rumour concerning conditions "outside," insofar as they might affect us personally, was sufficient to start off a flood of conjectures; all too frequently, such a flood was let loose without even having the basis of a rumour.'[9] To add insult to injury, when contact was made it was often of a nature to further undermine rather than bolster the already fragile morale – a classic example being a telegram from the Naval Officer in Charge at Stanley, in which he reprimanded Back for wrongly addressing a mete-orological report. 'That is the only sort of message they seem capable of sending, which is not cheering to chaps who have had no mail for over nine months.'[10]

While the storm lasted there could be no question of the sledgers depart-ing, and their growing impatience only added to the strain. Everyone watched the weather with almost obsessive interest and when 5 November dawned bright and calm Davies, Marshall, Russell and Ashton rushed from the hut at 5 a.m. to lay a small depot at the head of Duse Bay. Including a two-hour halt during which Marshall shot and buried some Weddell seals for dog food, it took them ten hours to make the return journey and by the time they arrived back at the hut the south-west wind had risen again, making them glad to reach shelter. The gale reached force 10 during the night and maintained a steady force 6 throughout the following day, making it seem that hopes of a change in conditions had been prema-ture. Then, gradually but unmistakably, the storm began to abate: fine and sunny conditions prevailed throughout the 7th and 8th and the mood in the hut lifted. With no deterioration on the morning of the 9th, Taylor decided that their moment had come: he, Russell, Davies and Lamb made final adjustments to their sledge loads, harnessed the two dog teams, and at noon, with Back, Matheson and Marshall helping them as far as Summit Pass, they were off.

They expected to be absent for approximately six weeks; otherwise, their plans remained vague. For the most part they would be covering old ground, and while they would undertake as much surveying and col- lecting as possible, they did not anticipate any startling new discoveries. Nonetheless, after so many weeks of incarceration, the journey would offer them some welcome novelty and they could expect the time before their relief to pass swiftly and energetically. The same could not be said for the men left at the base. If the weather continued to improve, they would no longer be trapped in the hut and would be able to venture further afield, but they could expect very little in the way of new experiences. Little wonder, then, if some at least felt resentful at not being included in the personnel of the second sledging expedition.

The spell of fine weather lasted five days and they spent much of it in the rookery, collecting eggs and observing the habits of the penguins, particularly the Adélies, which had returned in their tens of thousands. Although their incursions invariably produced an angry hiss which, 'like a gust of wind in the tree-tops would accompany any visitor right through the rookery',[11] the men found it remarkably easy to steal the penguins' eggs, and on 13 November Back, James and Blyth collected 1,300 in a single foray to the area around Andersson's hut. An amused Blyth noted that, 'David said these would last twenty-six households one year, we ate the lot in three weeks.'[12]

Meteorology also offered some slight novelty in the form of the hydro- gen-filled weather balloons used to measure wind speed and atmospheric pressure. On 10 November Back and James unpacked the equipment sent down for the 1945 season and on their first attempt observed one bal- loon reach an altitude of 7,000ft, which they considered 'quite good for a start'.[13] The work was made difficult by the fact that the red and white rubber balloons had to be carefully warmed before inflation in order to restore their elasticity, but before the weather closed in again they suc- ceeded in sending further balloons up to altitudes of 11,000 and 14,000ft. Their record ascent, achieved in early December, would be 19,500ft.

Although the field radio had been almost useless on the first sledge journey, Taylor had expressed the hope that it might prove more successful during the second – not least because it offered the only means by which to warn the sledgers of the ship's return. To everyone's surprise, his hopes were realised when, on 14 November, Donnachie picked up a message to the effect that Russell and Davies were en route to Hope Bay to pick up more supplies and to deliver the geological and botanical specimens so far collected. Not long afterwards the men themselves appeared, reaching Eagle House with both dog teams just as it began to snow.

Their tale was quickly told. In the five days since their departure from Hope Bay the sun had shone uninterruptedly, with temperatures barely below freezing point and hardly any wind. The surface, too, had been all but perfect: a few inches of snow topped with a wind-crusted surface that softened the inequalities of the sea ice and gave the dogs just the right amount of purchase to keep their 850lb sledges moving with ease. Indeed, for the early part of the journey the men had actually ridden the sledges for much of the time. For Davies, whose acquaintance with dog sledging had been limited to the movement of stores to the hut from Eagle Cove in May, the whole experience was one of unadulterated pleasure:

> Oh, they were marvellous fellows, those dogs, marvellous … you really did appreciate what the dogs were doing, having been man-hauling … Oh, it was great! They did the work, and all we had to do was ski along beside the sledge and just keep them on a straight course … we used to have to help them at times when the going was rough and the sledge was capsized and that sort of thing, but that was nothing compared to what they were doing for us.[14]

The landscape had been transformed as well: the barren ice of a few weeks earlier was now covered with hundreds of seals, which basked in the sunshine, hardly deigning to cast a glance in the direction of the sledgers as they made their way towards the newly named 'Eagle Archipelago' (not a gazetted name) at the far end of Duse Bay.

On 10 November they pitched camp on the moss and lichen-covered scree slopes of 'Sheppard Island' (not a gazetted name) before indulging in what Taylor described as a 'mild celebration' to mark Russell's birthday. The next morning they had separated, Russell and Davies returning to Hope Bay while Lamb and Taylor explored on foot Sheppard Island and its neighbours. The returning party did not follow a direct course; instead, in order to undertake the maximum amount of surveying possible, they had sledged south to Vega Island and then followed its northern coast to camp beside a penguin rookery discovered by Nordenskjöld's men in 1903. Here they had supplemented their rations with fresh eggs and then crossed the northern extremity of Crown Prince Gustav Channel to join the east coast of the peninsula. They then skirted the edge of Duse Bay before following the accustomed route up to Summit Pass. It was here that they had run into the only spell of bad weather so far encountered, with visibility rapidly deteriorating as a drift-laden south-west wind chased them up the glacier. Sensing that they were close to home, the two dog teams continued undismayed while Davies and Russell steered by compass. Whenever the dogs diverged from the chosen bearing, the driver had redirected them by throwing his whip alongside the team, so that the dogs instinctively veered away from it and back onto the correct path. The tactic worked perfectly – though Davies later admitted to being enormously 'surprised to find that at the end of the trip we actually landed where we should have landed. I was astonished because the compass was all over the shop … it really gave me faith in that method of navigation.'[15] Since 9 November they had covered a total of 85 miles.

The two sledgers had timed their return perfectly, for the blizzard raged throughout the next two days, and it was not until the 16th that they were able to set out with fresh supplies to rendezvous with Lamb and Taylor. The blizzard also marked the end of the fine weather at Hope Bay: the previously clear skies were now draped in a 'gloomy pall of stratus cloud',[16] which lasted until 7 December. Nonetheless, James admitted that he enjoyed the rest of November – not least because Back considered his toe sufficiently healed to allow him to undertake outdoor work once again.

Following Taylor's example of the previous year, he undertook a plane-table survey of the hut's immediate hinterland but, inevitably, his main focus was the dogs. All the fit adults and two of the adolescents were out sledging, but three pregnant bitches had been kept at the base and over the course of the next two weeks they bore a total of eighteen healthy pups. For James, this marked the achievement of a vitally important milestone:

> With eighteen pups growing apace, I felt reasonably happy about the dog position for the first time since I took over, for it seemed that at last we were past the vital threshold. In the requisition of stores for the following year we had asked for reinforcements; but even were these not to come, there was now an assurance of four or five teams, so that the future need not be crippled through shortage of transport as we had been.[17]

On the downside, he was forced to shoot a popular and hardworking dog called Jimmy 'under circumstances serving to emphasise that there is no course with huskies totally devoid of risk'.[18] During a cold night, Jimmy had caught his leg in his tethering chain and in struggling to free himself he had only succeeded in tightening the tourniquet still further. By the time he was discovered and released, frostbite had set in and this soon led to gangrene. Within a few days the withered paw hung only by a length of dead bone. James kept him just long enough to cover a bitch that was coming into heat – and then shot him. 'In theory this might be deemed gross cruelty, but the extraordinary thing was that he felt no pain; his tail, a certain indication of spirits, was carried erect to the end.'[19] In different circumstances, he might have kept the crippled dog, which limped along happily by his side during his survey work, but he knew too well that the pack instinct of the fit animals would result in his being first bullied and then torn apart soon after their return. A bullet seemed preferable by far.

The other men also occupied themselves as best they could and, by and large, the time did not weigh too heavily upon their hands as November gave way to December. Matheson paddled a second homemade boat around the cove and tried fishing, Ashton made new items of furniture and began to paint the hut, Back worked on the latest issue of the *Howler* and Marshall observed the returning birds and plotted their nesting sites and territories onto James' new plan of the area. With the hatching of the first penguin chicks on 8 December this became a particularly diverting activity, and the arrival of the chicks may have been an important factor in encouraging Marshall and James to undertake a complete census of the penguin rookery. Over the course of four days, they counted until their heads reeled, finally settling on a figure for the total population of 110,000. Walking to the various viewing points among the surrounding hills also became a favourite occupation for many – partly because it gave them an opportunity to stretch their legs, but more importantly because it enabled them to check on the ice conditions in the approaches to Hope Bay.

However, none of these pursuits served to suppress their frustration at being left in complete ignorance regarding the timing, or even the certainty, of their relief. 'Unless the present inactivity and apathy improves soon there is a definite chance we may have another year down here,' Back complained. 'Why on earth won't someone at home tell us something?'[20] Four days later he took mischievous delight in reporting that 'a Norwegian called Bugger has sent a telegram addressed to Deception asking for information. This blows the long obsolete security sky high and also raises hopes of whalers coming down. Three cheers for Mr Bugger who has renewed hope of mail and relief.'[21] Even James, with his constitutional cheerfulness and undiminished enthusiasm for the work of the expedition, admitted that 'A hundred-word signal sent any time during December explaining the position would have made all the difference to our capacity for work, our outlook and our enjoyment.'[22]

The mood darkened still further when the weather, which had been continuously dull and overcast since mid-November, took a turn for the worse. On 13 December 2½ft of snow fell and this was followed the next day by a stiff south-west wind and heavy drift, which blocked all the windows again and made lamps necessary indoors even at midday. 'We still have no news of our relief which is an intolerable state of affairs for there is not all that much summer left,' Back grumbled that evening. 'It is having a most adverse effect on the mental health of all here. People are getting annoyed with others and very touchy. The attitude of the authorities seems hard to justify; from here it looks like psychological persecution.'[23] The same day, he and Flett sent a telegram to the Falklands requesting that, at the very least, a concerted effort should be made to evacuate Bonner from Deception Island in view of his deteriorating health. This was not the first such request and no one expected that anything would result from the telegram – but for once they were wrong. On 17 December Donnachie received a terse signal advising them that the *Scoresby* should be expected in early January: 'News at last.'[24]

Unsurprisingly in the circumstances, Christmas proved to be a muted affair. They learned from the BBC that the mid-winter temperature in London was a balmy 42°F, compared with a mid-summer 32°F at Hope Bay, and in reply to various commentators' complaints about the lack of a white Christmas in England, James observed caustically that, with their hut still completely buried, 'we would willingly have exported them some of our spare snow and not charged a penny.'[25] But while the expedition was more than amply provided for, so far as snow was concerned, food was a different matter. As early as May, Taylor had commented that Berry's 'meals are not at all up to what they were last year, due perhaps to some extent to the loss of some of our stores on the *Eagle*'.[26] By December any cook would have found it challenging to conjure a representative Christmas dinner from the materials available. The best that he and Blyth could offer turned out to be a tinned steak and kidney pie followed by a tinned plum pudding. Alcohol had also been subject to strict rationing for some months, the drink-fuelled parties of earlier times all but forgotten. Nonetheless, they had managed to hoard enough to enjoy a glass of port at midday and that evening Back remarked that 'Sufficient liquor had been saved to remove some of the prevailing gloom and there was a small sing-song.'[27] Taken in the round, the doctor considered 25 December 1945 to be the 'least Merry Christmas I have ever spent due to lack of news, lack of mail, and lack of fresh food'.[28]

On 28 December Donnachie received a message from Taylor advising that the sledging party was now approaching the head of Duse Bay and that he and his companions would welcome some help in hauling their heavy loads from the sea ice up to Summit Pass. In response, at 10.20 p.m. Back, Marshall, Matheson and Blyth set off into the night with three dogs and a small sledge. By the time they reached the top of the glacier, the south-west wind was howling past their ears and 'a lurid sunset and sunrise sky to the south boded ill'.[29] Fortunately, the wind had swept much of the thick snow out into the bay and the surface enabled them to cover the 8 miles to the edge of Duse Bay in good time. They found the sledgers waiting for them, 'dirty and shaggy but fit and pleased to see us'.[30] The eight men squeezed into a tent that Taylor's party had just managed to erect in the face of the 40mph wind and together they enjoyed a meal of buns and pastries sent south by Berry. Next, they redistributed their sledge loads, leaving behind a depot containing just about everything except the collections they had made during the previous seven weeks. Since they had last visited this spot the sea ice at the foot of the glacier had been subjected to considerable pressure and new crevasses had opened up, revealing the sea some 20ft below. Over these crevasses, Taylor noted, 'there was considerable traffic until we had finished the repacking of the sledges.'[31]

At 4.30 a.m. on the 29th, they started back up the glacier. Conditions during the climb were even worse than those experienced by Davies and Russell on 14 November. Once again, a blinding, drift-laden wind swept across the ice, but this time the wind was from the north, blowing straight into their faces with such violence that it became difficult to stand, let alone pull. As they approached the pass, the two sledge teams became separated in the blizzard and the second team, driven by Taylor, Lamb, Blyth and Back, had great difficulty in keeping to the track and were forced, like Davies and Russell before them, to resort to navigating by compass. It took them four hours to reach Summit Pass, from where they caught a glimpse of the ghostly outline of The Pyramid. Even now, the cup of their misery was not quite full – as Taylor related: 'As if to add insult to injury, Nature, in this last wild display of her power at the conclusion of our trip, unloosed the floodgates, and we became thoroughly soaked in a cold driving rain.'[32] Up to this point, visibility had been less than 100yd, but at last it began to clear and soon they could see Hope Bay and the steel-grey waters of Antarctic Sound stretching out below them. As they came out on the steep hill immediately above the base, they released three of the dogs and then, leaping onto the sledge, 'tore down the hillside after them … swinging and lunging about as dogs, brakes and gravity in turn took control.'[33] Minutes later they drew up outside Eagle House.

During their fifty days in the field, the four men had travelled roughly 500 miles, making substantial additions and corrections to Nordenskjöld's maps by examining the coastline of James Ross Island from Cape Gage to Cape Broms and surveying all of the other islands in the area, as well as a small portion of the mainland coast not previously explored. In addition, they had returned with over a quarter of a ton of botanical and geological specimens, including many fossils collected mostly from James Ross Island; completed a good appraisal of the topography of the area; maintained daily meteorological observations; and gathered information on the glaciology, sea ice and wild life of the region. Finally, they had recovered the stores dumped on the sea ice of Erebus and Terror Gulf in September and 'left a number of small depots scattered about which may be of use to someone in difficulty'.[34] Except for the disturbed and often slushy sea ice in the area between James Ross Island and the Sjögren Glacier, surface conditions had been excellent for the most part, the two teams often travelling between 15 and 20 miles a day. Food had never presented a problem because seals were plentiful and the weather had been kind, with remarkably few involuntary halts. Photography had been frustrated by a frequent overcast sky, but even this disappointment had been balanced by a significant improvement in radio communication, with Taylor often able to talk to Layther at Port Lockroy, 200 miles away, 'as easily as one would over a city telephone'.[35] And yet Taylor was also forced to admit that the expedition had been 'not in the least sensational',[36] either in its experiences or its discoveries; instead, it had been representative of the kind of physically demanding geographically and scientifically useful, but fundamentally undramatic and unglamorous labour, which makes up so large a part of exploration in all parts of the globe.

Looking back, Taylor wrote that 'Not the least striking feature of the trip was the complete harmony which permeated every day's work, making it one of the most pleasant of such journeys that one could well experience.'[37] In contrast, on his return it must have been apparent that harmony was a commodity in very short supply within the walls of Eagle House. Without the beneficial distraction of sledging, Flett and his companions had had ample time to dwell on their predicament and there can be little doubt that they gave full vent to their feelings when the sledgers asked whether any definite news had been received concerning their relief. Since the message of 17 December, when they had been advised to expect a ship in early January, no further information had been vouchsafed regarding shipping movements and the probable date of their evacuation; indeed, the only communication open to a positive interpretation had been Stanley's request for weekly ice reports from all three bases. This at least seemed to indicate that plans of some kind were being formulated, though their exact nature remained obscure. Sharing his men's anger, Taylor immediately dispatched a particularly forthright message to Sir Allan Cardinall, complaining that:

> … the complete ignorance in which the Colonial Office is keeping us concerning the now imminent plans for our relief and of next season's work is incomprehensible to us. This has made the intelligent planning of the fieldwork unnecessarily difficult not to say hazardous, and has had a definite deleterious effect upon morale … On our behalf, could you please make representations to the Colonial Office requesting this information, for which we would be extremely obliged.[38]

That Sir Allan was a passionate advocate of the expedition, nobody doubted. Whether he held any great sway over the Whitehall mandarins, only time would tell.

Although Taylor's decision not to vary the personnel of the sledging teams had undoubtedly contributed to the tension in the hut, he acted quickly to diffuse the situation by asking Back, Marshall and Matheson to accompany Davies on an additional sledge journey to Sheppard Island, its main objective, ostensibly at least, being the collection of stores cached there during the last trip. In order to release Back, it was first necessary to request that a doctor at Stanley should be made available to provide advice by radio should Bonner's condition deteriorate still further but, to Back's immense relief, this request was granted by radio on New Year's Eve. After a series of delays caused by poor weather the four men set out with both dog teams at midday on 3 January 1946. The 65-mile return journey proved to be something of a baptism of fire for the novice sledgers, as the unaccustomed heat of the summer sun had melted the ice surface, leaving pools into which sledges, dogs and men fell repeatedly. Even when they switched to night travelling, in the hope that the lower temperatures would result in an improved surface, they found themselves trudging through slush and eventually they were forced to dump '100lb of useless garbage'[39] in order to keep moving.

Despite these problems, when he reached Eagle House on 8 January Back wrote of the trip that he had 'thoroughly enjoyed it',[40] and, from a psychological point of view, it had provided just the kind of variety that the men so desperately needed. However, the news awaiting them at the base quickly turned their initial elation first to surprise and then to fury. Perhaps as a result of Taylor's complaint to the governor, in the period since the sledgers' departure the volume of radio traffic between Stanley and Hope Bay had increased substantially. On 4 January, Taylor received the news that Surgeon-Commander Ted Bingham had arrived at Stanley and that 'he was taking charge of the entire operation to facilitate the changeover'.[41] Two days later, the explorers heard on a routine broadcast of the Falkland Islands radio station that the *Fitzroy* would sail for the South Shetlands on 9 January and that another motor vessel had arrived at Stanley en route to the Dependencies. This latter news so surprised them that no one caught the name of the second ship – though Taylor remarked with what must surely have been assumed amusement that 'It has not been given to many parties in the Antarctic to receive the first word of their relief in the manner in which we got ours.'[42] Finally, on 7 January, the day before the return of Davies, Back, Matheson and Marshall, another official communiqué confirmed that they should expect to be relieved within ten days. 'It is absolutely disgraceful after all these months of learning nothing to be pushed out like rubbish,' Back fumed on hearing the news. 'Taylor has been put under Bingham who commands new party. This is the culmination of our mistreatment by the authorities.'[43]

According to James, on hearing the news of their impending evacuation the explorers 'all went to panic stations as there is a hell of a lot of work to be cleared up'.[44] The apathy that had prevailed for so long now gave way to frenetic activity, the men dashing from place to place as they packed specimens and personal gear and tried desperately to complete their reports in the very limited time available. Commenting on the extent of the logistical nightmare they now faced, Taylor noted that 'the specimen boxes alone by this time amounted to seventy boxes',[45] while the rest of the stores to be shipped weighed nearly 3 tons. On 9 January they received another message, advising them that the *Scoresby* had sailed from Stanley that morning, and this announcement was followed by a flurry of signals from Bingham regarding the condition of the dogs and the availability of dog food. The only man of the twelve not packing for immediate evacuation was Russell, who, like Alan Reece at Deception Island and Frank White at Port Lockroy, had volunteered for a second year in the Antarctic. But Russell's decision did not excuse him from the general *mêlée*: as well as ensuring that his colleagues did not inadvertently pack items essential to the base's continued operation, he also had to obtain copies of charts, reports, cipher books 'and all the paraphernalia which went with the appointment of a postmaster'.[46] 'Rush, rush,' scribbled Back, 'and it seems so unnecessary.'[47]

On the evening of 11 January, Donnachie picked up a signal advising that the *Scoresby* would arrive at 8 a.m. the next day. But when the 12th dawned, a drift-laden wind reduced visibility to just half a mile and it seemed highly unlikely that the ship would be able to reach them. With their bags packed, their work completed and the weather preventing them from passing the time with a stroll up to the surrounding viewing points, the men had little option but to sit amongst the clutter of packing cases and kitbags, smoking and fidgeting, their desultory attempts at conversation rapidly dwindling into frustrated silence as they took turns to peer myopically through the blizzard. At last, at 8 p.m., they learned that the ship had retreated to Deception Island after encountering impassable pack ice. Similar conditions prevailed throughout the 13th and again the expectant men were forced to occupy their time as best they could.

When the long-anticipated relief finally came, it took them completely by surprise, arriving in the form of a heavily muffled Marchesi, who burst into their dormitory at 3.15 on the morning of 14 January, jolting them awake with a cry of 'Hey, you fuckers, don't you want to be relieved?'[48] In the face of a strong offshore wind, the *Scoresby* had nosed her way into Hope Bay at 3 a.m., her deck slippery with ice and her rigging glistening with frozen spray. Marchesi had ordered that the ship's whistle be sounded, but its screech was lost in the gale and besides the occasional howl of one of the dogs the base seemed deserted. Anxious to avoid becoming trapped by the pack ice that had forced him to abort his attempt to reach the bay on the 12th, Marchesi had told his first officer to continue steaming about the bay until his return and had then climbed down into a dinghy accompanied by Niddrie, a meteorological officer from the Falklands, and Dr James Andrew, the new medical officer sent to replace Back. Scrambling up the ice-covered rocks after a cold pull across Hut Cove, the three men had pushed their way into the hut only to find its occupants sound asleep – until, that is, Marchesi bellowed his greeting. 'Tumult broke loose then,' wrote Andrew, 'as everyone got up and was introduced, and there was a lot of scurrying around getting cases and specimens together, while the cook, Tom Berry, made cups of tea.'[49]

With the arrival of the *Scoresby*, the chaos that had reigned between 7 and 11 January again took possession of Eagle House. Marchesi's obvious nervousness regarding ice conditions only served to heighten the men's sense of urgency and soon all twelve were laughing and cursing in equal measure as they rushed from the hut to the shore, and back again, carrying boxes and sacks to the waiting boats. It was an unpleasant day – 'one of Hope Bay's better efforts' according to Back[50] – and in the driving snow and a temperature of 25°F it took nearly four hours and three boatloads to transport everything to the ship. Then came the handshakes and the brief, self-conscious, valedictory speeches as the ten men about to sail parted not only with Russell, who now took command of Base 'D', but also with James, who had volunteered to continue the meteorological observations until the arrival of the rest of the replacement personnel in a few days' time. Their farewells said, Taylor and his companions clambered into the waiting boat and, with two ratings and Donnachie at the oars, rowed through the heavy swell towards the waiting *Scoresby*. They climbed the ship's side and then lined her rails, waving and cheering as they looked through the swirling snow towards the hut and the three figures waving and cheering in reply. A great cloud of black smoke rose from the mouth of the funnel above their heads and they felt the deck beneath their feet vibrate as the engine's revolutions increased. The distance between ship and shore gradually increased and the men on the beach began to shed their individuality, becoming anonymous black specs against a bleak white and grey background. Soon they were invisible. The little ship turned in a wide sweep towards the mouth of Hope Bay, gave a long blast on her whistle and headed out into the choppy waters of Antarctic Sound.

From Tabarin to BAS

Within minutes of their departure from Hope Bay, the explorers had turned the *Scoresby*'s cramped wardroom into a shambles. Envelopes and mailbags were strewn across tables, chairs and deck as the ten men sorted and then devoured the letters that had accumulated since their last postal delivery early in 1945: 'there were dozens of letters for each of us, and over a hundred for some, many being dated back more than a year since they had been written.'[1] Occasionally, one of the explorers would break away to obtain a breath of fresh air and to watch the coast of Graham Land slipping by, but none paused for very long at the rail before diving back into the thickening fug of the wardroom to read or reread some portion of their long-awaited correspondence. In this fashion, the time passed swiftly and quietly, the studious silence broken only by the rustle of paper, by the delighted and boisterous consumption of fresh food from the galley, or by one of the men passing round a photograph or sharing a story from his personal budget of news.

Meanwhile, the *Scoresby* made rapid progress towards Deception Island. She encountered a belt of pack ice some 30–40 miles from Hope Bay, but a channel 5 miles wide separated the ice from the mainland coast, and she continued on her way without interruption. Gradually the weather moderated, the swell subsided and as they entered the remarkably ice-free waters of Bransfield Strait, the sun came out. Shortly after 7 p.m., the ship passed between the high cliffs of Neptune's Bellows and tied up against the rusty oil barge that had been towed into Whaler's Bay in January 1945. Two other ships lay at anchor in the bay: the *Fitzroy* and the 300-ton wooden sealer, *Trepassey*, which had been chartered to replace the badly damaged *Eagle* and was now commanded by Captain Sheppard. Taylor later wrote:

The barge was piled high with coal and other stores and along its decks we quickly picked out three figures from the crew of the *Eagle*, Bob Whitten and 'Sparks', in addition to Captain Sheppard. Before the lines were on the ship, they were down on the deck among us, and there was a great ceremony of handshaking all round.[2]

Another figure turned out to be Ted Bingham, now officially the commander of Operation Tabarin's successor, the newly established Falkland Islands Dependencies Survey (FIDS). A stocky, energetic Ulsterman, Bingham was a stickler for service discipline and he revealed no embarrassment at having been appointed above Taylor's head and, on his way home at last, Taylor diplomatically kept to himself any opinions he may have held on the subject. After allowing his subordinate a few minutes to swap anecdotes with Sheppard and his crew, Bingham invited Taylor into his cabin on the *Fitzroy* to hear his report and to outline his own plans. The *Scoresby* and the *Trepassey*, he announced, would proceed immediately for Hope Bay, where they would unload stores for the coming season, land Alan Reece and the new base personnel and collect David James. Two new bases would then be established, one at Marguerite Bay on the west coast of Graham Land and another in the South Orkneys. At the same time, the *Fitzroy*, with the retiring personnel from Deception Island and Hope Bay on board, would sail for Port Lockroy, where she would relieve Jock Lockley and his team before heading back to Stanley.

While this conference was underway, Lamb, Back, Matheson and Davies went ashore to have a last look at Base 'B', to inspect the new dog teams brought south to augment those left at Hope Bay and to be introduced to the new recruits for the various bases. They also met Sam Bonner. Throughout the course of the year Back had received regular reports on the deteriorating health of his patient, but Bonner's appearance still came as a shock to anyone who had seen him in happier days. Months of illness had left him pale, emaciated and obviously extremely weak. James Andrew and Stewart Slessor, the second of the new FIDS medical officers, had already conducted a full examination and had confirmed Back's tentative diagnosis of advanced cancer of the stomach. Clearly, Bonner had but a short time to live, but he seemed blissfully unaware of his prognosis and his obvious delight at his imminent return to his home in the Falklands was pitiful to witness. He died in the British hospital in Montevideo just a few weeks later.

That evening the whole party gathered in the wardroom of the *Fitzroy* for some 'mass drinking'[3] and to hear Bingham's formal expressions of gratitude for the work that the expedition had completed. 'Bingham is apparently surprised how much work we have done,' Back told his mother, 'as he had heard nothing about it. Eventually turned in in saloon

on settee 2 a.m.'[4] Hangovers notwithstanding, the *Fitzroy* put to sea at 8.30
the following morning, bound for the Gerlache Strait and Port Lockroy.
The voyage proved delightful, with the sea calm and the sun beaming
down from a clear blue sky to illuminate the mainland coast and the
islands of the Palmer Archipelago. The mineral-rich green rock of Anvers
Island's Copper Peak showed up particularly well as they passed down the
Neumayer Channel and shortly afterwards, at 10.30 p.m., they reached
Port Lockroy. 'Just like going home,' Back enthused, 'the little house looks
as nice as ever.'[5] The residents of Base 'A', Lockley, Layther, White and
Biggs, rowed over to the ship and the whole party spent the next day
in discharging stores and bringing aboard the men's gear and specimens
– including a crate of disconsolate-looking ringed penguins destined for
London Zoo.

Departing from Port Lockroy at 3 a.m. on 17 January, the *Fitzroy*
headed north-eastwards in fine, sunny weather. Passing Deception Island
some 20 miles to port in the evening, Captain Pitt then altered course
to east-north-east, towards Laurie Island in the South Orkneys. Except
for occasional bergs and growlers, the sea remained ice-free and on the
afternoon of the 18th the *Fitzroy* overtook the *Trepassey* and the *Scoresby*
on their passage from Hope Bay. All three then proceeded together. That
night a wide belt of pack ice to the north forced the convoy to change
direction and by the following afternoon they found themselves slightly
to the north and west of the South Orkneys. They corrected their course,
but as the ships began to roll in a beam sea that evening, an exchange of
signals with the governor resulted in a change of plans: '8 p.m. flapdoodle
as Governor is worried about Bonner,' Back noted tersely. '… decided to
turn for Stanley. Left other ships in 60°27' and headed across the 60th parallel and out of the Antarctic.'[6] To Back, who had made repeated pleas for a
ship to evacuate the dying handyman, this last-minute acknowledgement
of the seriousness of Bonner's condition and the accuracy of his diagnosis
must have seemed galling in the extreme.

As the ship pushed north, there was a perceptible rise in temperature
and the explorers were delighted to see and hear the melt water from snow
and icicles coursing down the ship's scuppers. They also saw birds in ever
increasing numbers, with flocks of cape pigeons fluttering about the ship,
joined occasionally by inquisitive whale birds and albatrosses. And then, at
about midday on 21 January, the lookout spotted the unmistakable loom of
the Falkland Islands on the horizon. An hour later the ship was passing low
tussock-covered islands as she made her way towards the narrows leading
into Port Stanley. To anyone arriving from milder climes, the treeless, rocky
islands with their pall of grey cloud might appear grim and uninviting. But
to Taylor and his companions they seemed almost unimaginably lush and

welcoming, the first sight of their flora and elements at least of their fauna giving rise to an excited hubbub on deck:

> We could smell the peat smoke and vegetation off the land [wrote Lamb] and were excited, after our two years sojourn amid snow and ice, to see green vegetation and human habitations again. The *Fitzroy* entered the narrows, and the town of Stanley appeared round the corner of the point, with its brightly coloured houses scattered on the hillside – a welcome and gladdening sight. At about 1330 hrs the *Fitzroy* docked against the public jetty, where a number of people were waiting. It gave us quite a thrill to see women again.[7]

The government surveyor, Colonel Woodgate, came aboard to welcome the expedition and to allocate accommodation to the explorers. Then two lorries appeared to ferry men and baggage to their billets and the numerous specimen crates to the warehouses of the Falkland Islands Company.

On disembarking the explorers were greeted like heroes or at the very least like lost sons, and they spent the next few days examining and repacking their specimens for onward transportation; eating fresh food, 'which was ambrosia after the years of corned beef and spam';[8] strolling about the islands; and, in the evenings, re-establishing old friendships and cementing new ones. Certainly Back, who had volunteered to help at Stanley's hospital, was swift to romantic action, as he revealed in a letter to his sister, Barbara: 'the people are wonderfully hospitable and life has been one party after another … Imagine your brother having an affair with a matron! But you should see this matron …'[9] A few days later it was the turn of Sir Allan Cardinall to express his gratitude to the retiring explorers, by throwing a party for the expedition at Government House, during which he 'made a speech saying what good chaps we were and how pleased he was with the work we had done'.[10] Formalities over, the younger men proceeded to a dance in the town's gymnasium, where they joyfully continued the process of fraternisation:

> These Falkland dances are great fun and everyone dances with much gusto although the band is no Harry Roy. In addition to the usual foxtrots and waltzes there are a lot of wild dances in which everyone whirls madly around and gets terribly hot … A group of people usually assembles for a preliminary stoking up and during the dance if you get too hot off you go to somebody's house for a cooling draught. The dance ends at 2 after which you usually join some gathering where drink is taken and talk ventilated far into the morning. It is all absolutely terrific.[11]

As well as being treated like honoured guests by the islanders, Back observed that his period at the hospital proved unusually busy because 'Most of the inhabitants seem to have decided … to have a look at me.'[12] But if he and his companions anticipated the same degree of appreciation and even celebrity when they reached England, they were to be sorely disappointed.

The first intimation of official indifference came when they departed from the Falklands on 11 February. For months, the explorers had been looking forward to once again sampling the delights of Montevideo, but now they learned that they would be allowed only five short hours to enjoy the sights and sounds of this vibrant and colourful city before sailing north. To add insult to injury, after having spent all their money 'under very high pressure buying conditions',[13] the party was split into two, those with military rank boarding the light cruiser, HMS *Ajax*, while their civilian colleagues took passage on the *Highland Monarch*. If these decisions revealed the authorities' inability to empathise with men who had lived in close companionship and in near-total isolation for more than two years, worse was to come. With his party reunited on the *Ajax* at Freetown, Taylor dispatched a telegram to London asking that his men be granted an advance on the arrears of their salaries. But the 'block and tackle brigade' failed to respond and when the cruiser arrived at Chatham at 4 p.m. on 9 March, the men found themselves all but penniless and their very existence apparently forgotten. After they had kicked their heels for a few hours, James Wordie appeared to greet them, but no arrangements of any kind had been made for their reception and three of the party – those who could not call upon the charity of friends or relations in London – were reduced to spending their first night in England sleeping rough in a disused air raid shelter. As Taylor remarked bitterly:

> … no government sponsored expedition into the Antarctic had ever set forth from the country of its origin so unostentatiously as had 'Operation Tabarin', when we left England in 1943, the entire operation shrouded in secrecy … [The] quietness of our departure was only exceeded by that of our return.[14]

It was a far cry from the kind of adulation heaped upon returning polar heroes like Scott and Shackleton at the beginning of the century.

Even more surprisingly, when Taylor tried to make his report to Brian Roberts – the man who, with Wordie and Neil Mackintosh, had done so much to make the expedition a properly scientific enterprise – he met with the same apparent indifference:

I went to see Roberts about one thing and another and he diddled me around. I just seemed to be waiting on things to happen and I had been away from home by that time for more than five years and my oldest son was born ... so I didn't want to spend an indefinite time diddling around with Roberts and I went down to Sussex where some friends that I had made while I was with the Second Division allowed me to work there and finished up what I had to do.[15]

During the previous fifty years, most returning expedition leaders had stepped from their ships into a bewildering whirligig of speeches, newspaper interviews, lecture tours and authorship. Not so Taylor. He simply completed the drafting of his reports and then sailed for Canada to be reunited with his family – and his experiences tallied precisely with those of his men. Indeed, Taff Davies probably summed it up best when he stated that, after more than two and a half years of service in the Antarctic, he and his colleagues were expected simply 'to disappear quietly, and keep our mouths shut'.[16]

This apparently cavalier treatment of the personnel of Operation Tabarin did not result from an ongoing need for secrecy: after all, the existence of the expedition had been public knowledge since April 1944. Nor was it borne of any lack of interest in Antarctic matters, either nationally or internationally. In fact, the austral summer of 1946–47 saw a huge resurgence of activity in the region, with *The Times* of 18 December 1946 reporting the preparation or launch of expeditions from Argentina, Chile and the United States, in addition to the maintenance of the British presence in Graham Land. The publicly avowed motivation behind these initiatives varied from nation to nation. The Argentine expedition, which sailed from Buenos Aires on the *Patagonia* on 4 January 1947, sought specifically 'to reaffirm Argentina's claim to sovereignty over the entire zone lying between the Argentine mainland and the South Pole'.[17] The Chilean naval expedition under Commander González Navarette made similar pronouncements and immediately began to overlay British place names with Chilean ones. In contrast, at a press conference on 27 December 1946, Acting Secretary of State Dean Acheson declared that the United States 'did not recognise any territorial claims by any nation in Antarctica' and 'reserved the right to contest such claims in the future'.[18] But in stating that 'the United States Government had never formally asserted any claims in the area on her own behalf', Acheson conveniently forgot to mention that Lincoln Ellsworth and Richard E. Byrd had both claimed thousands of square miles in her name – and that Byrd had been actively, though secretly, encouraged to do so by the pre-war administration of President Roosevelt. This ambivalence aside, the sheer scale of Operation Highjump, which ran from August

1946 to February 1947 and involved no fewer than thirteen US Navy ships and nearly 5,000 men, made it abundantly clear that the United States was quite prepared to flex her logistical, financial and military muscle to stamp her authority in the region.

A factor that distinguishes this post-war spurt of activity from that which succeeded the Sixth International Geographical Congress of 1895 is the degree to which the later expeditions were government sponsored. Of the sixteen expeditions launched between 1897 and 1921, almost all were made possible by substantial donations from private benefactors. This was also true of those led by Cope, Rymill, Ellsworth, Byrd and Wilkins in the inter-war years. However, the expeditions launched in the ten years from 1945 onwards were truly national in character, funded almost exclusively from the exchequers of their respective governments and thereby indicating a significant shift in perceptions of how their national interests might best be served. Of course, these developments could not be allowed to pass unnoticed in London. In April 1944 *The Times* had been the first newspaper to disseminate the official cover story for Operation Tabarin and in January 1947 it responded to the sudden burgeoning of international activity in the region in terms that might also have been dictated by Whitehall mandarins:

> ... it would be a misfortune if a tradition of friendly cooperation in Antarctica were to be broken by the intrusion of political rivalries, which only serve to interfere with genuine research. Certainly at this stage of history nationalist jealousy should not be allowed to find a field in the one continent where it has hitherto been lacking, and where material prizes are relatively insignificant. In the Antarctic there is room for many. Great Britain has nothing to fear from an impartial review of her own claims ... Antarctica is not a fit subject for national rivalries or political bargaining. Its future, if in doubt, should be decided by law and in the interests of science.[19]

Naturally, the nations least likely to be swayed by such statements were those intent on prosecuting their own claims, and the Colonial Office's continued insistence on the scientific and essentially altruistic purposes of the British expeditions – as articulated by *The Times* – convinced no one.

This fact was amply demonstrated on 4 March 1948 when, in the red salon of the Chilean Foreign Ministry in Santiago, the Chilean Foreign Minister and the Argentine Ambassador signed an agreement for the joint defence of Chilean and Argentine rights in the South American Antarctic zone. At a press conference in Buenos Aires the same afternoon, the Argentine Foreign Minister, Dr Juan A. Bramuglia, announced that 'Argentina would raise the question of these territories in the forthcoming

inter-American conference at Bogotá.'[20] When asked whether the
Argentine-Chilean Antarctic defence agreement included the potential
for military action, Bramuglia replied that Argentina and Chile intended
to 'exercise all rights derived from sovereignty'.[21] If, therefore, the British
government had anticipated that Operation Tabarin would bring to an
end any challenges to its authority over the Antarctic Peninsula, then
the operation had been a complete failure. But, as the Falklands War
of 1982 would reveal, far bloodier and costlier operations would be no
more effective in deterring Argentina from at least claiming sovereignty.
In reality, no one expected that Operation Tabarin would bring about a
decisive Argentine *volte-face*. Rather, the expedition was intended to bolster
a sovereignty that had been weakened by decades of apathy and indecision
by successive British administrations – and the fact that the Argentine and
Chilean governments continued to proclaim what they perceived to be
their rights over the region did not mean that the expedition failed in
that regard.

There is certainly no ambiguity over the expedition's success in terms of
the scientific and survey work it completed. Three meteorological stations
had been established with a near-continuous record maintained over the
entire two-year period. In addition, geological and glaciological work had
been undertaken at Deception Island and zoological and botanical investigations completed at Port Lockroy. Local surveys had also been made of
both sites. The undoubted jewel in the crown was the programme insti-
gated at Hope Bay. Despite the limited number of dogs, sledging journeys
totalling some 800 miles had been made between August and December
1945, adding significantly to the mapping of the area. Substantial work
had also been undertaken in the fields of botany, geology, marine biology
and glaciology, with a quarter of a ton of specimens collected, labelled and
shipped back to England for further study.

Unlike the work of earlier expeditions, this did not result in the publication of multi-volume scientific and survey reports. Nevertheless, by
practising the scientific rigour first exercised by Captain Scott and subsequently championed by the *Discovery* Investigations during the twenties
and thirties, the expedition helped to lay the foundation of an ongoing
commitment to collecting, documenting and analysing that became the
raison d'être of FIDS and its successor, the British Antarctic Survey (BAS).
Less than five years after the replacement of Operation Tabarin with FIDS,
the sheer volume of scientific data collected by its Antarctic bases had persuaded the Colonial Office that it must create a new body dedicated to
the collation, study and publication of this material: the FIDS Scientific
Bureau. Under the energetic direction of Dr Vivian Fuchs, the bureau's
reputation and its responsibilities would grow rapidly and, to their credit,

the bureaucrats of the Colonial Office quickly recognised that their crea-
tion had taken on a life of its own. At the end of its initial three-year term,
they decided to extend the bureau's life indefinitely. 'We were in business',
wrote a delighted Fuchs, '– and this time it was for keeps.'[22] In addition,
over the course of the coming decades, no fewer than fourteen new British
bases would be established throughout the Dependencies (redesignated
the British Antarctic Territory on 3 March 1962). The operation had come
a very long way since its inception, when the furthest extent of the government's ambition had been 'to send just a party of soldiers down there, a
sergeant and corporals, just to sit somewhere in the Antarctic'.[23]

The part played by the three bases of Operation Tabarin in the later life
of FIDS and BAS varied enormously. Despite a serious fire late in 1946,
which destroyed most of the inhabited portion of the old factory building, Deception Island continued to be occupied until 1969. Throughout
this period the base served as a meteorological station. More importantly,
it also became the hub of flying activity for FIDS, primarily because its
beaches offered by far the best available surface for runways. In 1955 the
island became the flying base of the Falkland Islands & Dependencies
Aerial Survey Expedition (FIDASE) which, over the course of two seasons, used a pair of Canso flying boats to photograph some 35,000 square
miles of territory.

Occupation of the base eventually came to an end in dramatic, indeed
cataclysmic, fashion. In April 1967, BAS base leader Phil Myers reported
that a series of minor earth tremors had been felt across the island.
They died away but then began again in November, gradually increasing in severity until 'there was a general impression of movement in the
ground rather like being in a bus that has its engine just ticking over.'[24]
At 10.40 a.m. on 4 December a jet of black ash and steam erupted many
thousands of feet into the air in Telefon Bay, followed by similar eruptions
at other points. Clouds of volcanic ash obscured the sun, turning day into
night and, to complete the apocalyptic picture, the waters of Port Foster
began to seethe and boil, rising and falling up to 5ft every minute. By
now, crockery and saucepans were jumping from shelves in the British
hut and black ash, like coarse sand, had begun to fall from the sky. In the
early hours of the following morning the personnel from the three bases
on the island – British, Chilean and Argentine – were safely evacuated by
the RRS *Shackleton*, the Chilean *Piloto Pardo* and *Yelcho* and the Argentine
Bahiá Aguirre.

Believing that the eruptions were a small-scale event unlikely to be
repeated for many years, a five-man party re-occupied the British base
at the end of 1968. Ominously, in February the following year the tremors began again. Then, at 3.30 a.m. on 22 February, the men were woken

by a powerful earthquake. As the buildings of the base began to buckle with the movement of the earth, base leader Dick Stokes contacted the *Shackleton* by radio to request immediate evacuation. An intense electrical storm broke over the men's heads as they rushed from their hut, followed by a fall of snow and then volcanic debris in pieces large enough to knock them down. Tearing sheets of corrugated iron from a disused shed to protect themselves, they decided to return to their hut to repeat their SOS – but they found the base in ruins: much of the derelict whaling station had been demolished and a cascade of mud and ice blocks had torn a hole 20ft wide through their own building. In the afternoon, conditions eased somewhat and eventually the party was rescued by helicopters from the *Piloto Pardo*, which had been closer than the *Shackleton*. Wisely accepting that if lightning could strike the same place twice, it might certainly strike a third time, BAS closed the base permanently.

The circumstances leading to the abandonment of Eagle House in Hope Bay were no less dramatic – but altogether more tragic. In November 1948, base leader Frank Elliott and three companions were surveying in the area of Cape Kater on the north-western coast of the Trinity Peninsula. For ten days neither Elliott nor Vivian Fuchs, at that time serving as overall FIDS field commander at Stonington Island, had been able to contact the three men still at Hope Bay. Although the interruption of radio signals by topography and weather conditions remained fairly commonplace, both men were becoming increasingly concerned, and on 18 November they agreed over the radio that Elliott's sledging party should return to Eagle House to establish the cause of the prolonged silence. Travelling fast, they covered the 85 miles in five days – and they were appalled by what they discovered. The hut upon which Chippy Ashton and his amateur helpers had lavished such attention in the early days of 1945 was now nothing more than a snow-filled skeleton of blackened timbers. Worse still, besides a solitary and empty tent erected close to the ruins, there was no sign of life. Increasingly anxious, the four sledgers walked over to the penguin rookery where, some weeks earlier, base doctor Bill Sladen had pitched an observation tent. The tent was still there and in answer to their calls a man appeared at the entrance. It turned out to be Sladen, deeply distressed and clearly suffering from the effects of severe shock. His companions, Dick Burd and Mike Green, were dead.

Sladen's story was quickly told. Sixteen days earlier he had been working at the rookery when he noticed a dense cloud of smoke rising from the north end of the base site. He ran back but found the hut already well ablaze and when he attempted to enter, he was driven back by the heat and by thick clouds of acrid black smoke. Nor could he obtain any answer to his 'frantic shouts made between breaths inside the window'.[25] With the fire spreading rapidly to all parts of the building and with small arms ammunition exploding within, Sladen eventually took cover in the tin galley, which was the only part of the original base left undamaged, before finally retreating to the observation tent all but overwhelmed by 'a feeling of great loneliness and deepest sorrow'.[26]

After this tragedy Hope Bay would not be reoccupied by FIDS until early 1952, when a replacement hut was built. However, the site did not remain unoccupied in the intervening years, as new base leader Dr George Marsh discovered when he tried to unload stores and building materials from the RRS *John Biscoe* on 1 February 1952. As the first boatload went ashore, a small detachment of Argentine soldiers appeared and fired shots over the heads of the British landing party. Marsh made his way to the Argentine huts near Seal Point, but his protest was brushed aside by the Argentine commanding officer and when more armed men were seen fanning out over the area, Marsh had no option but to return to the *Biscoe*. But the ship did not retreat. Instead, Captain Bill Johnston sent a coded message to the new Governor of the Falkland Islands, Sir Miles Clifford, who immediately boarded the frigate HMS *Burghead Bay* and set off in support of the *Biscoe*. Receipt of this news then enabled a gleeful Johnston to declare to the Argentine contingent 'in his booming Irish brogue, "The British Royal Navy is on its way and they will be settling your hash my fine fellows!"'[27] According to British eyewitness accounts, the response to this announcement was an instantaneous and no doubt humiliating climb down on the part of the Argentine troops. Before its eventual closure in 1964, considerable survey and scientific work would be completed from the new base, but the site would forever be marked by the tragic destruction of Eagle House and by the comedy of the first and, so far, only armed confrontation ever to take place on the Antarctic continent.

In some ways, the base with the most remarkable post-Tabarin history is Port Lockroy. In the years immediately after 1946, Bransfield House went through a depressing sequence of closures and re-openings driven partly by economic considerations, partly by the limitations of the base in terms of survey work – and ultimately by the realisation that Port Lockroy possesses a micro-climate all of its own, a fact which renders it all but useless for synoptic weather reporting. However, in an unusual instance of historical serendipity, a base set up in quite the wrong place for its original purposes was ultimately found to be perfectly located for other work of a much more wide-ranging significance. This development can be dated to March 1948, when work began to convert Bransfield House into an ionospheric recording station.

The ionosphere is a region of the Earth's upper atmosphere which is ionised by solar radiation and stretches from approximately 37 miles to

620 miles above the planet's surface. It affects atmospheric electricity and, as the work undertaken at Port Lockroy helped to demonstrate, profoundly influences long-distance radio wave propagation. The work that began early in 1948 involved the vertical transmission of radio signals into the ionosphere, and the subsequent recording of these signals as they bounced back from the different layers of ionised gas known to exist at certain altitudes. Crucially, the reflective quality of these layers is not constant, being affected by factors including latitude, the geomagnetic field, solar activity, such as solar flares and sunspots, the time of day and the season of the year. An improved understanding of these variables would do much to improve radio communications.

The radio transmissions from Port Lockroy commenced on 9 March 1948 and were repeated as far as possible (owing to the unreliability of the small Chore Horse generators) every sixty minutes, with the reflected signal trace read from a cathode ray tube and the results handwritten. In 1952 improved manually operated equipment was introduced and the following year the Union Radio Mark II Ionosonde was delivered, which automatically produced photographic records on rolls of 70mm paper film. In the words of David Price, who served at Port Lockroy during 1958 and 1959:

> Once the film was complete it would be processed in the base darkroom and after analysis (known as reduction) at site and conversion into numeric data it could be transmitted by normal radio signal to the Radio Research Station at Slough in England. These statistics were then collated and circulated to radio stations that wished to communicate over long distances, thus enabling them to predetermine the optimum frequency for the best reception for any desired location at a given time.[28]

The study of ionospheric physics was also a key component of the scientific programme of the International Geophysical Year (IGY) of 1957–58, and the work undertaken at Port Lockroy and at other stations, including the Amundsen–Scott base at the South Pole, would help to dispel the hypothesis that six months of winter darkness would cause the ionosphere to disappear altogether. The ionospheric sounding programme continues to this day, having been moved the short distance from Port Lockroy to the FIDS station (Base 'F') on the Argentine Islands when Base 'A' was closed. The programme is now the responsibility of the Republic of Ukraine, which took over Base 'F' in 1996.

In addition, during the preparations for the IGY, in 1956 the Dartmouth Naval College in Hanover, New Hampshire,[29] had asked whether a specialist listening post could be set up at a British Antarctic base. FIDS agreed and suggested Port Lockroy because it was the only British base with a twenty-four-hour electricity supply, used to power its ionospheric equipment. The purpose of this listening post, and of similar US facilities at Ellsworth Station on the southern coast of the Weddell Sea and on Ross Island in McMurdo Sound, would be to monitor and record a natural phenomenon known as 'whistlers'.

Whistlers had first been heard over long telephone wires towards the end of the nineteenth century. Later, during the First World War, German military engineers attempted to eavesdrop on enemy telephone conversations by placing copper spikes in the ground near British trenches. They then used long wires to connect these spikes to an audio amplifier behind their own lines. Back in the safety of their dugouts, what the German boffins heard was not the hoped-for exchange of information between British officers but a series of intermittent and seemingly meaningless pulses. Many years were to elapse before scientists began to understand that these pulses were actually the result of the bursts of electro-magnetic energy released when a lightning strike occurs. The surge of energy caused by a strike then travels from one hemisphere to the other along the Earth's magnetic field lines. On a suitably tuned radio receiver, the sound of the local initiating strike is heard as an abrupt tonal crack or 'bonk' and the discharge of energy is often powerful enough to cause the signal to bounce backwards and forwards several times between the hemispheres, with the sound in the opposite hemisphere to the strike being heard as a more musical low-frequency 'whistle' lasting a few seconds. Given that the Earth's magnetic field lines, which serve as the whistlers' pathway, stretch some 5,000 miles into space, it was quickly realised that the study of the whistlers' behaviour could shed new light on the composition of the upper atmosphere.

As the phenomenon began to be understood, whistler research became just one of many elements in the study of the Earth's near-space environment and complemented the aims and objectives of the IGY. Whistler recording equipment was flown from the United States to Montevideo, collected by a US Navy ice-breaker and transferred to HMS *Protector*, which arrived at Port Lockroy on 11 February 1957. The equipment comprised a power supply, a receiver, an electronic clock and two reel-to-reel tape recorders. Within twenty-four hours of its arrival at Base 'A' testing began. Daily recordings started shortly afterwards, with the electronic clock placing a marker on to the tape every ten seconds. These tapes would later be run side by side with recordings made in the United States, and the life of each individual whistler – from the initiating strike to the eventual fading of the signal – could be studied. In 1963, the study of whistlers resulted in the detection of the plasmapause, a quasi-permanent structure in the plasma conditions that occurs near geostationary orbit. The British Antarctic Survey maintained an active programme for many years at Base 'F' and continues to monitor that important region of our planetary environment from Rothera (to the south of Base 'F' and Port Lockroy).[30]

In a separate trial, also dating to the time of the IGY, attempts were made to establish the viability of communicating with submerged submarines through the use of Very Low Frequency (VLF) transmitters that had originally been set up to broadcast standard time signals.[31] For this, an additional receiver was supplied to Port Lockroy in 1960, although at that time the true purpose was not stated. Michael L. Trimpi, who worked on the project at Stanford, has observed that 'In those days submarine communication was hush-hush. I had to get security clearance to work with the data ... it was against the rules to say that these VLF transmitters were used to communicate with submarines! We had a grant from the Navy to study these signals. We provided our own receivers.'[32]

It is to be hoped that Jimmy Marr, who tortured himself over his failure to establish his base at Hope Bay and always viewed Port Lockroy as a poor compromise, may have learned of the facility's significant role in the study of the ionosphere and whistlers. Such knowledge might have enabled him to look with more satisfaction upon his achievements. But if Port Lockroy's contribution to the IGY would have pleased him, there can be little doubt that its later history would have left him utterly astonished. After its eventual closure in 1962, Bransfield House inevitably fell into disrepair and, by the time the British Antarctic Survey undertook a conservation survey in 1994, its deterioration had reached chronic levels, with portions of the roof collapsed, windows broken and penguin faeces everywhere. Recognising that urgent action was required if the hut was to be preserved, Base 'A' was immediately designated as 'Historic Site and Monument Number 61' under the terms of the Antarctic Treaty. In 1996, a comprehensive programme of restoration and conservation began with the intention of returning Bransfield House to its 1962 condition. Once this vital work had been completed the building opened as a museum, with the seasonal staff dividing their time between guiding visitors and research. The post office, first opened on 23 March 1944, also came back into operation, with around 70,000 postcards and letters now posted every year. Remarkably, as a result of a combination of position and logistics, this small base, built under the strictest conditions of wartime secrecy and located quite accidentally, has now become the most popular tourist destination on the whole of the Antarctic continent, with 18,000 visitors in the 2012–13 summer season, compared with around 400 annually at the Heroic Age huts of Scott and Shackleton.[33]

After his own departure in December 1944, Marr never returned to Port Lockroy. Indeed, he never again visited the Antarctic after 1945.

After a period of recuperation, he resumed his work with the *Discovery* Investigations and then, in 1949, he joined the National Institute of Oceanography as Principal Scientific Officer – a post he held until his death on 30 April 1965. Throughout this period his main interest was in completing his magisterial 460-page *Natural History and Geography of the Antarctic Krill*, which was published just three years before his death. But while the value of this work was immediately recognised in zoological circles, Brian Roberts believed that Marr's leadership of Operation Tabarin would ultimately be recognised as his most important endeavour:

> His Antarctic experiences began in the dying phase of the 'Heroic Age' of adventurous personal enterprise and ended at a time when these same activities, often no less adventurous, had largely become a routine government commitment. During the Second World War the rapid transition from one age to another was not easy for the few who were actively concerned with Antarctic affairs. The part which Marr played during this transition may well come to be regarded as of more far-reaching significance than his biological researches.[34]

At the time of his death, Marr would almost certainly have disagreed with Roberts' assessment of the comparative importance of his life's work and Operation Tabarin. Had he lived twenty or even thirty years longer and witnessed the burgeoning of BAS's activities, he might have been convinced otherwise.

As for the other Tabarin explorers, like millions of demobbed servicemen the world over, the majority found themselves thrust back into civilian life and in urgent need of paid work. They dispersed rapidly and, inevitably given their differing backgrounds and experience, they went on to a wide variety of jobs –very few of them continuing to work at high latitudes. Taylor intended to leave the army, but when he reached Ottawa in June 1946 his superiors in the Royal Canadian Engineers persuaded him to turn his hand to other cold weather projects, this time in the Arctic. He served first as an observer on a joint American and Canadian reconnaissance exercise called US Naval Task Force 68, during which he travelled around the Queen Elizabeth Islands in the far north. Next, he joined the Snow, Ice and Permafrost Research Establishment, where he became so expert in the compaction of snow for roads and runways using power-mixers and flamethrowers that he and his team could convert a pristine wilderness into a fully functional airfield within twenty-four hours. On retiring from the army, he set up his own surveying business, and during the mid-1950s the American government employed him to assist in the establishment of the Distant Early Warning (DEW) Line network of radar stations in the

Canadian Arctic. In his spare time he became a prolific, but unpublished, amateur author and wrote two lengthy accounts of Operation Tabarin. In these books, he sought to paint a balanced and unemotional picture of the expedition – but in private he would continue to rage against the authorities' neglect of the expedition in general and himself in particular, telling an interviewer from BAS in 1987 that he had been treated like 'a dog on that tour'.[35] He died in 1993, but his anger continues to sear the pages of his voluminous correspondence and memoranda, now kept by the University of Manitoba.

One man who refused to disappear quietly and keep his mouth shut was David James. As a result of what he described as 'an incredible stroke of good fortune',[36] shortly after his return from Hope Bay James was asked by film director Michael Balcon to act as technical adviser on the 1948 Ealing Studios production *Scott of the Antarctic*, starring John Mills. In this new role, he approached the Colonial Office and was granted permission to return to the Falkland Islands Dependencies with a camera crew to shoot suitable backgrounds for the film. Although Scott's tragedy took place on the opposite side of the continent, three months on location at Hope Bay gave the crew ample opportunity to film the scenes that give the film its impressive authenticity. These experiences also gave rise to a book, the best-selling *Scott of the Antarctic: The Film and its Making*. With a newly established taste for authorship, in 1949 James published a second volume. *That Frozen Land* is the only near-contemporary account of Operation Tabarin, but, perhaps fearful of the Colonial Office vetoing its publication, at no point did James use the name Operation Tabarin or refer to the mission's geo-political motives. He asserted instead that the expedition's primary goal was to 'continue the work of the BGLE'.[37] Thereafter, he focused his attention on politics, becoming a Conservative Member of Parliament in 1959, and on the restoration of his ancestral home, Torosay Castle. He died in 1986.

Other members of the expedition whose connections with the Antarctic continued after the return of Operation Tabarin included Reece, Blyth, Howkins and Lamb. After serving under Russell at Hope Bay during the 1946–47 season, Reece volunteered for the Norwegian-British-Swedish Antarctic Expedition of 1949–52 and over-wintered at Maudheim on the coast of Queen Maud Land. As well as taking part in the geological mapping of some 10,000 square miles inland of the Weddell Sea's eastern shore, during this expedition he also earned the dubious privilege of being only the second man, after Aeneas Mackintosh of Shackleton's 1907–09 *Nimrod* Expedition, to lose an eye in the Antarctic. Damaged by a rock splinter during geological work, the eye was surgically removed by the expedition's Swedish-American doctor, Ove Wilson. Unfortunately, Reece's misfortunes in the Polar Regions did not end there. After undertaking

further geological surveys in Greenland and Africa, in 1959 he took a job
with J.C. Sproule & Associates in the Canadian Arctic. On 28 May 1960,
while working from Resolute on Ellesmere Island, his light aircraft landed
on the sea ice to assist the crew of another aeroplane. On the flight back
to Resolute, Reece and his pilot both died when they crash-landed on
Cornwallis Island in whiteout conditions. He was just 39.

As for Blyth, he later wrote that 'from the moment of my arrival in Stanley
from Hope Bay in January 1946, I wanted to go back South, and often asked
myself, why the hell did I come back?'[38] His chance came in 1948, when
he was asked if he would like to serve at Port Lockroy for a second season.
He jumped at the chance and sailed south on the sloop HMS *Snipe*. This
last period in the Antarctic was uneventful to the point of monotony, but in
later years – and like many of his colleagues – he would remember his time
at Port Lockroy and at Hope Bay as 'the happiest days of my whole working life'.[39] On his return to the Falkland Islands, Blyth again took up his old
job at the Public Works Department. He eventually became a Justice of the
Peace and just two years before his death in 1995 he wrote a brief account of
his experiences in the Antarctic, now held in the archives of BAS.

Following demobilisation, Howkins returned to Stanley to undertake
meteorology on behalf of the Air Ministry. After several months Sir Miles
Clifford requested his secondment to FIDS, and eventually he served three
tours of duty, routinely visiting the British bases in the Falklands, on South
Georgia and on the Antarctic Peninsula. Awarded an MBE, he later went
on to become Assistant Director of Data Processing at the Air Ministry's
headquarters in Bracknell, a post he held until his retirement in 1979. Aged
95 at the time of writing, he is the last surviving veteran to have served
with the shore parties of Operation Tabarin.

Lamb, the man whom James and Russell both described as the
Dr Edward Wilson of the expedition, returned to academia, taking a job
as Professor of Cryptogramic Botany with the Argentine Instituto Lilloa
in Tucumán. Uncomfortable in the Argentine climate, in 1950 he and his
family moved to Ottawa, where Lamb accepted a post at the National
Museum of Canada. Three years later he became Director of the Farlow
Herbarium at Harvard, where he remained until his retirement aged 61.
It was during his directorship of the herbarium that Lamb again visited
the Antarctic, this time under the auspices of the US National Science
Foundation. The purpose of his visit to McMurdo Sound was to investigate the possibilities of studying Antarctic algae using scuba techniques,
and though he told Taylor that he found it 'slightly annoying to be treated
like an ignorant tenderfoot tourist',[40] this trip gave rise to a more prolonged expedition undertaken during 1964–65. As a result of this work
Lamb was awarded the US Polar Medal to accompany the British Polar

Medal that he had received in 1953 for his part in Operation Tabarin. The later expedition, humorously referred to as Operation Gooseflesh by Lamb, benefited from logistical support from the Argentine Navy and it is curious to speculate on whether the Argentine sailors who assisted him knew of his earlier exploits in the disputed territories of the Antarctic Peninsula. Lamb retired to Costa Rica in 1972 after undergoing gender reassignment surgery and died of motor neurone disease in 1990.

Although Taylor had accused him of being 'totally lacking in energy or initiative',[41] Freddy Marshall also went on to a highly successful academic career. After returning to the University of Hull to work with the distinguished oceanographer Sir Alister Hardy, Marshall soon moved to the Natural History department of the British Museum. He stayed there for fifteen years, writing numerous influential books and papers on marine fish, his works based on his wide experience of deep-sea oceanography. In 1971 he was awarded the Rosenstiel Gold Medal for services to oceanography, and the following year he took the Chair of Zoology at Queen Mary College, London University, where he remained until he retired to Saffron Walden in 1977. Professor Norman Bertram 'Freddy' Marshall died in 1996.

According to James, Tom Berry became a chief steward on the Newfoundland run after the expedition. In later life, and a few days before a Tabarin reunion, Taylor would state that Berry:

> was a wonderful cook and I have often thought since [that he] did more to contribute to the success of our expedition than any one person. I didn't realise it at the time, but I realise it now … we've lost track of him completely. We don't know where he is. I would like nothing better than if old Tom could appear on Friday with us.[42]

But by the time Taylor made these placatory remarks Berry was dead A Londoner by birth, he died in Bexley in 1978 aged 82. There is no record of whether he felt equally forgiving.

Like Andrew Taylor, Victor Marchesi stayed in uniform after the expedition, working initially in the Royal Navy Hydrographer's office. Anxious to return to general service – known to naval officers as 'salt horse' – he refused command of a surveying motor launch and instead went on to take part in a chemical weapons exercise named Operation Hornet. As First Lieutenant of the aircraft carrier HMS *Unicorn*, he spent two years in the Far East during the Korean War before becoming Senior Operations Officer and Fleet Atomic, Bacteriological and Chemical Defence Officer on the staff of the Commander-in-Chief, Mediterranean. After a period as staff officer of the RNVR in Northern Ireland, he retired from the Navy at 45 with the rank of lieutenant-commander. Thereafter, he spent a period working with the Bass brewery ('just a shore job, you know, prop the foresail'),[43] before becoming captain of the historic tea clipper *Cutty Sark*. He died aged 92 in 2007.

In 1946 the 53-year-old Jock Matheson rejoined the Merchant Navy, serving as bosun on the MV *Elysia* carrying cargo between Glasgow and New York. Thereafter, in order to spend more time with his ailing wife, he found work with the Lagavulin Distillery at Port Ellen on the Isle of Islay. Not surprisingly, after more than three decades at sea, Matheson found it impossible to sever all links with his old life and he continued to sail small boats around the Scottish islands, on one occasion causing David James to call out the coastguard when, after a storm, he failed to arrive on time for a visit to Torosay Castle. In fact, when the weather worsened, Matheson and his brother had put in to a small bay, where they anchored safely. When they saw the lifeboat, they waved cheerfully and received an equally cheerful wave in return before the lifeboat crew continued their search for a 'yacht in distress'![44] Matheson died in 1970.

Gwion 'Taff' Davies also returned to the sea on the basis that 'it was the only work I knew.'[45] Initially, he worked on a coaster, but after taking a course in agricultural science he joined the Fisheries Department, where he spent many more happy hours conducting research into the herring fisheries off the coast of Scotland. Although he never visited the Antarctic after Operation Tabarin, he continued to be profoundly influenced both by his experiences in the far south and by Marr, whom he continued to idolise. Transferring to the Fisheries Experimental Station in Conway, he specialised in problems connected with mussel farming, focusing in par-ticular on means by which to maximise food production:

> ... being in the Antarctic ... made me very concerned about food supplies.
> You were always hungry when you were out sledging: [it] made you realise
> that there must be a lot of people in the world [who] were always hungry,
> and they never could come back and have a good feed up in the base hut,
> like we could, at the end of it.[46]

He also discussed with Marr the potential for farming krill for human consumption, but his attempts to undertake research on a whaler in the South Atlantic, where he could obtain fresh samples, came to nothing. Taff Davies died at his home in North Wales in 2005.

Another member of the expedition who followed a career in fisher-ies – though in rather more exotic locations – was Jock Lockley. After his return from the Antarctic, he accepted a job as Fisheries Officer, working for the Colonial Office in Tanganyika. Subsequent postings took him to Kigoma and Dar es Salaam. When Tanganyika gained its independence in December 1961, Lockley – by now the recipient of an OBE for his services to the Tanganyikan fishing industry – moved on to Nassau and then Nairobi. Finally, he took another fisheries post in Wellington, New Zealand, where he died in 1990.

After ten years at sea and two in the Antarctic, James Edward Butler Futtit 'Fram' Farrington settled down to life on shore. On his return to England, he became a scientific officer with the Telecommunications Research Establishment at Malvern. Two years later he moved to the new electronics division at the Atomic Energy Research Establishment in Harwell, where he worked on radiation detection. He retired in 1975 and, in 1989, returned to his native Northern Ireland. He died in 2002.

The expedition's New Zealand radioman, Norman Layther, became a commercial pilot after the war, flying in Malaya throughout the fifties and sixties. By 1969 he was a chief pilot with Gulf Air. When defective hearing forced him to retire, he moved to Wimbledon, where he died in 1983. The last of the three radiomen to join the expedition, Tommy Donnachie, returned to Glasgow and then to the sea. Thereafter he disappeared from view.

Lewis Ashton, whom Taylor considered 'one of the most popular and capable people we had',[47] was the only member of the personnel to be employed for any lengthy period on expedition matters by the Colonial Office, working on the sorting, labelling and cross-indexing of the hundreds of photographs taken between 1944 and 1946. This work kept him in London for many months, where he was able to meet regularly with other ex-members of the expedition, though James admitted that his companions were 'never quite sure that it is the same chap without his bushy black beard'.[48] His later career is obscure; Taylor reported that he had died of complications arising from breathing in the dust of the flourmill where he worked.

Victor Russell went on to a highly successful career in the oil industry, working in the Middle East from 1949 to 1960 as a surveyor for the Iraq Petroleum Company (IPC). Thereafter he returned to Britain, continuing to work for the IPC until his retirement in 1972. Skiing, mountaineering and environmental protection remained hugely important to Russell throughout his life – as did his experiences in the Antarctic. He died in Invernesshire in December 2000.

William 'Bill' Flett, whom Russell had described as 'at times rather like a professor, but very good fun',[49] returned to his natural environment: the classroom. Immediately after the expedition he rejoined the staff of Glasgow University but then, in September 1947, he accepted the post of Senior Lecturer in Geology with the Mining Department of the Royal Technical College in Glasgow. He held this post until his retirement in 1965. On the basis of his contribution to geology, he was elected to Fellowship of the Royal Society of Edinburgh in 1952. He died in 1979.

Eric Back, whose diaries and letters form one of the most compelling and entertaining records of Operation Tabarin, moved from the Antarctic to the tropics – though it is unclear whether his memories of the chill south-westerlies of Hope Bay or the discomforts of post-war austerity England were the stronger influence behind this decision. Specialising in paediatrics, from 1952 he taught medicine at the University College Hospital in Kingston, Jamaica, becoming the first Professor of Paediatric Medicine at the University of the West Indies in 1963. Travelling widely in South, Central and North America, he also remained a member of the Royal Naval Volunteer Reserve for many years and, in 1961, participated in a hurricane relief mission to British Honduras. It was an experience he described as 'quite interesting',[50] despite the fact that he flew into a disaster zone with nothing but the clothes on his back and his medical bag. In 1972 he retired to Great Yarmouth on the Norfolk coast, where he became involved in National Health Service hospital building projects and management. His interest in Antarctic affairs continued throughout his life and between his retirement and his death in 1992 he was a regular attendee at the annual dinners of the Antarctic Club where, as a founder member of FIDS, he was accorded a seat at the top table.

None of the personnel of Operation Tabarin attained the celebrity of earlier polar explorers – hardly surprising given the Colonial Office's apparent embarrassment over their exploits. But too much can be made of the supposed 'neglect' that so irked Taylor. The explorers returned to England after a global conflict and at a period when the government was still deeply embroiled in the repatriation of hundreds of thousands of troops from every theatre of war. Little wonder, then, if the reappearance of a handful of Antarctic veterans failed to attract much attention in official circles. The award of the Polar Medal in 1953 was also not unduly belated – particularly when one considers that 1939–45 campaign medals were still routinely arriving through veterans' letterboxes in the 1960s. Though few members of the expedition expressed their frustration at being kept in ignorance as tartly as Back in the last months of 1945, he was also able to place his own experiences, irritations and discomforts in the wider context of a war which killed 60 million and displaced many millions more:

> … if it was uncomfortable, it wasn't as uncomfortable as being in the London Hospital during the blitz – and I wasn't being machine-gunned like my mother was, bicycling along the road … I had survived the war that my father was killed in, so that there really wasn't much to dislike.[51]

It was also the case that, despite their extraordinarily varied post-war careers, ranging from fisheries inspector to Bacteriological and Chemical

Defence Officer and from professor to MP, for many of the veterans their period in the Antarctic retained an importance disproportionate to its duration. Many polar explorers both before and after have felt the same way. Interviewed in 1986, Davies tried to explain something of the continent's strange attraction and its uncanny ability to seep into a man's bones:

> It was an unearthly kind of place really and you never forget it, you never forget it: it was beautiful in its grim way … the grandeur of it – it gets into you, you see. It's like when you look at the night sky and you begin to wonder what's up there; and it takes your mind outside this little earth … You never forget it, and it gives you a different outlook, somehow, on the problems of the world's peoples.[52]

But if the Antarctic affected the veterans profoundly, their influence on it has also been significant. Even the briefest glance at the huge mass of scientific and geographical work completed by the expedition and its successor bodies during the last seventy years – including an invaluable contribution to the new science of climate change – can leave no observer in any doubt that Operation Tabarin left an indelible and overwhelmingly beneficial mark on the Antarctic continent and on the planet as a whole. It is a legacy of which Marr, Taylor, Back, Lamb and their companions could be justifiably proud.

Select Bibliography

Anderson, W. Ellery, *Expedition South* (London: Evans, 1957)

Bagshawe, Thomas W., *Two Men in the Antarctic* (Cambridge: CUP, 1939)

Boothe, Joan, *The Storied Ice* (Berkeley: Regent Press, 2011)

Brennecke, H. J., *Ghost Cruiser HK33* (London: Futura Publications, 1974)

Charcot, Jean Baptiste, *The Voyage of the 'Why Not' in the Antarctic: The Journal of the Second French Polar Expedition, 1909–1910* (London: Hodder & Stoughton, 1911)

Christie, E. W. Hunter, *The Antarctic Problem* (London: George Allen & Unwin, 1951)

Churchill, Sir Winston, *The Second World War* (London: The Reprint Society, 1952)

Coleman-Cooke, John, *Discovery II in the Antarctic* (London: Odhams Press, 1963)

De Gerlache, Adrien, *Voyage of the 'Belgica': Fifteen Months in the Antarctic* (Norwich: Erskine Press/Bluntisham Books, 1998)

Dodds, Klaus, *Pink Ice* (London: I.B. Taurus, 2002)

Dudeney & Walton, 'From *Scotia* to "Operation Tabarin": Developing British Policy for Antarctica', *Polar Record Online*, 12 October 2011

Fisher, Margery & James, *Shackleton* (London: Barrie Books, 1957)

Fletcher, Harold, *Antarctic Days with Mawson* (London: Angus & Robertson, 1984)

Fuchs, Vivian, *A Time to Speak* (Oswestry: Anthony Nelson, 1990)

Fuchs, Vivian, *Of Ice and Men* (Oswestry: Anthony Nelson, 1982)

Glen, A.R., *Under the Pole Star* (London: Methuen, 1937)

Hardy, Sir Alister, *Great Waters* (London: Collins, 1967)

Helm & Miller, *Antarctica* (Wellington: R.E. Owen, 1964)

James, David, *That Frozen Land* (London: The Falcon Press, 1949)

King, H.G.R. & Savours, Ann, *Polar Pundit: Reminiscences about Brian Burley Roberts* (Cambridge: Scott Polar Research Institute, 1995)

Liversidge, Douglas, *White Horizon* (London: Odhams Press, 1951)

Marr, J.W.S., *The Natural History & Geography of the Antarctic Krill* (Cambridge: Cambridge University Press, 1962)

McIntyre, *Operation Mincemeat* (London: Bloomsbury, 2010)

Mott, Peter, *Wings over Ice: The Falkland Islands & Dependencies Aerial Survey Expedition* (Long Sutton: Peter Mott, 1986)

Nasht, Simon, *No More Beyond: The Life of Hubert Wilkins* (Edinburgh: Berlinn, 2006)

Nordenskjöld, Otto, *Antarctica, or Two Years amongst the Ice of the South Pole* (London: Hurst & Blackett, 1905)

Ommanney, F.D., *South Latitude* (London: Longman, 1938)

Pawson, Ken, *Antarctica: To a Lonely Land I Know* (Manitoba: Whippoorwill Press, 2001)

Price, David, *Tip of the Iceberg* (Cambewarra: David Price, 2007)

Robertson, R.B., *Of Whales and Men* (New York: Knopf, 1954)

Robson, John, *One Man in his Time* (Staplehurst: Spellmount, 1998)

Rudmose Brown, R.N., *A Naturalist at the Poles* (London: Seeley, Service & Co, 1923)

Rymill, John, *Southern Lights* (London: Chatto & Windus, 1938)

Scott, J.M., *Gino Watkins* (London: Hodder & Stoughton, 1946)

Shackleton, Sir Ernest, *South* (London: Robinson Publishing, 1999)

Smith, Michael, *Polar Crusader: A Life of Sir James Wordie* (Edinburgh: Birlinn, 2007)

Speak, Peter, *William Speirs Bruce, Polar Explorer and Scottish Nationalist* (Edinburgh: National Museums of Scotland, 2003)

Squires, Harold, *SS Eagle: The Secret Mission* (St John's: Jesperson Press, 1992)

Stewart, John, *Antarctica: An Encyclopædia* (Jefferson: McFarland & Co, 1990)

Thorne, Christopher, *Allies of a Kind* (Oxford: OUP, 1979)

Walton, E.W. Kevin, *Two Years in the Antarctic* (London: Lutterworth Press, 1955)

Worsley, Frank, *Under Sail in the Frozen North* (Santa Barbara: Narrative Press, 2003)

Notes

Prologue

1 Taylor, *Two Years below the Horn*, University of Manitoba, unpublished manuscript.

Chapter 1 The Shadow & the Substance

1 Churchill, Winston, *The Second World War*, vol. 2 (London: The Reprint Society, 1952), p. 472.
2 Brian Armstrong, edited transcript from *BBC WW2 People's War*.
3 Brennecke, H. J., *Ghost Cruiser HK33* (London: Futura Publications, 1974), p. 183.
4 James, David, *That Frozen Land* (London: The Falcon Press, 1949), pp. 41–42.
5 TNA, PREM 3/141, Most Secret Naval Cipher message to B.A.D. Washington, 23 March 1942.
6 Ibid.
7 Walter Lipmann to John Maynard Keynes, April 1942. Quoted in Christopher Thorne, *Allies of a Kind*, (Oxford: OUP, 1979), p. 149.
8 TNA, PREM 3/141, Prime Minister's Personal Minute to General Ismay for COS Committee, 1 April 1942.
9 TNA, FO 118/265, Haggard to the Marquess of Lansdowne, 5 January 1904. Quoted in Dudeney & Walton, 'From *Scotia* to "Operation Tabarin": Developing British Policy for Antarctica', *Polar Record Online*, 12 October 2011, p. 2.
10 Ibid.
11 See Dudeney & Walton, 'From *Scotia* to "Operation Tabarin"'.
12 Letters Patent of 21 July 1908. Quoted in E. W. Hunter Christie, *The Antarctic Problem* (London: George Allen & Unwin, 1951), p. 301.
13 Dudeney & Walton, 'From *Scotia* to "Operation Tabarin"', p. 5.
14 'Argentine and Chilean territorial claims in the Antarctic', *Polar Record* 4 (32), pp. 412–441. Quoted in Dudeney & Walton, 'From *Scotia* to "Operation Tabarin"', p. 7.

15 Speak, Peter, *William Speirs Bruce, Polar Explorer and Scottish Nationalist* (Edinburgh: National Museums of Scotland, 2003), p. 92.

16 TNA, FO 371/30313, W. Beckett, Memorandum, 16 September 1942. Quoted in Dudeney & Walton, 'From *Scotia* to "Operation Tabarin"', p. 8.

17 TNA, FO 371/30313, Anthony Eden, handwritten memorandum in response to minutes from J. Perowne concerning protests to Argentina, 19 September 1942. Quoted in Dudeney & Walton, 'From *Scotia* to "Operation Tabarin"', p. 8.

18 TNA, ADM 116/4670, C.H.M. Waldock, Letter to R.A. Gallop, 9 October 1942. Quoted in Dudeney & Walton, 'From *Scotia* to "Operation Tabarin"', p. 8.

19 TNA, FO 118/264, E. MacGregor, Letter from the Admiralty to Under Secretary of State at the Foreign Office, 26 March 1904. Quoted in Dudeney & Walton, 'From *Scotia* to "Operation Tabarin"', p. 3.

20 TNA, ADM 116/4670, Head of the Military Branch of the Admiralty, 27 September 1942.

21 TNA, ADM 116/4670, H.N. Morrison to Trafford Smith at the Colonial Office, 26 November 1942. Quoted in Dudeney & Walton, 'From *Scotia* to "Operation Tabarin"', p. 9.

22 TNA, PREM 3/141, Most Secret Cipher Telegram from Air Ministry to Mideast, 2 February 1943.

23 Ibid.

24 BAS, AD6/24/3.1, transcript of an interview with Gwion Davies recorded in 1986, part 1, p. 4.

25 Fuchs, Vivian, *A Time to Speak* (Oswestry: Anthony Nelson, 1990), p. 44.

26 Fuchs, Vivian, *Of Ice and Men* (Oswestry: Anthony Nelson, 1982), p. 23.

27 Ibid.

28 Churchill to Ismay, minute, 8 August 1943. Quoted in MacIntyre, *Operation Mincemeat*, (London: Bloomsbury, 2010), p. 56.

29 SPRI, MS 1308/22/1, hand-written note made by Brian Roberts over a telegram from the Governor of the Falkland Islands to the Secretary of State for the Colonies, 19 November 1943.

30 Glen, *Under the Pole Star*, (London: Methuen, 1937), p. 134.

31 The authors are indebted to Keith Holmes for permission to use his notes on Operation Tabarin.

32 Worsley, *Under Sail in the Frozen North* (Santa Barbara: Narrative Press, 2003), p. 5.

33 Ibid, p. 10.

34 Ibid.

35 Marr, J.W.S., 'Appendix A: A Short Zoological Report', in Worsley, *Under Sail in the Frozen North*, pp. 166–167.

36 Obituary of Dr J.W.S. Marr by Brian Roberts, *Polar Record*.

37 Marr, J.W.S., *The Natural History & Geography of the Antarctic Krill* (Cambridge: Cambridge University Press, 1962).

38 See Fuchs, *Of Ice and Men*, pp. 22–23.

39 Lamb, Ivan Mackenzie, 'How I came to the Antarctic', *Hope Bay Howler*, Vol. 1, No. 5, 21 October 1945.

40 Ashton, 'How I came to find myself in the Antarctic', *Hope Bay Howler*, Vol. 1, No. 2, 21 July 1945.

41 Ibid.

42 Flett, 'How I came to the Antarctic', *Hope Bay Howler*, Vol. 1 No. 6, 21 November 1945.

43 Helm & Miller, *Antarctica*, (Wellington: R.E. Owen, 1964), p. 125.

44 TNA, ADM1/18114.

45 Taylor, *Two Years below the Horn*, p. 7.

46 Reported as being a Royal Mail Steam Packet ship, the *Marquesa* does not appear on any shipping lists identified by the authors.

47 BAS, AD6/16/1986/4.1, transcript of an interview with Eric Back, 8 October 1986.

48 Davies, Gwion, 'John Matheson 1893–1970: A Tribute', *BAS Club Newsletter* No. 42, 1999, pp. 39–42.

49 BAS, AD6/16/1986/1.1, transcript of an interview with Victor Marchesi, 13 August 1985.

50 Davies, Gwion, 'J. W. S. Marr: An Appreciation'.

51 BAS, AD6/16/1986/1.1, transcript of an interview with Victor Marchesi, 13 August 1985.

52 BAS, AD6/16/1986/4.1, transcript of an interview with Eric Back, 8 October 1986.

53 Ibid.

Chapter 2 The Theatre

1   BAS, AD6/16/1986/1.1, transcript of an interview with Victor Marchesi, 13 August 1985.

2   *Journal of the Royal Geographical Society*, Vol. 3 (1833), pp. 105–112.

3   Adrien de Gerlache later identified the landing site from Biscoe's earlier description and named it Biscoe Bay on 8 February 1898.

4   *Journal of the Royal Geographical Society*, Vol. 3 (1833), p. 111. (Position now listed as 64° 47'S 63° 41'W).

5   W.S. Bruce's *Scotia* Expedition is excluded from this count of three as, despite over-wintering on Laurie Island, his main objective was exploration in the Weddell Sea.

6   Wilkins also served on the *Quest* Expedition, as ornithologist.

7   'Project of a British Antarctic Expedition', 7 January 1932, quoted in Scott, J.M., *Gino Watkins* (London: Hodder & Stoughton, 1946), p. 310.

8   Rymill, John, *Southern Lights* (London: Chatto & Windus, 1938), p. xiii.

9   See Christie, *The Antarctic Problem*, p. 241.

10 Hughes, Message from Secretary of State to Norwegian Minister, 2 April 1924. Quoted in Dudeney & Walton, 'From *Scotia* to "Operation Tabarin"', p. 6.

11 Roosevelt, Letter to the commanding officer of the US Antarctic Service, November 1939. Quoted in Dudeney & Walton, 'From *Scotia* to "Operation Tabarin"', p. 6.

12 See Dudeney & Walton, 'From *Scotia* to "Operation Tabarin"'.

13 Taylor, *Two Years below the Horn*, chapter 2.

14 Dawn Skilling (née Hooley), 'Memories of a Schoolgirl, There by Good Fortune', *BAS Club Newsletter*, No. 30, 1993.

15 BAS, AD6/1A/1944/B, Lamb, Operation Tabarin (Base A) Official Diary, 2 February 1944.

16 Hardy, *Great Waters*, (London: Collins, 1967), p. 161.

17 BAS, AD6/1/ADM (Item 22), Operation Tabarin Political Instructions, November 1943.

18 Ibid.

19 BAS, AD6/1A/1944/B, Lamb, Operation Tabarin (Base A) Official Diary, 3 February 1944.

20 Ibid.

21 Taylor, *Two Years below the Horn*, chapter 2.

22 Farrington, J.B. 'Fram', 'Memoirs of a Tabarin Wireless Operator', 4 October 1983. Courtesy of Gerry Farrington.

23 Taylor, *Two Years below the Horn*, chapter 2.

24 Marr to Cardinall, 6 February 1944.

Chapter 3 The Beachhead

1 BAS, AD6/1A/1944/B, Lamb, Operation Tabarin (Base A) Official Diary, 7 February 1944.

2 Ibid.

3 Taylor, *Two Years below the Horn*, chapter 3.

4 BAS, AD6/1/ADM 4.2, Marr to Cardinall, 13 February 1944.

5 Anderson, W. Ellery, *Expedition South* (London: Evans, 1957), p. 45.

6 BAS, AD6/1/ADM 4.2, Marr to Cardinall, 13 February 1944.

7 Ibid.

8 BAS, AD6/16/1986/1.1, transcript of an interview with Victor Marchesi, 13 August 1985.

9 Farrington to Mrs Eileen Farrington, 8 February 1944. Courtesy of Gerry Farrington.

10 BAS, AD6/16/1986/5.1, transcript of an interview with J.B. 'Fram' Farrington, 1–2 December 1986.

11 Dawn Skilling, 'Memories of a Schoolgirl', p. 69.

12 BAS, AD6/1/ADM 4.2, Marr to Cardinall, 13 February 1944.

13 Taylor, *Two Years below the Horn*, chapter 3.

14 *Sailing Directions for Antarctica*, US Hydrographic Publication 27, 1960, section 4.38.

15 Taylor, *Two Years below the Horn*, chapter 3.

16 BAS, AD6/1/ADM 4.2, Marr to Cardinall, 13 February 1944.

17 BAS, AD6/1A/1944/A, Marr, 'First Report on the Work of Operation Tabarin', 6 November 1944.

18 Ibid.

19 Taylor, *Two Years below the Horn*, chapter 4.

20 Dawn Skilling, 'Memories of a Schoolgirl', p. 70.

21 Taylor, *Two Years below the Horn*, chapter 4.

22 BAS, AD6/16/1986/4.1, transcript of an interview with Eric Back, 8 October 1986.

23 A second Boulton & Paul boatshed and store was erected at Port Lockroy in 1956–57; the company also supplied the base with a portal frame generator shed in 1957–58.

24 See BAS, AD6/16/1946/5, cine film taken by Ashton.

25 BAS, AD6/1/ADM 4.2, Marr to Cardinall, 13 February 1944.

26 Farrington to Mrs Eileen Farrington, 15 February 1944. Courtesy of Gerry Farrington.

27 Ibid.

28 Taylor, *Two Years below the Horn*, chapter 4.
29 Farrington to Mrs Eileen Farrington, 15 February 1944. Courtesy of Gerry
    Farrington.
30 Dawn Skilling, 'Memories of a Schoolgirl', p. 70.

Chapter 4 Island Life

1   Taylor, *Two Years below the Horn*, chapter 4.
2   BAS, AD6/1A/1944/B, Lamb, Operation Tabarin (Base A) Official Diary,
    17 February 1944.
3   Farrington to Eileen Farrington, 15 February 1944. Courtesy of Gerry
    Farrington.
4   Taylor, *Two Years below the Horn*, chapter 4.
5   BAS, AD6/1A/1944/A, Marr, 'First Report on the Work of Operation Tabarin,
    Part I: The Work at Base A, 1943–44', p. 3.
6   BAS, AD6/1A/1944/B, Lamb, Operation Tabarin (Base A) Official Diary,
    2 March 1944.
7   Farrington to Eileen Farrington, 23 March 1944. Courtesy of Gerry
    Farrington.
8   Taylor, *Two Years below the Horn*, chapter 4.
9   BAS, AD6/1A/1944/A, Marr, 'First Report on the Work of Operation Tabarin,
    Part I: The Work at Base A, 1943–44', p. 3.
10 Farrington to Eileen Farrington, 23 March 1944. Courtesy of Gerry
    Farrington.
11 BAS, AD6/1A/1944/B, Lamb, Operation Tabarin (Base A) Official Diary,
    6 March 1944.
12 Taylor, *Two Years below the Horn*, chapter 4.
13 Surgeon Commander (later Surgeon Captain) Edward William Bingham
    (1901–1993) was a member of Gino Watkins' British Arctic Air Route
    Expedition (1930–31) and John Rymill's British Graham Land Expedition
    (1934–37). He would later join the Falkland Islands Dependencies Survey
    (FIDS) as base leader at Stonington Island.
14 BAS, AD6/16/1986/4.1, transcript of an interview with Eric Back, 8 October
    1986.
15 TNA, ADM1/18114.
16 BAS, AD6/16/1986/4.1, transcript of an interview with Eric Back, 8 October
    1986.
17 BAS, AD6/1A/1944/A, Marr, 'First Report on the Work of Operation Tabarin,
    Part I: The Work at Base A, 1943–44', p. 4.
18 BAS, AD6/1A/1944/B, Lamb, Operation Tabarin (Base A) Official Diary,
    12 March 1944.
19 Ibid, 5 April 1944.
20 BAS, AD6/16/1986/2.1, transcript of an interview with Gwion Davies,
    13 September 1986.
21 Farrington to Eileen Farrington, 10 April 1944. Courtesy of Gerry
    Farrington.
22 Taylor, *Two Years below the Horn*, chapter 5.
23 Herbert Ponting's original cinematograph of the *Terra Nova* Expedition rather
    than *Scott of the Antarctic*, starring John Mills.

24 BAS, AD6/15/32, John Blyth, *Three Years in Antarctica: My Story*, unpublished manuscript, p. ii.
25 BAS, AD6/1A/1944/A, Marr, 'First Report on the Work of Operation Tabarin, Part I: The Work at Base A, 1943–44', p. 4.
26 TNA, ADM1/18114: some of these flags were fabricated in Naval Dockyards in England; others had been made at the base.
27 Victor Marchesi to Alan Carroll, 1999.
28 Quoted in Taylor, *Two Years below the Horn*, chapter 4.
29 BAS, AD6/16/1986/2.1, transcript of an interview with Gwion Davies, 13 September 1986.
30 Ibid.
31 BAS, AD6/1A/1944/B, Lamb, Operation Tabarin (Base A) Official Diary, 3 April 1944.
32 Farrington to Eileen Farrington, 5 April 1944. Courtesy of Gerry Farrington.
33 BAS, AD6/1A/1944/B, Lamb, Operation Tabarin (Base A) Official Diary, 24 March 1944.
34 Farrington to Eileen Farrington, 16 April 1944. Courtesy of Gerry Farrington.
35 What happened to the first bath salvaged from the whaling factory remains a mystery.
36 BAS, AD6/1A/1944/B, Lamb, Operation Tabarin (Base A) Official Diary, 17 April 1944.
37 TNA, FO371/37729, J.V. Perowne, Minute on Operation Tabarin activities and mail, 4 March 1944. Quoted in Dudeney & Walton, 'From *Scotia* to "Operation Tabarin"', p. 12.
38 *The Times*, 24 April 1944.
39 TNA, PREM 3/141, Prime Minister's personal minute to the Foreign Office, Serial No. M 462/4, 24 April 1944. It is assumed that 'solemn events' refers to Operation Overlord, the Allied invasion of Normandy.
40 TNA, PREM 3/141, Sir Anthony Eden to the Prime Minister, 27 April 1944.
41 Ibid.
42 See Margery and James Fisher, *Shackleton* (London: Barrie Books, 1957), p. 324.
43 Farrington, 'Memoirs of a Tabarin Wireless Operator', 4 October 1983. Courtesy of Gerry Farrington.
44 Ibid.
45 AD6/1A/1944/L, Taylor, 'Operation Tabarin Survey Report, 1944'.
46 Farrington to Eileen Farrington, 14 April 1944. Courtesy of Gerry Farrington.
47 Taylor, *Two Years below the Horn*, chapter 4.
48 Ibid.
49 BAS, AD6/15/32, John Blyth, *Three Years in Antarctica: My Story*, unpublished manuscript, p. 2.
50 Taylor, *Two Years below the Horn*, chapter 5.
51 Farrington to his father, 9 December 1944. Courtesy of Gerry Farrington.
52 BAS, AD6/16/1986/2.1, transcript of an interview with Gwion Davies, 13 September 1986.
53 BAS, AD6/1A/1944/A, Marr, 'First Report on the Work of Operation Tabarin, Part I: The Work at Base A, 1943–44', p. 1.
54 Ibid, p. 2.
55 Farrington to his father, 9 December 1944. Courtesy of Gerry Farrington.
56 BAS, AD6/16/1986/4.1, transcript of an interview with Eric Back, 8 October 1986.
57 Ibid.

58 BAS, AD6/1A/1944/A, Marr, 'First Report on the Work of Operation Tabarin, Part I: The Work at Base A, 1943–44', p. 5.

59 BAS, AD6/16/1986/4.1, transcript of an interview with Eric Back, 8 October 1986.

60 Taylor, *Two Years below the Horn*, chapter 7.

61 BAS, AD6/1A/1944/A, Marr, 'First Report on the Work of Operation Tabarin, Part I: The Work at Base A, 1943–44', p. 5.

62 Ibid, p. 4.

63 Farrington, 'Memoirs of a Tabarin Wireless Operator', 4 October 1983. Courtesy of Gerry Farrington.

64 University of Manitoba, Taylor, 'Private Report on Personnel'.

65 BAS, AD6/16/1986/1.1, transcript of an interview with Victor Marchesi, 13 August 1985.

66 BAS, AD6/16/1986/2.1, transcript of an interview with Gwion Davies, 13 September 1986.

67 BAS, AD6/16/1986/4.1, transcript of an interview with Eric Back, 8 October 1986.

68 Farrington to Eileen Farrington, 15 February 1944. Courtesy of Gerry Farrington.

69 BAS, AD6/16/1986/4.1, transcript of an interview with Eric Back, 8 October 1986.

70 Ibid.

71 BAS, AD6/16/1986/2.1, transcript of an interview with Gwion Davies, 13 September 1986.

72 University of Manitoba, Archived fonds, Box 10, Folder 20, Taylor, Memorandum dated 1 September 1989.

73 Farrington to Eileen Farrington, 10 April 1944. Courtesy of Gerry Farrington.

74 Taylor, *Two Years below the Horn*, chapter 5.

75 BAS, AD6/16/1986/4.1, transcript of an interview with Eric Back, 8 October 1986.

76 BAS, AD6/1A/1944/A, Marr, 'First Report on the Work of Operation Tabarin, Part I: The Work at Base A, 1943–44', p. 4.

77 Taylor, *Two Years below the Horn*, chapter 5.

78 Ibid.

79 Farrington to his father, 9 December 1944. Courtesy of Gerry Farrington.

80 BAS, AD6/1A/1944/A, Marr, 'First Report on the Work of Operation Tabarin, Part I: The Work at Base A, 1943–44', p. 4.

81 Ibid, p. 3.

82 BAS, AD6/15/32, John Blyth, *Three Years in Antarctica: My Story*, unpublished manuscript, pp. 1–2.

83 BAS, AD6/16/1986/2.1, transcript of an interview with Gwion Davies, 13 September 1986.

84 Farrington to Eileen Farrington, 6 April 1944. Courtesy of Gerry Farrington.

85 Taylor, *Two Years below the Horn*, chapter 5.

86 BAS, AD6/1A/1944/B, Lamb, Operation Tabarin (Base A) Official Diary, 24 July 1944.

87 Taylor, *Two Years below the Horn*, chapter 5.

Chapter 5 Wiencke Island

1 Ibid.
2 'Knife Edge Ridge' is not a gazetted place name. Similar in form to a sand dune, but made of snow, its position cannot be permanently fixed.
3 Taylor, *Two Years below the Horn*, chapter 6.
4 BAS, AD6/1A/1944/K, Marr, Narrative of Survey Journey on Wiencke Island, 20 September 1944.
5 Taylor, *Two Years below the Horn*, chapter 6.
6 Ibid.
7 Ibid.
8 BAS, AD6/1A/1944/K, Marr, Narrative of Survey Journey on Wiencke Island, 22 September 1944.
9 BAS, AD6/1A/1944/B, Lamb, Operation Tabarin (Base A) Official Diary, 22 September 1944.
10 BAS, AD6/16/1986/2.1, transcript of an interview with Gwion Davies, 13 September 1986.
11 BAS, AD6/1A/1944/B, Lamb, Operation Tabarin (Base A) Official Diary, 22 September 1944.
12 Ibid.
13 BAS, AD6/16/1986/2.1, transcript of an interview with Gwion Davies, 13 September 1986.
14 BAS, AD6/1A/1944/K, Marr, Narrative of Survey Journey on Wiencke Island, 22 September 1944.
15 BAS, AD6/1A/1944/B, Lamb, Operation Tabarin (Base A) Official Diary, 22 September 1944.
16 Taylor, *Two Years below the Horn*, chapter 6.
17 BAS, AD6/1A/1944/K, Marr, Narrative of Survey Journey on Wiencke Island, 22 September 1944.
18 Taylor, *Two Years below the Horn*, chapter 6.
19 Ibid.
20 BAS, AD6/1A/1944/B, Lamb, Operation Tabarin (Base A) Official Diary, 24 September 1944.
21 BAS, AD6/16/1986/2.1, transcript of an interview with Gwion Davies, 13 September 1986.
22 BAS, AD6/1A/1944/B, Lamb, Operation Tabarin (Base A) Official Diary, 24 September 1944.
23 Taylor, *Two Years below the Horn*, chapter 6.
24 Ibid.
25 Unadopted name.
26 Taylor, *Two Years below the Horn*, chapter 6.
27 BAS, AD6/1A/1944/K, Marr, Narrative of Survey Journey on Wiencke Island, 27–29 September 1944.
28 BAS, AD6/16/1986/2.1, transcript of an interview with Gwion Davies, 13 September 1986.
29 Taylor, *Two Years below the Horn*, chapter 6.
30 BAS, AD6/1A/1944/B, Lamb, Operation Tabarin (Base A) Official Diary, 6 October 1944.
31 Ibid.
32 Taylor, *Two Years below the Horn*, chapter 6.

33 BAS, AD6/1A/1944/K, Marr, Narrative of Survey Journey on Wiencke Island,
    6 October 1944.
34 BAS, AD6/16/1986/2.1, transcript of an interview with Gwion Davies,
    13 September 1986.
35 Ibid.
36 Ibid.
37 BAS, AD6/1A/1944/B, Lamb, Operation Tabarin (Base A) Official Diary,
    9 October 1944.
38 Taylor, *Two Years below the Horn*, chapter 6.
39 Ibid.
40 BAS, AD6/1A/1944/K, Marr, Narrative of Survey Journey on Wiencke Island,
    10 October 1944.
41 Ibid.
42 Taylor, *Two Years below the Horn*, chapter 6.
43 Ibid.
44 Ibid.
45 BAS, AD6/1A/1944/B, Lamb, Operation Tabarin (Base A) Official Diary,
    15 October 1944.
46 Taylor, *Two Years below the Horn*, chapter 6.
47 BAS, AD6/1A/1944/B, Lamb, Operation Tabarin (Base A) Official Diary,
    17 October 1944.
48 Taylor, *Two Years below the Horn*, chapter 6.
49 Ibid.
50 Ibid.
51 BAS, AD6/1A/1944/B, Lamb, Operation Tabarin (Base A) Official Diary,
    17 October 1944.
52 Ibid.
53 The survey of Wiencke Island was finally completed in 1948, when Blyth once
    again was serving at Port Lockroy.
54 Taylor, *Two Years below the Horn*, chapter 6.
55 Ibid.

Chapter 6 A Waiting Game

1 Ibid, chapter 7.
2 BAS, AD6/1A/1944/B, Lamb, Operation Tabarin (Base A) Official Diary,
   19 October 1944.
3 Taylor, *Two Years below the Horn*, chapter 7.
4 BAS, AD6/1A/1944/A, Marr, 'First Report on the Work of Operation Tabarin,
   Part I: The Work at Base A, 1943–44', p. 5.
5 Taylor, *Two Years below the Horn*, chapter 7.
6 Farrington to his father, 9 December 1944. Courtesy of Gerry Farrington.
7 Taylor, *Two Years below the Horn*, chapter 7.
8 Ibid.
9 BAS, AD6/16/1986/4.1, transcript of an interview with Eric Back, 8 October
   1986.
10 BAS, AD6/1A/1944/B, Lamb, Operation Tabarin (Base A) Official Diary,
   22 October 1944.
11 BAS, AD6/16/1986/4.1, transcript of an interview with Eric Back, 8 October 1986.
12 BAS, AD6/1A/1944/B, Lamb, Operation Tabarin (Base A) Official Diary,
   18 November 1944.

13 Ibid, 20 November 1944.
14 Ibid, 20 November 1944.
15 Ibid, 20 November 1944.
16 BAS, AD6/15/32, John Blyth, *Three Years in Antarctica: My Story*, unpublished manuscript, p. 4.
17 Ibid.
18 Taylor, *Two Years below the Horn*, chapter 7.
19 BAS, AD6/1A/1944/B, Lamb, Operation Tabarin (Base A) Official Diary, 21 November 1944.
20 BAS, AD6/15/32, John Blyth, *Three Years in Antarctica: My Story*, unpublished manuscript, p. 4.
21 BAS, AD6/16/1986/4.1, transcript of an interview with Eric Back, 8 October 1986.
22 Taylor, *Two Years below the Horn*, chapter 7.
23 BAS, AD6/1A/1944/B, Lamb, Operation Tabarin (Base A) Official Diary, 8 December 1944.
24 Farrington to his father, 9 December 1944. Courtesy of Gerry Farrington.
25 Taylor, *Two Years below the Horn*, chapter 7.
26 Ibid.
27 BAS, AD6/1A/1944/B, Lamb, Operation Tabarin (Base A) Official Diary, 11 December 1944.
28 In 2006 some of Lamb's 'retaining wall' boulders were still in place, but there was no evidence of imported soil or plant-life.
29 BAS, AD6/16/1986/2.1, transcript of an interview with Gwion Davies, 13 September 1986.
30 Gwion Davies to Alan Carroll, September 1999.
31 Ibid.
32 Ibid.
33 BAS, AD6/16/1986/2.1, transcript of an interview with Gwion Davies, 13 September 1986.
34 BAS, AD6/1A/1944/B, Lamb, Operation Tabarin (Base A) Official Diary, 12 December 1944.
35 Taylor, *Two Years below the Horn*, chapter 7.
36 Ibid, chapter 8.
37 BAS, AD6/1A/1944/B, Lamb, Operation Tabarin (Base A) Official Diary, 25 December 1944.
38 Taylor, *Two Years below the Horn*, chapter 8.
39 Ibid.
40 BAS, AD6/1A/1944/B, Lamb, Operation Tabarin (Base A) Official Diary, 6 January 1945.
41 Taylor, *Two Years below the Horn*, chapter 8.
42 BAS, AD6/16/1986/4.1, transcript of an interview with Eric Back, 8 October 1986.
43 Taylor, *Two Years below the Horn*, chapter 8.
44 Ibid.
45 Ibid.
46 Ibid.
47 On 8 March 1945, Lockley, Layther and White were joined by John K. Biggs, a Falkland Island handyman.
48 BAS, AD6/1A/1945/A, Lockley, Operation Tabarin, Base 'A' – Port Lockroy, February 1945 to January 1946, Preliminary Report.

49 Taylor, *Two Years below the Horn*, chapter 8.
50 BAS, AD6/1A/1944/A, Marr, 'First Report on the Work of Operation Tabarin, Part I: The Work at Base A, 1943–44'.

Chapter 7 Rendezvous

1 James, *That Frozen Land*, p. 62.
2 In December 1940 the coxswain of MGB No. 62 broke his back in just this fashion while en route to Fowey. See Robson, *One Man in his Time* (Staplehurst: Spellmount, 1998), p. 96.
3 Quoted in Robson, *One Man in his Time*, p. 124.
4 James, *That Frozen Land*, p. 62.
5 Squires, *SS Eagle: The Secret Mission* (St John's: Jesperson Press, 1992), p. 26.
6 Ibid, pp. 47–8.
7 Ibid, p. 60.
8 BAS, AD6/1B/1944/A, Flett, Operation Tabarin, Base 'B' Deception Island Report, 1944.
9 Ibid.
10 Ibid.
11 Ibid.
12 Gordon Howkins to Stephen Haddelsey, 4 July 2012.
13 Ibid.
14 Ibid.
15 Gordon Howkins to Stephen Haddelsey, 9 September 2012.
16 BAS, AD6/1B/1944/A, Flett, Operation Tabarin, Base 'B' Deception Island Report, 1944.
17 Ibid.
18 Ibid.
19 Ibid.
20 Quentin Bone, 'Obituary of Professor Norman Bertram Marshall, *The Independent*, 24 February 1996.
21 Taylor, *Two Years below the Horn*, chapter 8.
22 Ibid.
23 James, *That Frozen Land*, p. 20.
24 BAS, AD6/16/1986/5.1, transcript of an interview with J.B. 'Fram' Farrington, 1–2 December 1986.
25 James, *That Frozen Land*, p. 62.
26 Taylor, *Two Years below the Horn*, chapter 8.
27 BAS, G12/2/3, Back, diary, 7 February 1945.
28 BAS, G12/1/3/4, Back, 'Recommended treatment for Lt-Cdr JWS Marr, RNVR,' 8 February 1945.
29 BAS, AD6/10/1945/A, Taylor, Report to the Governor, December 1944–March 1945.
30 BAS, G12/2/3, Back, diary, 9 February 1945.
31 BAS, AD/6/1986/1.1, transcript of an interview with Victor Marchesi, 13 August 1986.
32 BAS, AD6/16/1986/2.1, transcript of an interview with Gwion Davies, 13 September 1986.
33 Ibid.
34 BAS, AD6/16/1986/4.1, transcript of an interview with Eric Back, 8 October 1986.

35 J. B. 'Fram' Farrington, 'Memoirs of a Tabarin Wireless Operator', 4 October 1983. Courtesy of Gerry Farrington.
36 James, *That Frozen Land*, p. 73.
37 University of Manitoba, Taylor, handwritten note, 7 September 1989.
38 Ibid.
39 BAS, AD6/16/1986/1.1, transcript of an interview with Victor Marchesi, 13 August 1985.
40 Taylor, *Two Years below the Horn*, chapter 9.
41 Squires, *SS Eagle*, pp. 67–68.
42 James, *That Frozen Land*, p. 75.

Chapter 8 New Horizons

1 Taylor, *Two Years below the Horn*, chapter 9, p. 147.
2 Squires, *SS Eagle*, p. 68.
3 James, *That Frozen Land*, p. 76.
4 BAS, AD6/1D/1945/C, Flett, Interim Report on the Establishment of Base D at Hope Bay, 5 March 1945.
5 The *Eagle's* original first mate, Abe Butler, had left the ship at Montevideo, suffering from a strangulated hernia.
6 Taylor, *Two Years below the Horn*, chapter 9, pp. 149–50.
7 James, *That Frozen Land*, p. 78.
8 Squires, *SS Eagle*, p. 72.
9 BAS, AD6/16/1986/4.1, transcript of an interview with Eric Back, 8 October 1986.
10 Ibid.
11 James, *That Frozen Land*, p. 83.
12 BAS, AD6/16/1986/5.1, transcript of an interview with J.B. 'Fram' Farrington, 1–2 December 1986.
13 Taylor, *Two Years below the Horn*, chapter 9, p. 163.
14 BAS, AD6/1D/1945/C, Flett, Interim Report on the Establishment of Base D at Hope Bay, 5 March 1945.
15 BAS, AD6/16/1986/2.1, transcript of an interview with Gwion Davies, 13 September 1986.
16 Taylor, *Two Years below the Horn*, chapter 9, p. 161.
17 BAS, G12/2/3, Back, diary, 5 March 1945.
18 James, *That Frozen Land*, p. 82.
19 BAS, AD6/1D/1945/C, Flett, Interim Report on the Establishment of Base D at Hope Bay, 5 March 1945.
20 Taylor, *Two Years below the Horn*, chapter 9, p. 154.
21 James, *That Frozen Land*, p. 83.
22 BAS, AD6/1B/1944/W, N. F. Layther, Report on Wireless Communication, Deception Island, 1944.
23 BAS, AD6/16/1986/5.1, transcript of an interview with J.B. 'Fram' Farrington, 1–2 December 1986.
24 Ibid.
25 BAS, AD6/16/1986/1.1, transcript of an interview with Victor Marchesi, 13 August 1985.
26 Taylor, *Two Years below the Horn*, chapter 9, p. 166.
27 J. B. 'Fram' Farrington, 'Memoirs of a Tabarin Wireless Operator', 4 October 1983. Courtesy of Gerry Farrington.

28 BAS, AD6/16/1986/5.1, transcript of an interview with J.B. 'Fram' Farrington, 1–2 December 1986.
29 Farrington to Eileen Farrington, 10 March 1945. Courtesy of Gerry Farrington.
30 Ibid.
31 TNA, ADM1/19509, Marchesi, Letter of Proceedings, No.7.
32 BAS, AD/6/1986/1.1, transcript of an interview with Victor Marchesi, 13 August 1986.
33 James, *That Frozen Land*, p. 86.
34 Squires, *SS Eagle*, p. 79.
35 Lamb, diary, quoted in Taylor, *Two Years below the Horn*, chapter 9, p. 169.
36 James, *That Frozen Land*, p. 86.
37 Ibid, p. 84.
38 Ibid, p. 87.
39 Squires, *SS Eagle*, p. 78.
40 Ibid, p. 83.
41 Ibid, p. 84.
42 Ibid, p. 86.
43 Quoted in James, *That Frozen Land*, p. 90.
44 Ibid.
45 Taylor, *Two Years below the Horn*, chapter 10, p. 175.
46 Ibid, pp. 175–6.
47 BAS, G12/2/3, Back, diary, 17 March 1945.
48 BAS, AD6/16/1986/2.1, transcript of an interview with Gwion Davies, 13 September 1986.

Chapter 9 The Witches' Cauldron

1 Lamb, diary. Quoted in Taylor, *Two Years below the Horn*, chapter 10, p. 169.
2 Taylor, *Two Years below the Horn*, chapter 10, p. 177.
3 Ibid, p. 178.
4 James, *That Frozen Land*, p. 91.
5 BAS, G12/2/3, Back, diary, 20–23 March 1945.
6 BAS, AD6/15/32, John Blyth, *Three Years in Antarctica: My Story*, unpublished manuscript, p. 9.
7 Taylor, *Two Years below the Horn*, chapter 10, pp. 179–81.
8 James, *That Frozen Land*, p. 84.
9 Taylor, *Two Years below the Horn*, chapter 10, p. 182.
10 Quoted in James, *That Frozen Land*, p. 93.
11 Taylor, *Two Years below the Horn*, chapter 11, p. 190.
12 Marshall to Olga Marshall, serial letter, 3–14 April 1945. Courtesy of Justin Marshall.
13 James, *That Frozen Land*, p. 94.
14 BAS, G12/2/3, Back, diary, 15 April 1945.
15 Olga Marshall, Operation Tabarin album. Courtesy of Justin Marshall.
16 Marshall to Olga Marshall, serial letter, 3–14 April 1945. Courtesy of Justin Marshall.
17 Taylor, *Two Years below the Horn*, chapter 11, p. 189.
18 BAS, G12/2/3, Back, diary, 1 May 1945.
19 Ibid, 5 May 1945.

20 Taylor to Sir Allan Cardinall, 8 May 1945. Quoted in BAS, AD6/15/32, John Blyth, *Three Years in Antarctica: My Story*, unpublished manuscript, p. 8.

21 Captain Scott had considered taking wireless in 1910, but had decided against it because of limited space on the *Terra Nova*.

22 Taylor, *Two Years below the Horn*, chapter 11, p. 203.

23 BAS, AD6/16/1986/2.1, transcript of an interview with Gwion Davies, 13 September 1986.

24 BAS, G12/2/3, Back, diary, 7 May 1945.

25 James, *That Frozen Land*, p. 100.

26 Ibid, p. 101.

27 University of Manitoba, MSS 108, box 8, folder 22, Taylor, 'Report on Interview with Tom Berry', 24 May 1945.

28 University of Manitoba, MSS 108, box 8, folder 22, Taylor, 'Private Report on Personnel', 21 May 1945.

29 Ibid.

30 Ibid.

31 Ibid.

32 Ibid.

33 Ibid.

34 Ibid.

35 Ibid.

36 University of Manitoba, MSS 108, box 8, folder 22, Taylor, 'Report on Interview with Tom Berry', 24 May 1945.

37 Ibid.

38 University of Manitoba, MSS 108, box 8, folder 22, Taylor, 'Private Report on Personnel', 21 May 1945.

39 Ibid.

40 Ibid.

41 Ibid.

42 James, *That Frozen Land*, p. 110.

43 Ibid.

44 BAS, AD6/16/1986/4.1, transcript of an interview with Eric Back, 8 October 1986.

45 BAS, AD6/15/32, John Blyth, *Three Years in Antarctica: My Story*, unpublished manuscript, p. 10.

46 James, *That Frozen Land*, p. 97.

47 Ibid, p. 102.

48 BAS, AD6/15/32, John Blyth, *Three Years in Antarctica: My Story*, unpublished manuscript, p. 10.

49 BAS, AD6/16/1986/4.1, transcript of an interview with Eric Back, 8 October 1986.

50 Ibid.

51 Taylor, *Two Years below the Horn*, chapter 11, p. 211.

52 See BAS, AD6/16/1986/1.1, transcript of an interview with Victor Marchesi, 13 August 1985. Hamilton had served as biologist with the National Oceanographic Expedition of 1925–27, during which he had been based at the Norwegian whaling station at Grytviken, South Georgia.

53 Farrington, 'Memoirs of a Tabarin Wireless Operator', 4 October 1983. Courtesy of Gerry Farrington.

54 BAS, G12/3/1, Back to his mother, 25 August 1945.

55 Taylor, *Two Years below the Horn*, chapter 12, p. 217.
56 BAS, G12/3/1, Back to his mother, 28 July 1945.
57 Taylor, *Two Years below the Horn*, chapter 11, p. 196.
58 See BAS Club Newsletter 30, Taylor, 'Reminiscences of Operation Tabarin', summer 1993, pp. 33–42.
59 Taylor, *Two Years below the Horn*, chapter 12, p. 213.
60 James, *That Frozen Land*, p. 119.
61 BAS, G12/3/1, Back to his mother, 1 April 1945.
62 Ibid, 29 May 1945.
63 Taylor, *Two Years below the Horn*, chapter 12, p. 221.
64 Ibid, p. 221.
65 James, *That Frozen Land*, pp. 119–20.
66 BAS, G12/2/3, Back, diary, 28 July 1945.
67 James, *That Frozen Land*, p. 120.
68 BAS, G12/2/3, Back, diary, 30 July 1945.

Chapter 10 The White Warfare of the South

1 BAS, AD6/1D/1945/K1/Appendix S, James, diary, 8 August 1945.
2 Taylor, *Two Years below the Horn*, chapter 13, p. 234.
3 BAS, AD6/1D/1945/K1/Appendix S, James, diary, 9 August 1945.
4 Ibid, 10 August 1945.
5 Taylor, *Two Years below the Horn*, chapter 13, p. 232.
6 BAS, AD6/1D/1945/K1/Appendix S, James, diary, 12 August 1945.
7 Taylor, *Two Years below the Horn*, chapter 13, p. 239.
8 BAS, AD6/1D/1945/K1/Appendix S, James, diary, 14 August 1945.
9 BAS, AD6/1D/1945/K1/Appendix R, Russell, diary, 14 August 1945.
10 BAS, AD6/16/1987/2.1, transcript of an interview with Andrew Taylor, 14 October 1987.
11 BAS, AD6/1D/1945/K1/Appendix S, James, diary, 17 August 1945.
12 James, *That Frozen Land*, p. 130.
13 BAS, AD6/1D/1945/K1/Appendix S, James, diary, 18 August 1945.
14 Ibid, 20 August 1945.
15 BAS, AD6/1D/1945/K1/Appendix R, Russell, diary, 20 August 1945.
16 BAS, AD6/1D/1945/K1/Appendix S, James, diary, 20 August 1945.
17 BAS, AD6/1D/1945/K1/Appendix Q, Lamb, diary, 21 August 1945.
18 Taylor, *Two Years below the Horn*, chapter 13, p. 254.
19 Ibid, p. 258.
20 BAS, AD6/1D/1945/K1/Appendix S, James, diary, 23 August 1945.
21 Taylor, *Two Years below the Horn*, chapter 13, p. 258.
22 BAS, AD6/1D/1945/K1/Appendix S, James, diary, 24 August 1945.
23 BAS, AD6/1D/1945/K1/Appendix R, Russell, diary, 24 August 1945.
24 Ibid, 27 August 1945.
25 Taylor, *Two Years below the Horn*, chapter 14, p. 265.
26 Ibid, pp. 265–266.
27 Ibid, p. 266.
28 Ibid, p. 267.
29 Ibid, p. 270.
30 Ibid, p. 270.

31 BAS, AD6/1D/1945/K1/Appendix S, James, diary, 28 August 1945.

32 BAS, AD6/1D/1945/K1/Appendix R, Russell, diary, 29 August 1945.

33 BAS, AD6/1D/1945/K1/Appendix Q, Lamb, diary, 29 August 1945.

34 BAS, AD6/1D/1945/K1/Appendix S, James, diary, 29 August 1945.

35 Taylor, *Two Years below the Horn*, chapter 14, p. 276.

36 James, *That Frozen Land*, p. 148.

37 BAS, AD6/1D/1945/K1/Appendix R, Russell, diary, 30 August 1945.

38 James, *That Frozen Land*, p. 149.

39 BAS, AD6/1D/1945/K1/Appendix S, James, diary, 30 August 1945.

40 BBC 2LO-5XX-S.B., F. H. Bickerton, transcript of his broadcast: *Australian Antarctic Expedition*, 17 March 1927, p. 4.

41 Taylor, *Two Years below the Horn*, chapter 15, p. 285.

42 Ibid, p. 286.

43 Ibid, p. 288.

44 Ibid, p. 288.

45 BAS, AD6/1D/1945/K1/Appendix S, James, diary, 1 September 1945.

46 BAS, AD6/1D/1945/K1/Appendix Q, Lamb, diary, 1 September 1945.

47 BAS, AD6/1D/1945/K1/Appendix S, James, diary, 2 September 1945.

48 Ibid.

49 Taylor, *Two Years below the Horn*, chapter 15, p. 290.

50 Ibid, p. 291.

51 BAS, AD6/1D/1945/K1/Appendix S, James, diary, 3 September 1945.

52 Ibid, 3 September 1945.

53 Taylor, *Two Years below the Horn*, chapter 15, p. 293.

54 Ibid, p. 294.

55 Ibid.

56 BAS, AD6/1D/1945/K1/Appendix S, James, diary, 4 September 1945.

57 Taylor, *Two Years below the Horn*, chapter 15, p. 296.

58 Ibid.

59 BAS, AD6/1D/1945/K1/Appendix S, James, diary, 4 September 1945.

60 BAS, AD6/1D/1945/K1, Taylor, Report on the First Sledge Journey, 15 November 1945.

61 Taylor, *Two Years below the Horn*, chapter 15, p. 298.

62 BAS, AD6/1D/1945/K1/Appendix S, James, diary, 5 September 1945.

63 Ibid.

64 Taylor, *Two Years below the Horn*, chapter 15, p. 299.

65 BAS, AD6/1D/1945/K1/Appendix S, James, diary, 6 September 1945.

66 BAS, AD6/1D/1945/K1/Appendix Q, Lamb, diary, 6 September 1945.

67 Ibid, 7 September 1945.

68 BAS, AD6/1D/1945/K1/Appendix S, James, diary, 8 September 1945.

69 Taylor, *Two Years below the Horn*, chapter 15, p. 304.

70 Ibid, pp. 304–5.

71 BAS, AD6/1D/1945/K1/Appendix S, James, diary, 9 September 1945.

72 BAS, AD6/1D/1945/K1/Appendix R, Russell, diary, 9 September 1945.

73 BAS, AD6/1D/1945/K1/Appendix S, James, diary, 9 September 1945.

74 James, *That Frozen Land*, p. 166.

75 Taylor, *Two Years below the Horn*, chapter 15, p. 307.

76 BAS, AD6/1D/1945/K1/Appendix S, James, diary, 11 September 1945.

77 BAS, AD6/1D/1945/K1/Appendix Q, Lamb, diary, 11 September 1945.

78 BAS, AD6/1D/1945/K1/Appendix S, James, diary, 11 September 1945.

79 Taylor, *Two Years below the Horn*, chapter 15, p. 308.
80 Ibid, p. 308.
81 BAS, AD6/1D/1945/K1/Appendix S, James, diary, 11 September 1945.

Chapter 11 The Long Retreat

1   Taylor, *Two Years below the Horn*, chapter 16, p. 310.
2   Ibid, p. 311.
3   James, *That Frozen Land*, p. 171.
4   Taylor, *Two Years below the Horn*, chapter 16, p. 326.
5   Back, *Hope Bay Howler*, October 1945. Quoted in James, *That Frozen Land*, p. 174.
6   BAS, G12/3/1, Back to his mother, 16 August 1945.
7   BAS, G12/2/3, Back, diary, 4 November 1945.
8   Taylor, *Two Years below the Horn*, chapter 16, pp. 324–5.
9   Ibid, p. 324.
10 BAS, G12/2/3, Back, diary, 19 November 1945.
11 James, *That Frozen Land*, p. 178.
12 BAS, AD6/15/32, John Blyth, *Three Years in Antarctica: My Story*, unpublished manuscript, p. 10.
13 BAS, G12/2/3, Back, diary, 10 November 1945.
14 BAS, AD6/16/1986/2.1, transcript of an interview with Gwion Davies, 13 September 1986.
15 Ibid.
16 James, *That Frozen Land*, p. 179.
17 Ibid, p. 180.
18 Ibid, p. 180.
19 Ibid, p. 181.
20 BAS, G12/2/3, Back, diary, 1 December 1945.
21 Ibid, 5 December 1945.
22 James, *That Frozen Land*, p. 186.
23 BAS, G12/2/3, Back, diary, 14 December 1945.
24 Ibid, 17 December 1945.
25 James, *That Frozen Land*, p. 186.
26 University of Manitoba, MSS 108, box 8, folder 22, Taylor, 'Private Report on Personnel', 21 May 1945.
27 BAS, G12/2/3, Back, diary, 25 December 1945.
28 Ibid.
29 Ibid, 28–29 December 1945.
30 Ibid.
31 Taylor, *Two Years below the Horn*, chapter 19, p. 397.
32 Ibid, p. 398.
33 Ibid.
34 Ibid, pp. 398–399.
35 Ibid, p. 337.
36 Ibid, p. 398.
37 Ibid, p. 399.
38 Taylor to Sir Allan Cardinall. Quoted in BAS, AD6/1D/1945/B3, Lamb, diary, 30 December 1945.
39 BAS, G12/2/3, Back, diary, 7 January 1946.

40 Ibid, 8 January 1946.
41 Taylor, *Two Years below the Horn*, chapter 20, p. 402.
42 Ibid, p. 401.
43 BAS, G12/2/3, Back, diary, 8 January 1946.
44 James, *That Frozen Land*, p. 189.
45 Taylor, *Two Years below the Horn*, chapter 20, p. 402.
46 Ibid, pp. 402–3.
47 BAS, G12/2/3, Back, diary, 10 January 1946.
48 BAS, AD6/1D/1945/B3, Lamb, diary, 14 January 1946.
49 James Andrew, diary, 14 January 1946. Transcribed by Keith Holmes.
50 BAS, G12/3/1, Back to his mother, 18 January 1946.

Chapter 12 From Tabarin to BAS

1   Taylor, *Two Years below the Horn*, chapter 20, p. 405.
2   Ibid, p. 405.
3   BAS, G12/3/1, Back to his mother, 18 January 1946.
4   Ibid.
5   BAS, G12/2/3, Back, diary, 16 January 1946.
6   Ibid, 19 January 1946.
7   BAS, AD6/1D/1945/B3, Lamb, diary, 21 January 1946.
8   BAS, G12/3/1, Back to Barbara Back, 8 February 1946.
9   Ibid.
10 BAS, G12/2/3, Back, diary, 29 January 1946.
11 BAS, G12/3/1, Back to Barbara Back, 8 February 1946.
12 BAS, G12/2/3, Back, diary, 25 January 1946.
13 Taylor, *Two Years below the Horn*, chapter 20, p. 411.
14 Ibid, p. 412.
15 BAS, AD6/16/1987/2.1, transcript of an interview with Andrew Taylor, 14 October 1987.
16 Gwion Davies to Alan Carroll, 4 September 2002.
17 *The Times*, 6 January 1947.
18 *The Times*, 28 December 1946.
19 *The Times*, 11 January 1947.
20 *The Times*, 5 March 1948.
21 *The Times*, 5 March 1948.
22 Fuchs, *A Time to Speak*, p. 217.
23 BAS, AD6/16/1986/2.1, transcript of an interview with Gwion Davies, 13 September 1986.
24 Walter, Deception Island Base Report. Quoted in Fuchs, *Of Ice and Men*, p. 288.
25 Sladen, report on the fire at Eagle House, Hope Bay. Quoted in Fuchs, *Of Ice and Men*, p. 113.
26 Ibid.
27 Davy Simmons to the author, 18 November 2004.
28 David Price, *Tip of the Iceberg* (Cambewarra: David Price, 2008), pp. 52–3.
29 Now the Thayer School of Engineering.
30 I am most grateful to Dr John Dudeney and Dr Mark Clilverd, of BAS, for their assistance in describing the ionospheric and whistler research undertaken at Port Lockroy in the post-war years.
31 Robert A. Helliwell, *Whistlers and Related Ionospheric Phenomena* (New York: Dover, 2006; 2nd updated edition).

32 Michael L. Trimpi, Dartmouth College, New Hampshire, to Alan Carroll, 12 December 2015.
33 Visitor numbers courtesy of the UK Antarctic Heritage Trust.
34 Brian Roberts, 'Obituary of Dr JWS Marr', *Polar Record*, 1965.
35 BAS, AD6/16/1987/2.1, transcript of an interview with Andrew Taylor, 14 October 1987.
36 James, *That Frozen Land*, p. 193.
37 Ibid, p. 60.
38 BAS, AD6/15/32, John Blyth, *Three Years in Antarctica: My Story*, unpublished manuscript, p. 12.
39 Ibid, p. 18.
40 Lamb to Taylor, quoted in George A. Llano, 'Obituary of Ivan Mackenzie Lamb', *The Briologist* (The American Briological and Lichenological Society), Vol. 94, No. 3, 1991.
41 University of Manitoba, MSS 108, box 8, folder 22, Taylor, 'Private Report on Personnel', 21 May 1945.
42 BAS, AD6/16/1987/2.1, transcript of an interview with Andrew Taylor, 14 October 1987.
43 BAS, AD6/16/1986/1.1, transcript of an interview with Victor Marchesi, 13 August 1985.
44 Story recounted by Margaret Cameron, Matheson's daughter, to Alan Carroll, March 2013.
45 BAS, AD6/16/1986/2.1, transcript of an interview with Gwion Davies, 13 September 1986.
46 Ibid.
47 BAS, AD6/16/1987/2.1, transcript of an interview with Andrew Taylor, 14 October 1987.
48 James, *That Frozen Land*, p. 190.
49 Russell to his parents, 28 October 1945. Courtesy of Madeline Russell.
50 BAS, AD6/16/1986/4.1, transcript of an interview with Eric Back, 8 October 1986.
51 Ibid.
52 BAS, AD6/16/1986/2.1, transcript of an interview with Gwion Davies, 13 September 1986.

Index